Donated by

Károly Fazekas

Adelaide — 1977

THE TIMELESS NATION

THE HISTORY, LITERATURE, MUSIC, ART AND FOLKLORE OF THE HUNGARIAN NATION

By ZOLTÁN BODOLAI Dip.Ed., Ph.D. (Budapest)
Tutor of Hungarian History and Culture, University of Sydney,
Head of the Language Department, S.G.H.S.

HUNGARIA PUBLISHING COMPANY
SYDNEY — 1978

First edition 1977

Second edition 1978

Wholly set up and printed in Australia by New Life Printery Pty. Ltd.,
54 Renwick Street, Marrickville, N.S.W., 2204. Tel.: 55-6184.

COVER ILLUSTRATION BY OLGA KARDOS A.S.T.C.

National Library (Canberra). Cataloguing in Publication data.

Bodolai, Zoltán, 1917 —
 The timeless nation.

 Index.
 ISBN 0 9596873 2 7.
 ISBN 0 9596873 1 9 Paperback.
 1. Hungary — Civilization. I. Title.

943·9

They ignore the logical sequence of time. Though they had formed a viable nation before Abraham left Ur, they are still searching for their national identity today. They possessed modern social and political institutions a thousand years ago — and in the present century they still live by a medieval code of naive chivalry.

They defy the dictates of History. Whether it is a life-and-death struggle or a period of lazy prosperity, the present exists for them only as a timeless transition from a glorious past into a magnificent future.

Born at the misty dawn of antiquity, having outlived the lifespan of countless empires, this nation hopes to survive till the end of Time.

They are truly timeless.

The Hungarian Coat of Arms

THE UNSUNG SAGA

The Great Pyramid had already been ruling the desert for a thousand years and Tammuz, the lover of Inanna, had already become a legend among the Sumerian god-kings of Kish, but the treacherous beauty of Helen had not yet launched a thousand angry ships when somewhere in the immense steppes on the borderland of Europe and Asia an unknown, unsung people set out in search of a warmer, richer, freer homeland.

Their millenia-long search brought them into contact with many races: some related, some strange, some aggressive, some peaceful. The wanderers seemed to possess a strange magic affecting friend and foe alike. Neither their conquerors, nor their subjects or allies could resist this mysterious attraction: one after the other they joined them. After centuries of this expanding progress the united tribes created a large, multi-racial but viable and dynamic nation which, eventually, found the long-sought haven in the Carpathian basin. There they settled and have fought, dreamt and lived for over thirteen centuries.

*   *   *

" . . . The enchanted stag lured Nimrod's two sons, Hunor and Magor, and their two hundred companions for seven days and seven nights, through treacherous swamps and bottomless marshes, until, at the end of the seventh day, they reached a land of exceeding beauty, a land of rich, velvety meadows, sparkling brooks and beautiful forests, abundant in fish and teeming with game . . . Here the white stag leaped into a pond and disappeared forever . . ."

5

*"The two brothers and their men pitched camp near the pond
and fell asleep. In the middle of the night they were awakened
suddenly by the sound of heavenly music. The full moon shone
in the sky. Cautiously following the sounds through a small
grove of willow trees, the two brothers suddenly beheld a scene
so beautiful that, for a moment or two, their very hearts stopped
beating. On the shore of the little pond, on the exact spot where
the white stag had disappeared, clad only in the silvery moon-
light, the two beautiful daughters of King Dul were dancing,
surrounded by two hundred maidens."*

*"In one second the two brothers fell in love with the two
lovely princesses and took them for their wives. The two hundred
warriors married the two hundred maidens and they all settled
on the new land."*

*"Thus the descendants of Hunor and his men became known
as the Huns in years to come, while the descendants of Magor
and his men were destined to be called Magyars."*[1]

*So ends the popular legend explaining the origins of the
Hungarians or Magyars. There is, of course, no historic truth
in it but it gives a poetic reason for their millenia-long quest
for a new homeland. It also tells us a few things about the
ancestors of the Hungarians: that they were strictly monogamous,
that they were good mathematicians, (just observe the equation:
202 warriors = 202 maidens), that they were interested in music,
dancing and spectator sports, that hunting was one of their
favourite sports and that they have probably invented the "stag
party" . . . Apart from this, it is a truly incredible story.*

*The reader of this book will soon find, however, that Hung-
arian history — documented, true history — is full of incredible
happenings. He will learn of archbishops leading cavalry charges,
of a Palatine (Prime Minister) dressing in his king's armour to
attract the enemy's charge, thus saving the king at the cost of
his own life. He will read about a Catholic Prime Minister
committing suicide in order to call the world's attention to his
country's tragedy. And he will read of a Prince of the Holy
Roman Empire, the richest man in Hungary, who once led a
rag-tag army of peasants fighting for his country's independence
from the same Empire.*

*The reader will also notice an incredible medley of conserva-
tive thought and progressive ideas, of astuteness and naivety.*

Witches were declared "non-existent" 700 years before Salem and the Hungarians had democratic Parliaments "before they had chairs to sit on" (the members attended on horseback), 1000 years before the French Revolution. On the other hand, Latin was still the official language of legislation in the middle of the XIXth century. Hungary had book-printing three years before England and a university twenty years· before Germany — and yet some of the great national leaders could scarcely speak Hungarian because they had been educated abroad. One of the greatest military disasters of Hungarian history was prompted, to a great extent, by the Hungarians' decision not to attack the Turks (who outnumbered them ten to one) as they laboriously dragged their cannons through swampy terrain. Only when Suleiman the Magnificent had properly deployed his immense army did the Hungarians attack. They were destroyed — mainly by the Turkish cannon-fire. On another, more peaceful occasion, the Hungarian nobles offered their "life and blood" to an attractive Habsburg queen who addressed their Parliament with tears in her eyes, a baby on her arms, equipped with wily feminine psychology and considerable acting talent. Though she represented the dynasty which, only a generation before, had tried its worst to destroy the Hungarians, on that occasion she did look like the Holy Virgin with Jesus — right out of the national flag of Hungary. Needless to say, the resemblance was entirely intentional . . .

The reader may well ask, how the Hungarians endured as a people during their long centuries of struggle. This book suggests one answer: they are mankind's most durable artists of survival.

7

I. THE MILLENIAL QUEST

The origins and migrations of the Hungarians

The mystery of the origins of the Hungarians has been a question debated since the first appearance of the warlike nation in Central Europe. Hungarian linguists have indicated the cold, northern regions of what is Russia today as their possible birthplace. Hostile opinion of the IXth-century Europe suggested a much hotter place of origin (and wished them back there). Other Hungarians have proposed more imaginative theories, claiming descent from such widely different races as the Etruscans, Romans, Atlanteans, Mayas, Incas and dwellers of Mu (wherever that was).

During the study of this question, we shall refer to the ancestors of modern Hungarians as "Proto-Hungarians", that is the Hungarian or Magyar people before their settlement in the Carpathian basin. The following summary represents the consensus of most serious historians concerning the origins and prehistory of these Proto-Hungarians. The opinions of various researchers differ in certain details, but for our purposes, it should be sufficient to present the general picture without the debatable details, which would seem irrelevant to the non-Hungarian reader anyhow.

1. The language

The Proto-Hungarians were at least bi-lingual. Some of them spoke a Finno-Ugrian type of language, others a West-Turkic (Turanian or Onogur) tongue and some others probably an Iranian-Mesopotamian type of language. Gradually a new, composite language evolved, based on the grammatical structure of

9

the Finno-Ugrian component, a logical, simple, agglutinating tongue. It retained the simplest basic words of that language, with the Turkic-Onogur and the Mesopotamian-Iranian elements enriching its vocabulary.

The name the Hungarians apply to themselves, "Magyar", derives from the Ugrian "Mansi- or "Magy-" with the addition of the Turkic "-eri", forming "Megyeri" – "Magyeri" – "Magyar", which became the name of the largest tribe. Both particles mean "men". The name given to them by the western historians, "Hungarian" (Latin: "Hungarus"), is a variation of the name "Hun-Ogur" – "Onogur" – "Hungur" used since the fifth century by foreign chroniclers, a reminder of their association with Turkic-Onogur-Hun peoples.

2. Racial composition

Anthropometric measurements carried out on skeletons from the settlement period indicate a racially composite people. The main components were the Turanoid (Turkic-Onogur), the East-Baltic (Finno-Ugrian), the Uralian or Ugrian (the eastern branch of the Finno-Ugrian) with substantial components of Caucasian, Anatolian, Nordoid, Dinarian, Mediterranean and Alpine racial types.

3. Ethnogenesis

This linguistically and racially composite nation has obviously evolved from the successive amalgamations of clans, tribes and groups of various racial and geographical origins. The Proto-Hungarian people were made up of some *nordic* tribes of Ugrian origin who came from the Volga-Kama-Ural region and of a (probably larger) *eastern* component of Turkic-Onogur (Turanian) people who came from the Caspian region. These Turkic elements included Scythian, Hunnic and Avar types as well, and later some Khazars. To these came the third, *southern* segment, the Caucasian (Sabir, Alanian) and Iranian-Mesopotamian elements.

It has been proven that all these races, cultures and languages contributed to the formation of the Magyar or Hungarian people and from their amalgamations arose during the first centuries of the Christian era a remarkably colourful, complex and viable nation, not unlike today's evolving nations, the Australians or the Americans. The latent dynamism of this young

10

people urged them to move on in search of a safer, more suitable homeland. These migrations lasted many centuries.

4. The chronology of the migrations constitutes the most debated field of Hungarian prehistory. The general consensus is the following:

(a) *IIIrd and IInd millenia B.C.* The Ugrians leave the Finno-Ugrian conglomeration in the north of (modern) Russia. The largest group of the Ugrians, later to be called "Magyars", detaches itself from the other tribes and begins to move to the south.

Ornaments used by the Avar-Magyars.
(IXth century).

(b) *1st millenium B.C.* In the border area of Asia and Europe the Ugrians (Magyars) contact Turkic-Turanian peoples and form unions with them. A large group of Magyars remains however at the confluence of the Volga-Kama rivers (today: Central Russia) where they form a well settled nation which exists until the XIIIth century (the time of the Mongol invasion).

(c) *At the beginning of the Christian era* the Proto-Hungarians' southward movement brings them into contact with the Kharezm-Iranian empire. More Turkic-Hunnic-Scythian elements join them in the Caspian region.

11

(d) During the *Vth-IXth centuries A.D.* the Proto-Hungarians move westward. In the Black Sea-Caucasus area they maintain trade and cultural links with Caucasian cultures and are joined by Alans and Sabirs. They also meet the Avars in this area, called "Levedia" by foreign chroniclers. Here the evolving nation remains, for a while, in close contact with the Khazar "empire". It is probably from this area, during the VIIth century that a large contingent of Magyars (of the more peaceful, Ugrian race) move ahead and settle in the Carpathian basin: these were the "Late-Avars" or "Early Magyars". The more aggressive Turkic type Onogur-Hungarians remain in the area and participate in the campaigns of the Khazars as their allies or vassals, until the collapse of that empire, at the beginning of the IXth century.

(e) A dissident *Khazar tribe,* the "Khabar", joins the Proto-Hungarians and together they move further west to the area called *"Etelköz",* the "Region between the Rivers" (Dniestr, Dniepr). During this last stage of their westward movement, at the end of the IXth century A.D., they organise themselves into a nation of eight tribes, elect a hereditary ruling dynasty and prepare themselves for the occupation of the Carpathian basin.

5. The Carpathian basin

During the first centuries of the Christian era, the future homeland of the Hungarians was a power-vacuum, with no cohesive or durable State structure. The semi-independent, autochtonous tribes of Sarmatan, Yazygian, Gothic, Alanian and Germanic races lived under the erratic and loosely organised rule of the Romans (in certain areas) or of the Celts. In the IVth century the Huns moved in and united the area into a powerful but short-lived empire which collapsed after the death of Attila (453).

The evidence of anthropometry and foreign chronicles indicates that the first groups of Proto-Hungarians arrived in the basin during the Vth century. After the collapse of the Hun empire some Huns and groups related to them remained in the area. The best-known of these remnants are the Székelys, who lived in Transdanubia and Transylvania.

The VIth century marks the arrival of the Avars (also known as "Proto-Avars", "Uar-Huns" and "Varchonites") from the

Caucasus area, where they had been in contact with the Proto-Hungarians. At the same time the first Slavonic immigrants arrived in the basin.

The dress of a IXth century
Magyar woman.

The VIIth century brings the arrival of the people who, until now, had been called "Late-Avars", but who are now known to have been Proto-Hungarians ("Early Magyars") [1]. They were peaceful agriculturalists, probably of the northern (Ugrian) type. It is reasonable to assume that they had detached themselves from their more warlike brothers in the "Levedia" area and chose the sanctuary of the Carpathian region. This was probably not the first, and certainly not the last dissension among Hungarians.

6. The "Sumerian connection"

At this stage we should say a few words about the question of Sumerian-Proto-Magyar connections. Whilst the idea of the Mesopotamian-Sumerian origin of the Hungarians is not new, the question became the object of prolific (but often amateurish) research by Hungarians outside the frontiers of present-day Hungary after World War II. The scientists of the "old country" have, at the same time, refused even to consider such a possibility.

Sumerian ceased to be a spoken language around 2000 B.C. (the time of the Akkadian conquest), but lived as a written language until the beginning of the Christian era. From their original homeland, in the south of Mesopotamia, the highly civilised, but not very numerous Sumerians exerted a disproportionately large cultural influence over vast regions, from Greece to Iran-Turkestan. Sumerian writings have been found as far west as Transylvania (Hungary).

The following facts form the basis of the "Sumerian origin" theories: Sumerian, the oldest written language of mankind, used a cuneiform notation, reminiscent of the writing of the Proto-Hungarians and Hun descendants (Székelys etc.), but also of many other cultures. The Sumerian language belonged probably to the Ural-Altai language family (to which Ugrian-Magyar and Turkic also belong). Its agglutinating grammar shows many similarities to certain structures of the similarly agglutinating Hungarian language, such as the lack of genders, transitive and intransitive verb endings and the use of prefixes and suffixes. Some Hungarian researchers claim to have collected from 300 to 1,000 words in Hungarian which are supposed to derive from Sumerian words, but some of these derivations are hotly contested. At any rate, the linguistic similarity cannot be proven without thorough examination and evaluation of the Sumerian scripts, something the Hungarian researchers have not achieved yet.

There is however a real possibility of the influence of post-Sumerian culture upon the Proto-Hungarians at some stage of their migrations in the Caucasus area, through the Alans, Sabirs or through Iranian contacts.

2. "A WAY OF LIFE..."

The Hungarian character

We shall find it easier to understand the history and civilisation of the Hungarians, if we look at first at some interesting traits of their national character.

The Hungarians who settled in the Carpathian basin represented a composite, multi-racial, multi-cultural and multi-lingual nation. This complexity was the result of prolonged contacts of varying intensity with many European and Asian races and cultures during the centuries of their migrations. The Proto-Hungarians had also come under the influence of several ephemeral nomadic "empires" and had remained for periods of various length "submerged" in these empires. During these periods they were usually referred to by foreigners by the name of the leading, most aggressive segments of the "empire" in question: Turks, Khazars etc. The amazing fact is, however, that after each such period of national anonymity they always emerged again, stronger in numbers, enriched in culture and language, their national identity seemingly strengthened by the experience of "submersion."

It is logical, therefore, to assume that the Proto-Hungarians developed a durable and strong national identity at the earliest stage of their migrations. The original tribal group, which had set out on these migrations during the last millenium B.C., must have formed a viable nucleus for the future nation.

This heterogeneous racial and cultural structure, superimposed on a millenia-old national identity, had provided the Hungarians with certain recognisable national characteristics, some of which may seem to be of a contrasting nature. These vastly different features have, during the last thirteen centuries of their Central-

European existence, mellowed into a surprisingly rich, colourful but harmonious national character.

Though elusive and hard to define, this *national character* exists without visible physical racial characteristics. Magyars do not belong to any particular race, they do not present any noticeable religious, political or social conformity — in fact, the very diversity in these fields seems to be one of the typical characteristics of this people. The definition of their national "ethos" is therefore a very complex task. For one thing, Hungarians are usually too emotional to be able to form impartial judgments of themselves while foreigners are rarely familiar enough with their culture and history to form valid conclusions.

The answer to this question requires a compromise solution, similar to the answer to their origins. The nation's multi-ethnic origin suggests a synthesis of many deep-rooted qualities. No single epithet will adequately describe a Hungarian and those who only see one particular aspect of the many faces of their character will be just as wrong as those who insist that they are descendants of one single ("pure") race. Thus the basic traits of the national character can be traced back to the original "donors", the racial components, from which those qualities may have originated.

The Hungarians inherited from their *Turkic-Turanian-Onogur* components their organising talent in military and political matters. This talent enabled them to resettle and reorganise their previously nomadic tribes in Central Europe, to create a western, Christian state and to maintain it for thirteen centuries among hostile nations. Akin to this military talent are their emotional heroism and mercurial instability.

These aggressive qualities are tempered by the legacy of their nordic *Balto-Finno-Ugrian* ancestors. These peaceful, fishing-hunting-pastoral (later agricultural) tribes bequeathed to the present-day Hungarians the basic structure of their language along with their taste for a placid, agricultural existence and pastoral occupations. The love of the native soil is so deep-rooted that even the best "assimilated" Hungarian migrants treasure a handful of soil of their native country among their cherished souvenirs. Magyar folksongs present an endless display of nostalgic expressions of the love of the soil and native environment.

16

These two, seemingly contrasting features combine to present an interesting attitude of the Hungarian soldiers on the battlefield. They can fight well when they are defending the frontiers of their own country, protecting, as it were, their own homes and families. Aggressive campaigns beyond the country's frontiers have, however, rarely inspired Hungarian soldiers to heroic deeds. The greatest Hungarian general, John Hunyadi suffered his only two defeats during campaigns far from the frontiers of the country.

The well-known artistic talent of the people is the synthetic product of Central-Asian (Turkic-Avar-Scythian) influence in folklore and folkmusic, Finno-Ugrian heritage in folk poetry and *Mesopotamian-Iranian-Caucasian (Sumerian?)* contacts (e.g. interest in mathematics, science, decorative folk-art, certain types of folk music, etc.). Their Caucasian heritage manifests itself also in their preference for intellectual interests, such as literature, art, music, chess and discussion.

Their conservative *moral philosophy,* respect for women, elders and ancestors, is a legacy of their gentle Ugrian ancestors. The pre-Christian religion of the Magyars also reflects the mentality of their northern forebears: it was a monotheistic, monogamous, family-centered, ancestor-worshipping creed.

Another typical quality of the Hungarians is their ability to assimilate foreigners and integrate themselves into other nations. This two-way flexibility is an attribute acquired during the migrations. The hard core of the nation formed a magnetic nucleus attracting and assimilating smaller foreign groups, thus increasing the nation during its progress. During the XVIIIth and XIXth centuries the numbers of the Magyars increased ninefold, mainly through assimilation. On the other hand, it is a well-known fact that Hungarians make excellent settlers in any country. Though they are proud of their ethnic heritage and share it prodigally with anyone interested, they form no cultural ghettoes and inter-marry freely with any ethnic group.

Honour — personal and national — is a cardinal virtue in their moral spectrum. Keeping one's given word is an obligation over-riding all other considerations, including political expediency. This is why the Hungarians never changed sides during international conflicts, however advantageous it may have been to do so.

17

In the courtyard of a "Matyó" house. (Cf. Chapter 27).

O. Glatz: Mother and child (Cf. p. 209)

"For alien nations do not understand
His guileless heart, his good and stainless hand,
His unoffending love, his ploughman's life
So blest with leisured song, so free from strife . . ."

(E. Szép)

There are, of course, many *negative aspects* of the Hungarian character. The proverbial Magyar dissension and their lack of perseverance are probably the legacy of those Turkic tribes which frequently formed short-lived nomadic empires bent on the conquest of the world and soon in collapse for no apparent reason. The dreamy, unrealistic optimism, the expectation of miracles is, perhaps, a tradition handed over by the star-gazing poets of Mesopotamia. The Hungarians' volatile temper — easily aroused, easily pacified — their periodical complacency and smug conservatism also point to Mesopotamian sources.

Their proverbial love of *freedom and independence* often hardens into rugged individualism which rejects guidance or discipline, military or political. Only leaders with great personal appeal can unite them for any considerable length of time. When formal rejection of an authoritarian rule is not possible — though given half a chance they would rise against it — their resistance finds verbal expression in the form of political satirical humour — probably a Hungarian invention.

Another national vice, their excessive *pride* — a Turkic legacy — causes them to look down upon those they consider "inferior", whether other Magyars or foreigners, such as national minorities.

All these qualities have a common denominator, a basic attitude toward life and mankind. When searching for such a quality, the Hungarians like calling themselves the *"Defenders of Christian Europe"* for having fought the eastern and southern pagan aggressors for a thousand years. Such religious altruism is hardly an immanent characteristic of these formerly pagan nomads. Nor did they choose this role out of proselytic fervour in order to "expiate" their former pagan aggressiveness. This task was rather imposed upon them by their unfortunate geographical situation. It is true that they did fight with stubborn gallantry for centuries in the gateway of Christian Europe. It is also a fact that on many occasions these powerful aggressors offered to the Hungarians an alliance against the West, which had treated them with selfish cynicism anyhow. The Hungarians, as a nation always rejected these approaches, not because of their mythical mission as the "bastion of Christianity", but because the moral and social ideology of the Mongols and Turks was alien to their conservative morality and freedom-loving individualism.

20

Thus their "militant Christianism" must have deeper roots in the national character. When searching for this fundamental quality, one is struck by a symbolic coincidence. The little tribe which, during the long centuries of migrations, formed the nucleus of the future nation, called itself "Megy-eri" – "Magyar". Both particles of this word mean "MAN" — in Ugrian and Turkic respectively. This word seems to point, in a symbolic way, to their basic quality: *humanism*.

Humanism, under its definition expressed by the philosophers of the Renaissance (the Hungarians' favourite period), is a reaction against religious or secular doctrines which tend to subordinate men to abstract concepts of a philosophical, political or social nature. Humanism attaches primary importance to man, to his faculties and well-being. It is a social attitude as well: respect for one's fellow-human is compatible with the concern for one's well-being.

The Hungarians' humanism is based on the racial, cultural, moral and social concepts inherited from their ancestors in Asia and Europe. Therefore we may justly call their particular philosophy *Euro-Asian humanism*.

How does this basic attitude reveal itself in Hungarian history and civilisation?

Hungarians have always been known for their thirst for knowledge: an important humanistic attribute. Their attitude towards foreign cultures has always been that of sympathetic curiosity: they accepted their inspiration and adapted them to their own tastes. The proverbial Hungarian *hospitality* is akin to this cultural curiosity. They are probably the only western nation which truly loves foreigners and treats them with the old-fashioned respect only found among more primitive Asian tribes. This respect for foreigners was codified by the founder of Christian Hungary, King St. Stephen, who admonished his son to welcome foreigners" . . . because the nation of one language is weak . . . " He and his successors welcomed immigrants of all nationalities, including pagan refugees fleeing from the Mongol invasion, Jews fleeing from German pogroms (medieval and modern), Slavs and Vlachs escaping from Turkish domination, Poles escaping from Russian and German invaders etc.

Hungarian statesmen frequently fell prey to the intrigues and machinations of international diplomacy. Though efficient organ-

21

isers in military and political matters, their naive faith in human goodness and *credulous innocence* left them defenceless against the wily methods of their machiavellian opponents. Their vitality, optimism and flexibility assured their survival, but their guileless diplomacy always prevented them from playing an important role in Europe. The outspoken Magyar writer, Dezsö Szabó once said: "We Hungarians have been the greatest suckers in the world . . ."

Their soft-hearted humanism is well illustrated by their behaviour in wars. They are incapable of using guerilla tactics, kill unsuspecting or trapped enemies. (Hungary is probably the only country in Europe which produced no effective armed "Resistance" during World War II). They cannot use terror methods, retaliations against civilians and other inhuman methods of warfare. The lower half of the Hungarian Crown was given to the Hungarian King by a Greek emperor, because the Magyar troops had treated their Greek prisoners humanely.

The *social structure* of the nation has also been based on humanitarian principles. Being human, it was, of course, characterised by fragmentation into classes, though not "feudal" in the western sense of the term, but it possessed a great degree of vertical mobility. Promotion from the lower class to the higher was denied to no one. Peasants of Magyar or other nationality often rose to the highest offices.

Folk music, art and folklore present remarkably humanistic characteristics. The Magyar folk poet is a down-to-earth realist: his imagination is tinged with earthly colours. Flowers, trees, domestic animals, the sky, the rivers and his crops interpret his basic emotions. His beloved is a "turtle dove" and when he is separated from her, he envies the birds that are free to fly to their mates. When he leaves his village, nature itself weeps with him, the dust of the road spins his protective cloak and the stars pity his sorrow. His religion is anthropomorphic: the Child Jesus is the little prince of the shepherds, the Holy Virgin is the mother of all Magyars. The Saviour (" — if only He had been born in Hungary . . . —") and Saint Peter visit the Great Plain and talk to the outlaws there. Death holds no terror for him, it is nature's destiny: the crop dies when ripe. He believes in immortality and resurrection — but he would prefer to be awakened by his girl's kisses instead of the archangel's trumpet. He is no mystic: secrets of the after-life do not interest

22

Peasant girl dressed for a "Bethlehem" play.
"An aristocracy of virtue and talent . . ." (Jefferson).

him. At any rate, Heaven cannot be as beautiful as Hungary, so there is no hurry to get there . . .

Even *religion* seems to offer many examples of Hungarian humanism. Among the 40 Hungarians canonised by the Catholic Church (and one canonised by the Buddhist faith) there are no mystics: they were all practical men and women, martyrs, fighting priests, soldiers, kings, hard-working women. Even Princess Margaret chose the lowly tasks of a scullery maid in a convent as her sacrifice for Hungary's liberation from the Mongols in the XIIIth century — in an age when mysticism and prayer seemed to be the straightest way to Heaven.

*   *   *

The Hungarians have never built pyramids, ruled slave empires, conquered new worlds. They are a proud, strange and lonely people. They live in the Carpathian basin and just about everywhere else, engaged in all possible (and some impossible) occupations. No two Hungarians are alike, and yet the magnetism of their diversity seems to bring them together: they seem to be united by their differences. When they meet, they greet each other like long-lost brothers, laugh, dream and sing together for a while, then discover some of the innumerable, specially Hungarian differences and go their own, lonely ways, working and dreaming (they are very good at both): fourteen million Don Quixotes in search of new windmills to fight.

It is said that all Australians claim to be equal, some even more equal than the others. Hungarians are all different and each one claims to be more different than the others. They deny having common characteristics — yet they all present the same attitude towards life and things beyond. — One is inclined to believe the American saying: "Hungarian is not a nationality, it is a way of life."

They believe in God. They also believe in miracles, in beautifully useless ideals, but first of all they have unlimited faith in themselves. They love women, music, poetry, romantic history (their own), pure mathematics, applied humour, sumptuous dresses, dignified or fiery dances, melancholic music — but most of all their unique language, a flowery relic of bygone ages with its strange mixture of oriental colour and nordic majesty.

They have survived at the crossroads of history where more numerous nations had perished. Strangers came by the millions to join them and to die for them, attracted by that strange magic which is Hungary. They have survived and with them has survived a unique, complex culture, the synthesis of ancient Euro-Asian humanism and modern, western Christianity.

3. ANCIENT ECHO

The origins and development of Hungarian folk music

Like their ancient language, the folk music of the Hungarians has maintained its basic structure through centuries of migrations and more than a thousand years of statehood in Central Europe. The structure of their folk music underwent certain superficial changes during these centuries. Ornamentations, modern, richer tonalities, western scales and rhythm patterns have been added to the original pentatonic scale and simple structure, without obliterating the distinct, ancient characteristics of this unique form of artistic expression.

The movement of these melodic elements can be traced from China to the Danube, from the Arctic Sea to Mesopotamia, mirroring the influences and contacts which shaped the racial, cultural and artistic character of the Hungarian people during their long migrations before their final settlement in the Carpathian basin. Thus the evolution of the Hungarian folk music began in the prehistoric mist of antiquity somewhere on the immense Euro-Asian plain, where a multi-racial group of tribes amalgamated into a more or less united people of heterogeneous racial and cultural composition. This composite ethnic structure accounts for the various sources of inspiration in their folk art in general and folk music in particular.

The systematic study of Hungarian folk melodies, carried out by Kodály, Bartók and their associates during the last seventy years, revealed two distinct types of folk tunes: the "ancient strata" or old style and the "new style" which evolved from this during the last two centuries.

The main characteristics of the *"ancient strata"* are:

(a) The pentatonic scale: only five tones are used instead of the seven known in western music. The second and sixth tones ("a" and "e") are missing, though they may appear in the form of unaccented, passing notes in ornamentation.

(b) The melody is repeated a fifth lower later in the song. This is called the "fifth construction" and it usually occurs in a "descending structure."

(c) The rhythm is "parlando" (recitativo) or "rubato" (free) to suit the singers' mood and the occasion. Quicker ("giusto") tempo is used with dance melodies and group singing. The slower rhythms accept all forms of ornamentation, as well as decorative, individual variations.

(d) The song-structure usually consists of four lines of equal length, the second of which may carry the repeated melody five tones lower.

The pentatonic scale, probably the oldest melodic structure used by mankind, is found in the folk music of peoples who could not possibly have had cultural contacts with each other, such as the Celts, the Chinese, the Incas etc. However, a comparison of Hungarian and Central Asian, Northern European (Ugrian) and Caucasian folk music reveals other similarities of melodic structure and rhythm as well as other components which exclude the possibility of sheer coincidence or natural development along the same lines. It is obvious from these investigations that the basic Magyar folk music represents the westernmost area of a great Euro-Asian musical heritage. Furthermore, this specific musical form, with its harmonious and distinct structure, shows no similarity to the folk music of any of the Central European neighbouring peoples (Slovaks, Serbs, Rumanians) and no influence from their melodic types. If anything, the Hungarian music has influenced these neighbours, especially Rumanians, in areas where there was close contact between these nations.

Closer study of the old-type tunes reveals interesting facts about their possible origins. Thus the song "Fuj, süvölt . . .", an old pentatonic melody recorded by Kodály in 1905 in Northern Hungary, can be traced to similar melodies among the Mari (Cheremis) and Chuvas peoples (Upper Volga, Eastern Russia),

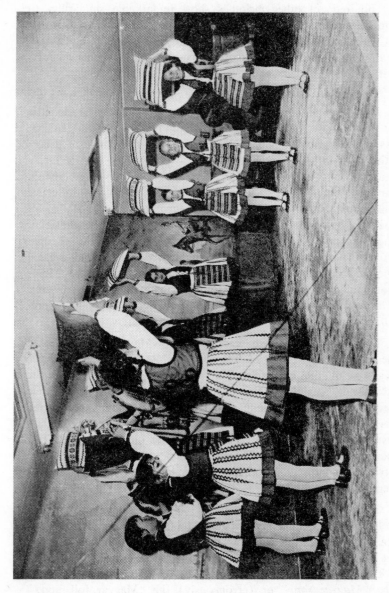

"The Pillow Dance" (children's song and game).

the Kalmuk in Western Siberia, the Tartars in Central Asia and to some Chinese folk melodies.

Hundreds of other melodies show remarkable similarities to the folk music of people as far apart as the Western Siberian Ostyaks and Voguls, the Central Asian Nogai Tartars, the Eastern European Bashkirs and the Anatolian Turks, indicating contacts with Ugrian, Turkic and Central Asian cultures.

The extent of the Transcaucasian or Mesopotamian influence is less clear. Folklore research in these regions has made little progress, consequently there is insufficient material for comparison. As the influence of these cultures is clearly detectable in decorative folk art and other aspects of Hungarian culture, it is reasonable to expect a similar effect on the development of folk music. Zoltán Kodály, when studying the Gregorian influence on certain Transylvanian melodies, suggested the possibility of melodic influences of "pre-Gregorian" nature on the music of the Magyars' ancestors (Proto-Hungarians) before the occupation of the Carpathian basin. The cultures which had created the antecedents of Gregorian music were those of the Mesopotamian region: Sumerian, Babylonian and Semitic cultures. The folk ballad "Istenem, Istenem . . . " seems to point to pre-Gregorian (Mesopotamian) inspiration.

During the last two centuries the Magyar people have developed a *new style* of folk music while preserving the basic features of the old style. The new style has maintained the pentatonic scale in many melodies and short, pentatonic sequences in others, along with Doric, Mixolydian, Aeolian and modern minor and major scales. The "fifth construction" is usual and the rhythm is as free as in the old style songs. This new style is a purely Hungarian creation; nothing similar in style or character has been found in the Central European region.

This more modern form of the folksong, together with the soldiers' dance-song type, called "toborzó" (recruiting dance), and certain western elements helped to create, at the beginning of the XIXth century, the artistic popular song, usually performed by gypsy musicians and known all over the world as the *"Magyar song"* or (erroneously) the "Magyar folk song". This pleasant, but rather hybrid style has since been mistakenly identified with genuine Hungarian folk music by such eminent composers as Liszt, Schubert, Brahms, Tchaikovsky and Ravel. In Hungary this urban "folkish" song became the favourite musical style of the middle classes, mainly through the production of countless stereotyped "Magyar songs" by urban composers and operetta composers, such as Lehár, Kálmán and Kacsóh.

The *gypsy orchestras* have been the best known interpreters of this song and music type. The gypsies — a people of east-Indian origin — came to Europe during the Middle Ages. They have found in each country certain volatile occupations as tinkers, showmen, dancers or musicians. In Hungary they almost entirely replaced the folk musicians whom we only find in remote areas playing mostly woodwind and string-percussion instruments. The gypsies have formed orchestras made up of a large number of string instruments, woodwind instruments and the "cimbalom" (dulcimer) a string percussion instrument. The band, led by the "primás" (prime violinist, conductor) performs according to the tastes of the audience, playing the tunes with an excess of ornamentation and variations with typical "gypsy" style in variable "rubato" tempo. They do not compose the music they play. Instead, they perform — sometimes rearrange — popular urban songs, operetta arias, internationally known light compositions and, of course, genuine folksongs. It is wrong, therefore, to speak of "gypsy music" which (like feminine logic) is quite delightful but does not exist.

The researchers of folk songs have also classified the melodies according to their social role and use. Thus, in addition to the songs of general, lyric nature, there are many tunes used in connection with special occasions: marriage, death, harvest, vintage and other festivals (some of pagan origin), children's songs, games and ditties, religious songs and minstrels' songs ("regös"). The melodies of folk ballads usually belong to the old strata. These occasional tunes have conserved their original melodic forms, being associated with certain ancient customs, or — in the case of the children's songs — with pantomimes, games and dances. Some children's songs preserve very old melodic forms: the three-tone, pre-pentatonic scale. Their ancient, classic simplicity makes them eminently suitable for the purpose of elementary musical education by the well-known "Kodály method."

As the various themes and topics of lyric, epic, festival and children's songs are expressed in their texts as well as melodies, we shall divide the various areas of folk poetry in later chapters and examine the contents as well as the poetic and melodic forms in each thematic group.

On the initiative of Kodály, Bartók and their fellow researchers a rich treasure of about 100,000 folk melodies has been collected in Hungary. Many Hungarian and foreign composers have used the inspiration of the Magyar folk song in their compositions or the artistic orchestral or choral arrangements of these tunes. As it is, Bartók and Kodály saved the treasures of the Hungarian folk music in the eleventh hour. In a few decades, urbanisation and industrial progress would have destroyed all traces of this magnificent treasure.

4. THE SETTLEMENT

(The occupation of the Carpathian basin.

The IXth-Xth centuries)

In the "Etelköz" settlement area (modern Bessarabia), the seven Onogur-Magyar tribes (Nyék, Megyer, Kürtgyarmat, Tarján, Jenö, Kér, Keszi) and the Khabar tribe established a firm federation under a hereditary ruler. In a covenant called the "Blood Treaty" the tribal chiefs, representing the nation, codified their national constitution. They elected Árpád, the chief of the largest tribe (Megyer), and his descendants as their hereditary rulers. They also agreed that the land obtained by common effort should be shared justly by all members of the nation. Thus, shortly before their exodus from the Etelköz area (895-896 A.D.), the Hungarians laid the foundation of a progressive, liberal constitution. The elected sovereign was to rule by the will of the nation (not by the "Grace of God"), and land was to be held by the individuals as their rightful property, not in fief from their lord: thus they rejected the medieval principle of feudalism.[1]

The leaders of the nation became interested in the power-struggles of the Byzantian and Western (German) Empires and allied themselves with one and the other on various occasions. As allies of the German emperor, Arnulf they were instrumental in the destruction of the shortlived "Moravian Empire" of Svatopluk (892-894). During these campaigns they had ample opportunity to reconnoitre the Carpathian basin, which their legends had already indicated as their inheritance from Attila. The constant harassment of their eastern neighbours, the Pechenegs (Besenyö), made them realise how unprotected their Etelköz homeland was. So they decided to settle behind the Carpathians.

31

The movement of the entire nation was planned and directed by Prince Árpád and took place in 895-896 in the form of a gigantic pincer movement: the bulk passed through the North-Eastern Carpathians and a smaller contingent entered Transylvania from the south.

Hungarian historians call this operation "Honfoglalás" ("Occupation of the Homeland), or simply "Bejövetel" (Entry). This was truly no "conquest". Even imaginative medieval chroniclers fail to make much of the occasional skirmishes that took place during this rather peaceful resettlement operation. One cannot help admiring Árpád's sense of timing: the area was, at this period, truly a "power vacuum" without an effective central state structure.

Most of the population of the central area consisted of Avar-Magyars and other closely related races which greeted the Hungarians as their brothers. The southern areas were still nominally part of the Bulgarian empire, already crumbling under Byzantian attacks. The northern mountains were settled by Slavonic tribes, e.g. Slovaks. After the collapse of Svatopluk's empire, these scattered settlers (themselves rather recent arrivals: see Chapter 1), were left to fend for themselves. They surrendered to the Hungarians, or rather accepted the status of allies and vassals. They were allowed to keep their own feudal social structure, national and cultural identity and religious freedom — and the Slovaks did survive eleven centuries of Hungarian "domination".

During the tenth century, Árpád and his successors reorganised their heterogeneous nation. The latest arrivals provided the nation's leaders, while their tribal members represented the pastoral occupations and animal husbandry. The "old settlers", such as the Avar-Magyars and related groups, retained their role as agriculturalists. The non-Magyar elements found their role and position in the nation's social structure according to their skills, feudal status and property. The land was divided among the tribes and each free member of the nation was given land to own, not in fief.

With the task of reorganisation completed, the power of the paramount ruler (Prince) declined, though Árpád (895-907) and his successors, Solt (907-?) and Taksony (?-972), were recognised as the supreme authority, but the semi-independent tribal chiefs became practically absolute rulers of their

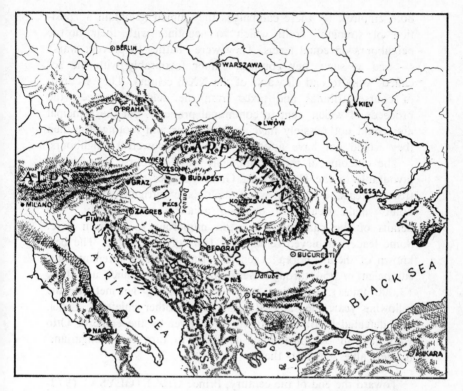

Hungary, encircled by the Carpathians, lies in the heart of Europe.

segment of the nation. They carried on independent internal, religious, external and military policies and concluded alliances with their neighbours or fought them independently. Thus the chief of the "Keszi" tribe (settled in Transylvania), who held the second highest hereditary office of the "Gyula", maintained independent relations with Byzantium and accepted Christianity long before the conversion of the western tribes.

This leads us to the examination of the so-called *raids*. The Hungarians, though not exactly new arrivals, were still considered outsiders, even intruders, by their powerful neighbours, the Germans and the Byzantians. The fact that the Hungarians retained their pagan religion was considered a further offence by their neighbours. So the Hungarians decided to assert their rights in the settlement area they had chosen. For more than 70 years they fought deterrent, preventive campaigns against both empires. By these campaigns they aimed to obtain a "position of strength" from which to negotiate with their hostile neighbours on equal terms. They were "battles to prevent wars" — and as such they compare rather favourably with the so-called "wars to end all wars" of the XXth century. They secured, of course, tributes and taxes from the defeated princes, the proceeds of which went to communal property, but the principal aim could not possibly have been plunder and looting, for then they would not have attacked their most powerful neighbours.

The outcome of these campaigns was, of course, not always favourable to the Hungarians. Great victories turned into disastrous defeats, especially when diplomatic intrigues (the Hungarians' main weakness) changed alliances unexpectedly. The details of the campaigns are too numerous to mention here. Some leaders achieved remarkable feats of generalship. The best known of them, "horka" (general) Bulcsu, led a seven months' campaign in 954 through Germany, Holland, France and Italy (3,000 miles), defeating every western army he met. In the following year, the same Bulcsu, with another chieftain, Lehel, was defeated in Bavaria, at the Lech river by the emperor Otto who had, in the meantime, managed to turn the Hungarians' former allies against them.

Toward the end of the century, Prince *GÉZA* (GEYSA) (972-997) began to strengthen his authority as the hereditary leader of the nation. He married the daughter of the Gyula, the second most powerful chief, then proceeded to assert his authority over the other tribal chiefs by putting an end to the campaigns and concluding a peace treaty with the Emperor, Otto I, the victor of Lech, on equal terms. With deep understanding of the process of power consolidation in Europe, he decided to claim his nation's place as a member of the western Christian civilisation. As he had already noticed the signs of decline in the Byzantian empire, he asked for western missionaries, had his entire family baptised and encouraged the Hungarians to convert to Christianism. His only son and heir, Vajk (baptised Stephen or "István"), married the sister of the future emperor of Germany, Gisela (the granddaughter of the conqueror of Lechfeld).

The "show of strength" of the preventive campaigns had paid off. No longer despised "outsiders" the Hungarians were ready to join the European community as equal partners.

34

5. THE CROSS AND THE SWORD

(Christian Hungary under the Árpád kings: 1000-1301)

The task of Christianisation, unification and consolidation was left to Géza's heir, **ISTVÁN I** (SAINT STEPHEN) (997-1038), who inherited his father's political wisdom and his mother's (Sarolta, daughter of Gyula) deep Christianity. During his reign Hungary became a strong, independent Christian Kingdom, maintaining friendly relations with the German empire without becoming its vassal.

Stephen turned to Pope Sylvester II, asking for his recognition as an independent Christian king and implying that he did not wish to become the vassal of the emperor. The Pope sent him a crown and bestowed upon him the title of "King by the Grace of God", thus acknowledging his independence from the German empire. He also sent Stephen an apostolic cross, the symbol of authority over the state as a religious unit, and granted him the permission to establish a national church (hence the title of "Apostolic King"). The crown (the upper part of the present Holy Crown) was placed on Stephen's head on Christmas Day, 1,000 A.D. Since that day the Holy Crown remained the symbol of supreme authority in Hungary.

Stephen now proceeded to consolidate his authority in the nation against protests by some malcontent chieftains. Among these were his uncle, Koppany (Kupa) and Ajtony, the Gyula of the Transylvanian Hungarian tribe. At times he resorted to measures which seem harsh by today's standards but were usual in his time. The result was the decline of the tribal system and the creation of a strong, united, prosperous nation.

He established a Catholic hierarchy by founding two archdioceses, eight dioceses, abbeys, monasteries and parishes. Among

King Saint Stephen (997-1038).

"Preserve everything that is Hungarian.
Without a past a nation has no future."

(From his "Admonitiones" to his son).

The Holy Crown

the heads of the dioceses, the archbishop of Esztergom has remained the head of the Catholic Church in Hungary ever since. The state organisation was based on the establishment of the "counties" ("comitatus": "megye" in Hungarian), which consisted, at first, of the domains of the crown (the properties of the king, enlarged by the properties confiscated from the rebel chiefs). They also included the uninhabited frontier areas, mostly wooded land. Each county was administered by a "count" ("comes"), appointed by the king. The number of these counties rose to 45 in Stephen's time and to 73 by the twelfth century, covering eventually the entire area of the country, not only the crown estates.

Stephen invited knights, priests, scholars and artisans from the western nations and provided them with privileges and estates for their services. Most of these "guests" stayed in the country and founded historic Hungarian families. The king's power was unlimited, similar to that of other medieval kings, but he listened to the advice of the leaders of the church and people. He maintained friendly political and family ties with many European rulers. One of his daughters, Agatha, married Edmund the Ironside's son, Edward, and became the mother of Queen Saint Margaret, wife of Malcolm III of Scotland.

There were few foreign wars during Stephen's reign. He dealt swiftly with an unprovoked German attack in 1030. Unfortunately, his only son to reach adulthood, (Saint) Imre (Emery) died in a hunting accident and Stephen's death (August, 1038) was followed by a period of internal strife.

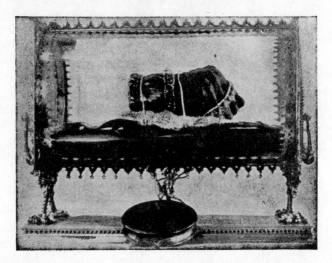

The preserved Holy Right Hand of St. Stephen.

While Stephen's successors (Peter, Aba Samuel, Endre I, Béla I, Solomon and Géza I) were busy quarelling about the succession, the ambitious German emperor, Henry III, seized his opportunity to make Hungary the empire' vassal. After many attempts, he eventually succeeded in making young king Peter swear loyalty to him in 1044. This cowardly act had, however, hastened Peter's downfall and his successor, Endre I, defeated the Germans and reasserted Hungary's sovereignty, which remained unchallenged until the XVIth century.

King **LADISLAS (LÁSZLÓ) THE SAINT** (1077-1095), son of the able but short-lived Béla I, a heroic and popular figure, represented the finest virtues of the medieval knight during his many battles against the eastern pagan invaders (Cumanians, Pechenegs, etc), whom he subsequently Christianised and resettled in the frontier areas. To counter this eastern danger, he

King Saint Ladislas (1077-1095).
(Silver herma by the Kolozsvári Brothers, cf, ch. 10)

encouraged the total Hungarian settlement of the unpopulated, wooded portion of the eastern region of the country (Transylvania) by founding two bishoprics there and granting privileges to the frontier settlers, the Székelys. He re-established internal order and by his clever family politics incorporated Slavonia and Croatia as autonomous provinces. At a Hungarian Church Council (in 1083) he decreed the canonisation of Saint Stephen and Saint Imre. The Pope immediately approved of this decision.

His nephew and successor, **COLOMAN (KÁLMÁN),** called **THE WISE** ("BOOKLOVER") (1095-1119), extended the power of the Hungarian state to the ports of the Adriatic. Kálmán was an enlightened man who modernised the country's laws. He forbade, among other things, the persecution of the "strigii" (a type of witch) who, he stated "did not exist" ("quae non sunt . . .". He died after a long illness, during which he became easy prey to the intrigues of his court and his family. The blinding of his brother Álmos, and of his nephew, Béla (for alleged conspiracy), was obviously not approved by this lenient and pious king. His wife's disgraceful behaviour may have given Kálmán second thoughts about the "witches that did not exist . . ."

After his death there was another period of internal struggle for the crown. The "Blood Treaty" — the basis of the Hungarian Constitution — had only stipulated that the sovereign should be a descendant of Árpád, but did not specify whether he should be the deceased king's brother or son. The renewed ambitions of the last great Byzantian emperor, Manuel (a grandson of Saint Ladislas by his daughter, Piroska or Saint Irene), added external problems to the internal ones.

The Byzantian pressure suggested closer contacts with the West, especially with France. Géza II (1141-1162), an ally of Louis VII of France, invited French monks (Cistercians) to settle in Hungary and encouraged Hungarians to attend French universities. During his reign many German, French, Italian and Flemish tradesmen, merchants and artisans settled in Hungary. The Vlach (Rumanian) shepherds began also to settle in the hitherto uninhabited mountain areas of Transylvania during this period.

Under the reign of **BÉLA III** (1172-1192) Hungary became the leading power in Central Europe, extending its frontiers beyond the Carpathians and well into the Balkan peninsula and the Adriatic coast. He maintained close family, cultural and political ties with France and ruled wisely over a nation which presented the best characteristics of a universal European culture, having assimilated the best of Italian, French, German and Byzantian contributions.

During the first two centuries of the Árpád kings, the central power of the king, firmly established under Saint Stephen, had gradually been reduced, with the diminution of the royal estates as a result of land grants to deserving subjects.

Thus, by 1222, the nobles, supported by the heir to the throne, Prince Béla, were strong enough to force king *ENDRE II* (1205-1235) to issue a charter of rights, called the GOLDEN BULL, which guaranteed personal freedom and other basic rights to all free members of the nation. This narrowed the gap between the rich barons and the poorer nobles and free men. The nobles — i.e. the nation — were also granted the right to resist illegal royal acts. This charter brought forth a rapid improvement of the position of the lower classes. Endre's other memorable achievement was his Crusade, for which he received the title of "King of Jerusalem". During one of his absences the Queen Gertrude was killed under obscure circumstances, possibly during a rising of the Hungarian nobles against the Queen's hated German courtiers.

When Endre died, Hungary had a population of over three million. This nation was a composite one: even the original settlers came from different races at different times as we have explained in chapters 1 and 3. The non-Magyar autochtonous population of the Carpathian basin joined the nation, but the largest group, the Slovaks, retained their national identity.

King Saint Stephen and his successors welcomed foreigners: they invited certain groups of western settlers and allowed the gradual immigration of others (eastern pagans, Slavs, Vlachs). Though originally all non-Magyars were serfs, their descendants could gain nobility or high offices in Church, military or royal service and many did. Many non-Magyars who lived in larger settlements, kept their national identity in matters of culture, language and religion but did not form separate political units.

Thus the Hungarian nation of the XIIIth century, blissfully ignorant of the legal and political complexities of national "minority" problems, lived in multi-lingual communities, the members of which considered themselves Hungarians, whether they spoke Magyar or Slovak or German or — as most educated people did — Latin. They all owed loyalty to one king and all had equal prospects of prosperity and advancement in their chosen country.

BÉLA IV (1235-1270) began his reign by attempting to restore a healthy balance of the rights of the various classes of the nation: he reasserted the power of the king and the right of the poorer freemen against the abuses of the rich barons. His honest efforts, however, alienated the barons — at a time when the nation faced the greatest danger in its European existence: the Mongol invasion.

The *Mongols* (erroneously called "Tartars" or "Tatars"), a Central Asian people related to the Turks, were members of a small, but crafty and violent tribe. Their chieftain, Ghengis

(Jengis) Khan (1162-1227), conquered the neighbouring (Tartar) tribes and extended his empire over most of Central and Northern Asia. His successor Ogotai (Ogdai) sent his nephew, Batu Khan, into Europe to fulfil the great Khan's dream of conquering the world. Batu crushed the Russian princes and by 1240 his huge army was ready to attack Poland and Hungary, the two great bulwarks of Christian Europe.

The studious and enlightened Béla knew more than most European princes about the Mongols and their intentions. He sent four monks to search for the Hungarians who had remained in the upper Volga-Kama area centuries before (see Chapter 1). Brother Julian did actually reach this "Magna Hungaria" and found that the population there had preserved their Hungarian language in spite of several hundred years of separation from their western brothers. Béla sent Julian back with missionaries — but it was too late. The Mongols had destroyed the Volga-Hungarian nation. The southern Cumanians were luckier: their king and some 40,000 families were able to escape the Mongols and, joined by other refugees, managed to reach Hungary. Here they were given refuge by the king.

Having gathered sufficient information about the Mongols, Béla began to prepare the country for the onslaught. He sent envoys to the Pope and the western kings, urging them to organise a crusade against these enemies of civilised mankind, but received only offers of prayers and good wishes in reply. The king's warnings were similarly ignored by most of Hungary's magnates: the sulking lords refused to mobilise their private banderia. So the king only had his royal army and the banderia of his office-bearers and prelates.

The Mongols regrouped their army outside the Carpathians. The bulk, under the leadership of Batu himself, was to attack Hungary from the east, the left wing, under Bedjak khan, to attack the Hungarians from the south (Transylvania) and the right wing (Orda khan) was to destroy the Germans and Poles (which they eventually did at Liegnitz), then to turn against Hungary, the main enemy. In March, 1241, Batu destroyed Palatin (Chief Minister) Dénes' troops defending the passes and crossed the Carpathians. On seeing the wounded Palatin — practically the only survivor of the battle — the lords began to mobilise their banderia. Duke Frederick of Austria, who had come with a small escort to "assist" Béla, captured a Mongol soldier during a skirmish. The soldier turned out to be a Cumanian (obviously one of the many auxiliaries the Mongols forced to march with them). Frederick, however, argued that the Cumanians were on the Mongol side and managed to incense the Hungarian nobles so much that they killed the Cumanian king. The Cumanians, furious at this treachery, rose against the Hungarians, then collected their families and left the country. Thus the Hungarians lost a potential ally, one familiar with the Mongol fighting methods.

Béla and his lords turned against the Mongols, who had reached the Danube north of Buda and had taken and completely destroyed the episcopal city of Vác, massacring the entire population. When attacked by the main Hungarian army of about 50,000, the raiders retreated swiftly — their usual strategy — enticing the Hungarian army toward Batu's main army.

Batu chose the area between two small rivers (Sajó and Hernád) near the village of *Mohi,* manoeuvring the Hungarians on to the swampy plain while the Mongol troops occupied the surrounding forested hills. The Hungarians who had not fought a major battle in centuries, failed to realise the trap and set up a hastily reinforced camp in the plain. Batu's seasoned troops moved according to the master plan and managed to surround the Hungarian camp unnoticed during the night. When the day of the battle dawned — April 11, 1241 — the Mongols attacked and Béla's heavily armoured knights were completely overwhelmed by the strange, oriental tactics of the enemy. The Mongols' fast-riding units moved in complete silence directed by mysterious signals only and supported by rockets and other puzzling devices, such as horsemen disguised as terrifying giants. They were aided by batteries of precision-shooting archers and they all fought like machines, with death-ignoring bravery. The Hungarians' medieval fighting methods and heavy armour were an added hindrance in the swampy terrain.

On that day, the arrogant lords, selfish prelates, quarrelling nobles and disgruntled knights of a divided nation found unity. loyalty and Christian humility during the magnificent hours of Mohi. They died bravely for a nation they had served so poorly during their lives. As they died, one after the other, the battle raged on. It was no easy victory for the Mongol. In fact, at one stage, Batu wanted to retreat and only the timely arrival of an encircling column kept him from giving the order.

One of the first Hungarians to die was the nominal commander, archbishop Ugrin of Kalocsa. The archbishop of Esztergom, Matthias, head of the Church followed him soon, and so did the other bishops and magnates. The Templar knights died to the last man without retreating an inch. Dénes Tomaj, the Palatin ("Nádor": Chief Minister) put on the king's regalia and rode against the Mongols at the head of the bodyguard into certain death: the Mongols wanted the king at any price. Béla, dressed in a simple soldier's armour, managed to slip through, accompanied by a few young nobles of his guard. All but two of the nation's high office-bearers died that day.

*   *   *

The Mongols, realising their mistake, set out in hot pursuit of the king and his wounded brother, Kálmán, king of Croatia. One after the other the nobles, escorting the king, gave up their horses, when the king's fell and stayed behind to delay the pursuers at the sacrifice of their own lives. Béla eventually reached the safety of the Danube.

In the meantime, the southern Mongol army overran Transylvania and the Great Hungarian Plain, annihilating the population to the last infant when they met resistance. An eye-witness, Canon Rogerius, who lived through the devastation hiding in the marshes, gave a harrowing account of the nightmarish atrocities of the Mongols in his "Carmen Miserabile".

Batu's victory was not complete: he wanted the Hungarian king, knowing that for the Hungarians the person of their sovereign was the symbol of the nation's independence. On arriving at the Danube, the king accepted the "hospitality" of his "ally", Frederick of Austria, who immediately imprisoned him and demanded, as his ransom, three counties of Hungary. After Béla's release, Frederick quickly plundered these three counties before the Mongols could "claim" them. Frederick's intervention was, incidentally, the only western "participation" in Hungary's life-and-death struggle. The Pope, the Emperor and the western kings were busy fighting each other. In fact the Emperor actually suggested that Béla "forget" the Mongols and join him in fighting the Pope . . .

Béla defended the Danube line against the Mongols skilfully until February 1242. Then, during the coldest winter the country had had for a century, the Danube froze and the mounted Mongols crossed it at several points. Unable to resist further, Béla fled to the Dalmatian coast. There, after a furious chase, he took refuge in an island fortress which the Mongols could not capture. Batu overran Transdanubia, but several fortresses managed to resist and survive.

Then blind fate — or Providence — came to the rescue of the lonely nation. Suddenly, in the spring of 1242, the Mongols turned around and began to leave the country. They moved as swiftly as they came, burning, looting and killing on their way; they drove with them herds of slaves, most of whom they killed when they left Hungary. Duke Frederick soon followed them in Transdanubia, completing the destruction of the western counties of Hungary.

Several reasons have been suggested for the Mongols' unexpected withdrawal. They may have found that they could not feed their army and horses, having wantonly destroyed their hinterland. They may have wanted to regroup and refresh their elite Mongol troops which had been decimated during their Hungarian campaign. We know that the great Khan, Ogatai, had died in 1241 and that Batu was one of his likely successors. This explains why he hastened back to Karakorum, their Asian capital, but it does not explain why he had to evacuate the country he had just conquered at such horrendous loss. In fact, most of the Mongols remained in southern Russia for many decades. They even made several attempts to return to Hungary during the following years.

Béla returned to find a devastated Hungary, populated by the pathetic survivors of the once great nation: they had taken refuge in swamps, inaccessible mountains or the few fortified towns the Mongols could not take, or in the loyal southern provinces of Hungary, such as Dalmatia, where the king had also found safe refuge.

Béla is rightly called the second founder of Hungary. The task of *reconstruction* was incredibly difficult. Knowing that the Mongols intended to return, he had fortresses and fortified towns built, encouraging the magnates to do the same and to equip their banderia. He granted municipal self-government to the larger towns with fortifications. Later he repeatedly rejected the Mongols' offers of an alliance against the West, knowing quite well that in the case of a renewed attack Hungary would be left to fight alone again.

His youngest daughter, Margaret (born during the Mongol siege), spent her life in a convent in voluntary sacrifice for the liberation of Hungary. She is known in the Catholic Church as Saint Margaret of the Árpads.

Béla welcomed foreign settlers as migrants to the devastated areas, among them the Cumanians, Jazighs and Pechenegs, refugees from Mongol devastated regions in the east.

*   *   *

After Béla's death in 1270 three weak kings allowed the magnates to recover their privileged status. Among these kings, *Ladislas IV* (1272-1290), called the "Cumanian" (his mother was a Cumanian princess), achieved a feat of great international significance but of doubtful benefit to Hungary. He defeated the Czech king, Ottokar, in 1278 in alliance with Rudolf Habsburg, thus helping to establish Habsburg hegemony in Central Europe.

By the death of *Endre III* (1301), the last of the Árpád kings, the barons were in the process of consolidating their feudal rule over their own lands. This development, though normal in medieval Europe, had harmful effects in Hungary which, being situated at the frontiers of the Christian world, did not enjoy the peaceful safety of sheltered Germany, France or England and needed therefore a strong central government.

The *dynasty of Árpád* ruled Hungary for 400 years. The five princes and 24 kings of the dynasty gave to the nation a new land, a new religion and a new civilisation and to the Church some twenty saints. During their reign Hungary remained a national state with its own independent policy and with a civilisation which was truly European and Christian but still characteristically Hungarian.

6. "I HIDE IN SONGS . . ."

(The ancient roots of Hungarian folk poetry)

Saint Stephen, in establishing western Christianism in Hungary, realised the dangers of the pagan poetic inheritance, the interpreter of the ancient religion. He countered it with western, Latin literacy and religious Latin-based education. His harsh action doubtless spared the nation the long, weakening agony of hesitation between the old and new cultures. A strong nation was needed to hold its own among the new nations of Europe, and it could not be fettered by lingering memories of eastern pagan traditions alien to the Hungarians' new environment.

Stephen had succeeded in creating a strong and vigorous nation, but in the process he and his Christian successors were instrumental in destroying a valuable poetic treasure which was the heritage of 2000 years of migrations. Fortunately, the destruction was not complete: there still remained some indestructible elements of the creations of the rich soul of this ancient people. Fragments of ancient songs, legends, chants, fairy tales and ballads continued to live by word of mouth only, often still containing words and phrases which have remained unintelligible.

Many of these fragments are found among the so-called *minstrel-songs*. Minstrelsy ("regölés" in Hungarian) is an old heathen custom, known to many ancient cultures in Europe, but Hungarian minstrelsy contains practices unknown elsewhere. One interesting fact is that it is still being practised in some villages (in Transdanubia and Transylvania).

Mysterious in itself is the Magyar word "regös", the name of the performer or singer. This obsolete word is a derivation of the verb "rejteni" (:to hide): thus: "regös" is the person who hides something, an interpreter of hidden things. He was once a singer endowed with talent akin to wizardry who could fall into a trance and foretell the future; he could communicate with the spirits of the dead and interpret their wishes. (Ancestor-worship was part of the ancient Magyar religion).

A "regös" song as sung today in Transdanubia presents an interesting text, full of half-forgotten pagan allusions and mentioning a "miraculous stag". It ends with the "regös" identification: "I hide in songs . . ." [1] The Transylvanian variation from the Székely region mentions the winter snowfall as "regös" singing is usually connected with the Christmas-New Year period. This, too, is mainly a good-wish song and the mention of the "ancient ones" and the "old law" clearly refers to the "ancient religion." [2] Christian elements are often mixed with allusions to pagan rituals. The Transdanubian song, for instance, refers to a "thousand mass-candles."

There are similarly mixed Christian and pagan elements in the Transdanubian "Whitsun-Queen" chant. At Whitsuntide (Spring in Europe) the girls elect a little girl "Queen", crown her with a flower-patterned head-dress and accompany her in a procession from house to house, chanting a well-wishing song similar to the "regös" song. Among references to the Christian significance of the day, they also sing about the Queen who "was not born of a mother . . . and grew up with the Whitsun dews of the rose-tree . . ."

The "shaman" — the wizard priest-doctor of the ancient Magyar religion — used to heal with chant and music. This ritual is remembered in the common children's ditty "Stork . . .", known everywhere in Hungary.[3] The Summer Solstice festival (June 22, St. Ivan's Day) has preserved the mating song about the "rutafa", a plant credited with magic qualities. This plant (whose botanic name is "Artemisia") is of a sub-tropical nature and does not grow in Hungary. This indicates a southern source of inspiration for some Magyar traditions, possibly Meso-potamia. [4]

The so-called "flower-songs" contain elements of more recent inspiration (XVIth century) but some of their allusions stem from a more ancient, pagan ideology. In one song, the flowers connected with Christian ceremonies are compared — unfavour-ably — with the pansy, the pagan symbol of love.

*   *   *

The above examples display some amazing qualities of the most ancient elements in Magyar folk poetry. These songs (fully quoted in the Appendix), were recorded in various regions of the country (often quite distant). They show a remarkable similarity of wording and content, conserved, apparently, for more than a thousand years. This durability of the text suggests a closer examination of the methods of the *propagation and preservation* of folk poetry.

The poet is anonymous. His environment is the real creator of the poem. Thus the poet does not reserve his rights, does not forbid the changing of the words (which is rarer) or the application of different melodies (which is more frequent). Many folksongs have "interchangeable" texts and melodies: as long as the rhythm is identical, the same texts may be carried by different melodies, and the same melody may carry different texts. The folk poem is preserved by verbal tradition only: it is either sung or recited, not written down. The recurring rhythm and rhyme patterns aid memorization of the text, even when it is in prose, such as the folk tales or stories which still present recurring rhythm patterns as a solid frame carrying the content.

The propagation is the task of the self-appointed and anonymous bards: story tellers, poetry tellers and singers, rustic Homers who, at village gatherings or festivals, in the spinneries and inns, would often recite or sing the folk songs and stories. The bard passes his art to someone else, usually a very young child who has the necessary talent and interest. So a young child often hears these stories and songs from his grandparents, conserves this treasure throughout his life and then passes it on to his grandchildren. A talented bard ("versmondó" or "énekes") may span five generations — 120 to 150 years — with his poetic heritage. Thus the poetic tradition of a thousand years may be preserved through the talents of only a few generations of story-tellers.

The regional propagation of folk poetry is facilitated by exchanges and meetings between isolated communities: market-days, pilgrimages, seasonal workers' movements, military service, domestic employment, trade apprenticeships and other movements.

The live presentation (singing or reciting often accompanied by mime or dance) adds beauty to the content. Rhythm and rhyme fulfil their original Homeric role: they are the framework and the musical accompaniment of the poem.

49

Due to their tragic historic circumstances, the epic poetry of the Hungarian people could never be gathered into a continuous epic collection as happened with Finland's Kalevala saga. The Mongol, Turkish and independence wars and the long Austrian-German oppression destroyed what might have been the Hungarian Kalevala, the epic legend with a history much more exciting than that of the Finns. Only broken fragments have remained, songs, legends, tales, chants and ditties, found in the remote areas of Transylvania and Transdanubia.

7. THE UNKNOWN BARDS

(Hungarian literature before the XVIth century)

Hungarians take pride in many artistic and historical achievements. While some of these claims may be somewhat exaggerated, the unbiased observer cannot help finding at least two fields in which the genius of this unique people has created values equal to the greatest human achievements. These are the fields of music and poetry. But while Liszt, Kodály and Bartók are known universally, as their art does not require translation, the creation of the Hungarian poets appeals only to the speakers of Hungarian and to the few foreigners who have learnt the language. Heine, the great German lyric poet of the XIXth century, learnt the language with the sole aim of reading Hungarian poetry. Very few foreigners feel such a strong motivation nowadays. For the others translations offer the only access to Hungarian literature.

When translated, however, Hungarian poetry loses much of its characteristic flavour: its rich imagery, the impact of its figures of speech, the easy flow of its flexible vocabulary, the musicality of its alliterations and assonances and the wide spectrum of decorative adjectives. The harmonious sequence of the clear vowels and melodious consonants together with the unusual rhythm caused by the accentuation of the first syllable in each word produce the impression of a cool, pure, harshly beautiful musical language, somewhat reminiscent of the untamed freshness of the folksong.

The same applies, to some extent, to prose. Historic novels, the most popular genre in Magyar prose, are just as difficult to translate as poetry. Jókai, Gulácsy, Makkai and Füry wrote epic poetry in prose form. The enjoyment of their art not only requires a knowledge of the imagery and semantics of the language, but also a deep understanding of the emotional patriotism of the Hungarians and, by the same token, some knowledge of their history: the bitter pride and sorrow of their romantic Christianity and their constant struggle in the defence of an ungrateful Europe.

The understanding of the Hungarian character, art and history will, therefore, make it easier for the reader of this book, to enjoy even translated Magyar literature, such as the extracts quoted in the Appendix.

It is a remarkable fact that, while Hungarian literature is hardly known outside its country of origin, foreign authors have always been translated into Hungarian with an amazing degree of understanding. Shakespeare has always commanded the Hungarians' admiration and the greatest poets made it their task of pride to translate some of his works. More Shakespeare plays are produced in Budapest than anywhere else in the world. French, Italian, Spanish and classical Greek and Latin poets are also popular and available in excellent Hungarian translations. The mysticism of the Germans and Russians does not seem to appeal to the same extent. The Magyar language is a particularly suitable vehicle for poetry translations. It can render both modern metres based on accent and ancient metres based on syllabic quantity and rhyme because of its flexibility of vocabulary and its clever use of prefixes and suffixes.

Another barrier between Hungarian and non-Hungarian readers is that of evaluation and emphasis. To the Hungarian, poetry is the bread and butter (bread and wine?) of the arts. No festival is complete without a recital of poetry. Editions of poetry run to the hundreds of thousands in a nation of 14 million and even so there seems to be a constant shortage of classics. There is not always a clear dividing line between prose and poetry. Many passages of novels, short stories and essays read like poetry and descriptive, narrative poetry — a very popular genre — often resembles, in its contents if not in its form, passages in novels or short stories.

Hungarian writing — poetry or prose — is the most cherished heirloom of Magyars everywhere in the world: it represents for them that mystic, unidentifiable notion which is Hungary.

*   *   *

Three poems, chosen from poets of various periods and differing themes, are given in the Appendix in Hungarian and English in order to give the reader a foretaste of the great wealth of Hungarian poetry.

The first, *"THE END OF SEPTEMBER"*,[1] is a love-elegy by the fiery poet of the Hungarian struggle for freedom, *Sándor Petöfi* (1823-1849). He wrote it to his young bride on their honeymoon, one of the few poets who wrote love poems to his own wife. His melancholic prophecy in the poem came true: he died in battle not two years afterwards and his wife did "abandon his name" — she remarried a few months after the poet's death.

The second poem is from *Endre Ady* (1877-1919), the mercurial genius of modern Hungarian literature. He was a lusty, melancholic, scolding poet of fiery images and the possessor of a vast vocabulary (some of it of his own making). In the vivid poem entitled *"THE OUTCAST STONE"*, he expresses his feelings about his impulsive fellow-countrymen. [2]

In the third poem, *"FOR MY BIRTHDAY"*,[3] *Attila József* (1905-1937), the tragic modern poet of the city, pours his heart into a defiant satire of his own hopes and frustrations on his birthday — a few weeks before his self-inflicted death.

The beginnings of Hungarian literature

Folk songs, legends, ballads and references in contemporary chronicles bear witness to the fact that poetry and descriptive literature were the constant companions of the Hungarians even before their arrival in the Carpathian basin.

There exist, however, few written texts of Magyar literature before the XVIth century. There are two reasons:

(a) With the introduction of Christianity, the King and the Church made Latin the official written language. Chronicles, official documents and laws were recorded in Latin. The art of the Hungarian-speaking minstrels (the "regös" or "igric") was not in favour, as the Church feared that their pagan-inspired songs and legends might endanger the recently, and rather reluctantly, accepted Christian faith. All we find in Latin chronicles of these times are some scornful references to the "silly songs and legends" of the minstrels.

(b) The second reason — a more tragic one — is that Hungary was twice devastated during her history, in the XIIIth, then in the XVIth - XVIIth centuries. No one knows what literary treasures were destroyed during these periods.

It is beyond the scope of our examination to study the Latin literature extant in the chronicles of the first five centuries of Christian Hungary, though they present the picture of a very rich medieval and Renaissance civilisation. The Latin poems of the humanist bishop, Janus Pannonius (Cseznicei) (XVth century) were well-known in the humanist world.

The earliest surviving text in Hungarian dates from the end of the XIIth century. It is the "Funeral Oration", written by an unknown monk. It displays remarkable qualities of style, proving that Magyar language literary activity must have reached a fairly advanced degree at that period.

The earliest written example of Hungarian *poetry* is the "Lamentations of the Blessed Virgin" ("Ómagyar Mária Siralom") from about 1270. It is an inspired hymn, characteristically in honour of the Virgin Mary, "Our Lady of Hungary". Legends of Saint Margaret (daughter of King Béla IV) and of other Hungarian saints were also written in Hungarian at the end of the XVth century.

Book printing began in Buda in 1473 (three years earlier than in England), while the first university was founded in 1367 (20 years before Heidelberg, Germany's oldest university). The first Hungarian translation of the Bible dates from 1430. A verse legend of Saint Catherine and hymns about Saint Ladislas are among the texts extant from this period . . . The impressive Hungarian re-creation of the popular "Dance of Death" poem in a codex (copied and possibly translated by a nun called Lea Ráskai) illustrates in its rhythmic prose the poetic potential of the medieval Magyar language.

Secular topics are treated in a few remaining examples of court poetry of the XVth century. The satire of Ferenc Apáti (around 1520) directs its witty criticism against prelates, aristocrats and peasant alike, unwittingly heralding the imminent great tragedy of Hungarian history, the defeat at Mohacs (1526).

8. THE MAGNIFICENT TWILIGHT

(The era of the Anjou and Luxemburg Kings)

After the death of the last Árpád King (Endre III) lengthy disputes followed in Hungary, but eventually the majority of the nation accepted Charles Robert of Anjou, Prince of Naples, as its ruler.

This was a fortunate choice, for *CHARLES ROBERT* (1307-1342), a descendant of Árpád on his mother's side and of the French Capetians on his father's side, became a good king and the founder of a short-lived but truly Hungarian dynasty. At the beginning, many rich magnates opposed his election and Charles had to enforce his rule with arms in several cases. In this task he received the enthusiastic support of the lesser nobles and freemen, who had been suffering from the tyranny of the semi-independent feudal barons during the preceding decades. Charles rewarded his loyal followers with the highest offices, giving the nation an entirely new, honest government of poor nobles.

In the characteristic Hungarian variant of the medieval State structure, the free members of the nation owed services to the King not through feudal tenure of their estates (for it was their freehold) but by virtue of the King's power, conferred on him by a nation which had freely elected him. A "feudal" relationship in the western sense existed only between the free members of the nation and their serfs, who worked as tenant (share-) farmers, paid one tenth of their produce to the landlord share-) farmers, paid one tenth of their produce to the landlord and one tenth to the Church. (They were better off than today's taxpayers). Otherwise they were free to change their landlords or enter ecclesiastical or military careers (as many did).

Charles Robert reorganised the nation's finances. By the economical use of the country's mineral wealth — almost all of it crown property — he made the Hungarian florin the most stable currency in Europe. Related by birth to the French and Spanish dynasties and by marriage to the Polish and Czech royal families, he used his family connections to extend Hungary's authority well beyond the frontiers. Under his rule Hungary became the most respected power in Central Europe, a leader of economic and political alliances such as the Czech-Polish-Hungarian bloc, a medieval "common market" created to counter German economic domination. The Polish-Hungarian alliance proved itself also during the common campaigns against Poland's pagan enemies and the quarrels with the Teutonic Knights.

His sumptuous court at Visegrád (north of Buda) represented the best of the western and Hungarian ideals of Christian chivalry and became a centre of late-gothic culture and knighthood.

*   *   *

Charles Robert's son, *LOUIS I (THE GREAT)* (1342-1382), inherited the crown of a prosperous, strong country. He was called the last of the knight-kings a truly Christian monarch, like his ideal, Saint Ladislas. He saw the danger of the Osmanli Turks' advance in the Balkans against the declining Byzantian empire. So he improved on his father's somewhat hesitant foreign policy and created in the south and north-east of Hungary a protective belt of vassal states under various degrees of Hungarian supremacy. After King Casimir's death, the Poles invited him to their throne (1370). During this successful (albeit short) personal union, the dual empire represented a giant zone of peace and prosperity between the east and west of Europe.

Ironically the Anjou kings of Neapolitan origin had little success in their dealings with their own home-state, Naples. Louis' brother, Andrew, had inherited the Neapolitan throne but he fell victim to the intrigues of the court (and of his own Neapolitan wife) and was eventually assassinated. Louis reluctantly led two campaigns into Italy to punish the criminals but achieved only partial success.

Louis was also a patron of arts and sciences, founder of the first Hungarian university at Pécs (1367).

Appointed by the Pope "Captain of Christendom" to head a crusade against the Turks, he led several victorious campaigns against them in Bulgaria with his Hungarian troops. He could

A knight of Louis I's court (mid-XIVth century)
(From the gothic statues found in Buda castle, cf Chapter 10).

not fully exploit these victories as the other Christian nations gave him no aid in the "crusade". Venice, the great sea-power actually supported the Turks.

Louis died in 1382 after a long illness, probably leprosy, which he had contracted during his campaigns. He had no male heir: only two daughters.

In the century which saw the twilight of the Middle Ages, the beginning of the Hundred Years' War at Crécy (1346), the internal wars in Italy, France and England, the struggle between the Pope and The Holy Roman Emperor, the "Black Death" (1347-1350) and the Turkish landing at Gallipoli, a prosperous and strong Hungary was the bulwark of stability, strength and peace in Europe.

*   *   *

As a mark of particular respect for Louis, the nation accepted, with some reluctance, the succession of twelve-year old *Mary* to the throne of her father. Her younger sister, Hedwig (Saint Jadwiga), inherited Louis' Polish throne. While the barons were looking for a suitable King-Consort for Mary, the temperamental dowager queen, Elizabeth, ruled in her daughter's name. This impetuous woman and her friend, the Palatin Gara, caused a series of tragic incidents. A pretender to the throne, the Neapolitan prince Charles of Durazzo, who was the favourite of the Croatian barons, was killed in Queen Elizabeth's court under obscure circumstances. In revenge, the Croatians abducted the two queens and eventually killed Elizabeth. On being freed from her captors, Mary married Prince Sigismund of Luxemburg, the son of the German emperor, who was thus accepted as King-Consort and, after Mary's death, as the ruling king.

SIGISMUND (1387-1437) was an energetic young man. Some Hungarian nobles refused to accept him for a long time, such as the legendary Kont of Hédervár and his 30 fellow nobles, who were executed for treason.

Soon after his ascension, Sigismund organised a crusade against the Turks with the participation (for the first and last time) of the great western powers: the French, the English and the Poles. However, the battle of Nicopolis (1396) was lost for the crusaders for lack of co-operation among the various Christian contingents.

After the defeat, Sigismund turned his attention to Germany. After the crown of Bohemia, he soon gained the crown of Germany and in 1414 was elected Emperor of the Holy Roman Empire. Upon his election he presided at the famous Council of Trent, trying to heal the ravages of the schisms, quarrels and internal wars of Christianity. He had the Czech reformer, John Hus, executed. This roused the Czechs and caused a long, bloody civil war in Bohemia, Sigismund's home-country.

Sigismund used Hungary's considerable economic, military and political resources in obtaining his goals in Germany, but cared very little for the country which gave him his strength. He gave up his plans to chase the Turks out of Europe. It was a tragic omission, as it was during this period that the Mongol ruler, Timur Lenk (Tamerlan) inflicted several crushing defeats upon the Turks in Asia and it would have been relatively easy to chase them out of Europe.

During his last years Sigismund tried to make up for his "absenteeism" and to befriend the Hungarians, but the resentful Magyars never quite accepted him as a truly Hungarian king.

*   *   *

János Hunyadi († 1456)

"We were enemies, but nevertheless, his death grieves me for the world has never seen a greater man".

(Sultan Mohammed II)

After Sigismund's death the Hungarians turned to their traditional friends, the Poles, and invited the brave Prince *Wladislas* (1440-1444) to the throne. Wladislas accepted the invitation and immediately undertook the struggle against the Osmanli empire with the assistance of the greatest Hungarian general, *JOHN HUNYADI.* This great soldier of the Turkish wars was a professional officer of humble origins. By 1441 he became the commander of the southern forces of Hungary and the richest landlord in the country. He used his immense fortune to finance his campaigns against the Turks. His victories contained the Turkish advance for decades. Hunyadi was the typical representative of the militant Christian Hungarian who united religious fervour with ardent patriotism.

By 1443 he had pushed the Turks back to Bulgaria and restored the rule of the friendly Serbian king, an ally of Hungary. Wladislas, following the Pope's call for yet another crusade, attacked the Sultan's army at Varna, in Bulgaria (1444). Though the Turks outnumbered the Hungarians and their allies four to one, Hunyadi's strategy seemed to win the day. Then the impetuous King charged the Turks at the head of his Polish and Hungarian cavalry — and lost his life as well as the battle. Hunyadi himself escaped with difficulty.

The infant Ladislas V (1445-1457) was elected king and during his infancy Hunyadi was elected Regent.

Sultan Bayazid conquered Byzantium (Constantinople, today Istanbul) in 1453. The Pope again urged the western nations to raise a crusade but this time no one came: the Hungarians were alone as Hunyadi wrote to the Pope: ". . . we only, left alone, have endured the fury of the war . . ." The Sultan led his huge army, reinforced with heavy artillery (a new feature on the battlefields of Europe) against Hungary.

Hunyadi and his friend, (Saint) John Capistrano, a Franciscan monk, hastily organised the Hungarians while the Pope ordered prayers all over Europe. Hunyadi's strategy, the blood of the Magyar soldiers and the prayers triumphed once more: the Turks were utterly defeated at *Nándorfehérvár* (today Belgrade) in 1456 and Europe could again breathe a sigh of relief. The Pope ordered that the bells should toll every day at noon in memory of Hunyadi's great victory.

There was rejoicing in Europe — but mourning in Hungary. On the morrow of the victory Hunyadi and his friend, the survivors of countless battles died, victims of the plague . . .

9. DARKNESS AFTER NOON

(Hungary's history from 1456 to 1540)

Matthias' "flamboyant" Empire

After Hunyadi's death in 1456, the king, Ladislas V, succumbed to the intrigues of his courtiers and perfidiously arrested and executed the great general's elder son, László. This understandably angered the nation so much that the king had to flee to Prague, the capital of his other kingdom, Bohemia. He took with him Hunyadi's second son, Matthias, as a hostage. A few months later king Ladislas died — ironically of the same plague that had killed John Hunyadi.

The nation, tired of the misrule of foreign kings and foreign courtiers, decided to elect the son of the country's greatest soldier as sovereign.

MATTHIAS I (or MÁTYÁS HUNYADI) (1458-1490) was only eighteen when he returned to Buda to become the country's greatest king. The brilliant and energetic young man began his reign by breaking up the cliques of some magnates opposing his election. He did this by using a judicious mixture of charm, strength and cunning: he simply moved his enemies to higher offices — away from the court, the seat of power. Thus he made his family's arch-enemy, Ujlaki, the king of Bosnia, Hungary's southernmost province. He had more trouble with his friends, especially with his domineering uncle, Mihály Szilágyi, who had been appointed regent during Matthias' minority. Matthias, made it abundantly clear that he was mature enough to rule alone and disposed of his impetuous uncle by making him Captain-General of the Turk-harassed southern frontier.

Then he dealt with the marauding Hussite Czech raiders in the north, recruiting the useful elements among the defeated raiders into his future mercenary army. From these adventurers he eventually formed the greatest mercenary troop of his era, called the "Black Army".

He stabilised the nation's *finances* by imposing upon the entire nation a fair and equitable system of taxation, based on each person's income, and complemented the royal revenue with the yield from the mines and crown-estates. In addition to these regular revenues, he also imposed special levies when the need arose. He was thus able to finance the "Black Army" and conduct his many campaigns without undue loss of Hungarian blood. The treasury, not the poor, bore the burden of his immense social and cultural expenditure, which raised the nation's economic and cultural standard above that of the rest of contemporary Europe.

Matthias understood the importance of urban development. By strengthening the status of the towns he added a powerful "third estate", the town burgesses to the other two estates (clergy and nobility). Promotion into this new "middle class" was made free to any serf who had the will and talent to improve his status. Had peaceful times followed Matthias' reign, Hungary would have built the most equitable and progressive social system in Europe. His legal reforms protected the lower classes, allowing them the right to appeal against the sentences of the baronial courts to the royal courts ("Tabula", "Curia"), which were headed by professional jurists (often of lower-class birth) or by himself.

Matthias' *foreign policy* disappointed those who expected him to continue his father's crusades against the Turks. He realised that the Magyar nation was not strong enough to chase the Turks out of Europe without bleeding to death in the process. He was also realistic enough not to count on the "help" of the West. So he prepared a long-range plan, aiming ultimately at possession of the crown of the Holy Roman Empire so that he could use the empire's military might to deal with the Turkish menace. As Hungary had never been a member state of the Empire, he tried to gain the crown of Bohemia which was one of the member states with the right to vote in the election of the Emperor. Thus he fought a long war against the king of Bohemia and his allies and also against

King Matthias (Mátyás) I (1458-1490)

Emperor Frederick, allying himself first with the one, then with the other. Eventually he managed to obtain the Bohemian crown — without the right to vote — and then he also conquered Austria from the Emperor — without decisively defeating him.

He also led short, mainly defensive campaigns *against the Turks* and managed to build up a defensive belt in the south with the inclusion of such vassal states as Bosnia, Serbia, Wallachia and others governed by his troublesome friends or placated enemies. He refused, however, to commit his beloved Magyars or expensive mercenaries to adventurous campaigns deep in Turkish territory.

Matthias, a son of the *Renaissance,* was a true and intelligent patron of art and literature. He had the castle of Buda rebuilt in French "flamboyant" style and gathered his humanist friends to court. His third wife, Beatrice, brought from Italy many artists and scientists who helped Buda to become one of the great centres of humanism. Matthias' library of illuminated codices, the "Corvina", was one of the largest in Europe. As part of his cultural programme, he founded a university in Pozsony (the third Hungarian university). Book printing began in Buda in 1473.

Matthias' apparent passivity in regard to the Turkish question, his obscure western policy and the increasing financial burdens resulting from his policies led to unrest among the magnates. Though Matthias managed to deal with these dissensions in his autocratic way, he soon found himself friendless among the barons.

Increasing loneliness cursed his *family life, too.* His first wife died while they were both still children. His second wife, Catherine, the daughter of the Bohemian king, died in childbirth together with the new-born child, a son. His third wife, Beatrice d'Este, Princess of Naples-Aragonia, bore him no children. Between his marriages he met Barbara Krebs, the daughter of the mayor of Breslau, who bore him a son. Matthias took his illegitimate son to his court, giving him a fine education and the title of a duke (John Corvinus). Not having any legitimate children, it was his wish to make the intelligent, courageous boy his heir and successor — an arrangement not unusual in those times.

By 1490 Hungary was a powerful state with a population of 4 million (the same as England) and Matthias, now fifty, was the most influential ruler of Central Europe. His far-reaching plans seemed to be approaching their realisation: he was king of Bohemia, Austria was a Hungarian province, the Turks had been chastised and he had powerful friends support-ing his imperial ambitions . . . Then, one day, while visiting

Hungarian-occupied Vienna, he fell ill and died under somewhat suspicious circumstances.

The dowager queen and the barons disavowed their previous promises and rejected John Corvinus, who would have made a better king than any of Matthias' successors — just as his mother would have made a better queen than any of Matthias' wives.

National self-destruction

The magnates wanted a weak king and the queen wanted a husband. Wladislas Jagello obliged in both respects and so he was elected king under the name *Wladislas II* (1490-1516). He married Beatrice in a sham ceremony, which was later annulled, disbanded the "Black Army" and promptly lost Austria. Otherwise he obligingly left the government of Hungary to the barons. The magnates, possessed by a madness of self-destruction, swept away the fine state structure of social justice and equal taxation, stripped the country of practically all revenues and defence ability. Instead they concentrated on endless and barren parliamentary debates with the representatives of the lower nobility over decisions which were rarely formulated and never respected. They then attempted to impose further tax burdens on the lower classes and the burgesses who refused to pay.

Then, in the face of the increasing Turkish menace, the Primate-archbishop, Cardinal Bakócz, received, in 1514, the Pope's authority to raise a crusader army. The poor nobles, over-taxed citizens of the towns and the serfs flocked to the army, which was placed under the command of an able officer, the Székely nobleman, *György Dózsa*. The barons became suspicious, besides they did not want to lose their serfs at the time of the harvest. They tried to restrict the recruiting and to penalise those who had already signed up. Soon clashes began and the crusaders (who called themselves "kuruc", a distortion of the Latin "crux": "cross") turned against the barons and prelates. Soon a full scale civil war broke out in the south between the barons of this region and the "kuruc". The Primate hastily withdrew the crusaders' commission but Dózsa still considered himself the king's commander and continued fighting the magnates who obstructed the army's movements with their own private troops. Battles of increasing vehemence were followed by retaliations of increasing cruelty on both sides. A few weeks later, the inexperienced kuruc army was crushed by the regular army of the governor of Transylvania, John Zápolya. The victor — who was destined to become one of the most fateful figures of Hungarian history — punished the captured leaders with the savage cruelty usual in the rest of Europe in those times, but which the humane Hungarians have found monstrous.

Subsequently the revengeful Diet — for once unified — inflicted various *restrictions upon the serfs,* whom they held responsible for the uprising (which, however, had been led by noblemen, burgesses and lower clergy). The worst of these measures was the abolition of the serfs' right to change their domicile. They were not condemned to "eternal servitude", as some prejudiced historians have mistranslated the words "perpetua rusticitas" (:"eternal farmwork"). The true meaning is that of their exclusion from other occupations, especially higher ecclesiastical careers. This was a censure of Cardinal Bakócz who was the son of a serf (as were many high dignitaries in Hungary). We also have to remember that at that time no European serf had a free choice of landlords; and they were all restricted to "farmwork", having much less chance than their Hungarian counterparts to gain higher offices. All these vengeful articles of law did was to deprive the Hungarian serfs of certain privileges they, and they alone, had enjoyed before the uprising.

The jurist Werböczi codified these and preceding laws in a remarkable legal work called *"Tripartitum",* a three- volume compendium of the *Hungarian constitution.* The work defines the "free nation" (i.e. the nobility), as one body, the "members of the Holy Crown", the symbolic source of all law and power. The nobles elect the King and invest him with sovereign powers through the coronation. Legislation is exercised in the Parliament (Diet) by the King and the nobles.

The less theoretical — and more unfortunate — part of the Tripartitum summed up the privileges of the nobility. Apart from repeating the legal safeguards already codified in the Golden Bull of 1222, the compenduum emphasises that the noble does not pay taxes and has no obligation to render military service, except in a defensive war. The right to resist "unconstitutional" royal acts was also reaffirmed.

The flexible interpretation of "defensive military service" and the exemption from taxes were soon to bring catastrophic results to the nation, which was by then facing the greatest trial of its existence: the onslaught of the Ottoman (Turkish) Empire. The Tripartitum and the nobles' vengeful attitudes, were stripping the nation of its ability to levy taxes, to raise an army and, especially, to rely on the patriotism of the oppressed peasant in war and peace.

Mohacs

LOUIS II (1516-1526) was only ten when he succeeded his father. During the years of his minority, his relatives and courtiers ruled the country in his name.

In 1521 Nándorfehérvár (then a Hungarian frontier town, today Belgrade), the scene of Hunyadi's great victory fell to the Turks. Even this key defeat failed to arouse the nation, which was in the grip of constant power struggles. The treasure was empty (the nobles did not have to pay taxes, the others could not). The barons refused to believe in the seriousness of the Turkish danger and refused to mobilise their own troops. Pál Tomory, a former professional soldier and Franciscan monk, now archbishop of Kalocsa, had been appointed Captain-General of the southern frontier. He had only his own finances and the help of the papal nuncio, Burgio, Hungary's true friend.

The destructive power-struggle was in no way an isolated phenomenon in Hungary. All over Europe class and religious wars, peasant wars and ferocious retributions of apocalyptic magnitude heralded the downfall of the gothic order of the Middle Ages. These senseless wars surpassed Hungary's mercifully short peasant war of 1514 both in cruelty and in duration. Any European country would have collapsed if the Turks had been able to turn their armies against them. It was Hungary's geographical tragedy to be situated in the path of the Ottoman aggression.

Convinced by Tomory of the magnitude of the danger, the intelligent young king began to send desperate messages to the Christian rulers of the West, asking for help against the Moslems. "His Most Catholic Majesty", Charles V, who ruled the largest empire the world had yet seen, the Holy Roman Empire, promised to pray for him, but he was too busy fighting France's Francis I ("His Most Christian Majesty"). Francis had already made a secret pact with the Turks, urging them to attack Charles' empire through Hungary. Henry VIII ("The Defender of the Faith") replied that he was having "domestic trouble" — the understatement of the century. The important "Christian" sea-power, Venice, had long been in open alliance with the Turks.

Hungary stood alone, divided, paralysed, condemned. In the spring of 1526, Suleiman the Magnificent set out from Istambul with an army of 300,000 to conquer the world. The Ottoman army crossed into Transdanubia practically unopposed. King Louis left Buda at the head of his guard — a pathetic 4,000. Some prelates and barons, on learning this, mobilised their own troops and joined the king. John Zápolya, the richest baron of the country, had 40,000 troops but showed no haste to join the royal army.

The Hungarians, totalling about 26,000 with late reinforcements and armed with 50 old cannon, decided to wait for the Turks on the plain of *Mohács,* near the Danube, in Transdanubia. Having decided that it would be "unchivalrous" to attack the Turks while they were struggling to cross the marshy terrain, they watched with detached interest the deployment of the huge army and 300 heavy cannon on the advantageous hilly part of the plain. They also decided not to wait for Zápolya's army but to attack the Turks immediately. Whatever other faults the Hungarians have, timidity has never been one of them.

It was the *29th of August, 1526,* the Feast of Saint John the Martyr. When the Hungarians decided to attack, the young bishop Perényi remarked: "Let us rename this day the Feast of 20,000 Magyar Martyrs."

Tomory's impetuous cavalry (the "hajdus") attacked and broke through the first Turkish lines. In that moment, the young King, (he was 20), exuberant with the strength of his newly found confidence, took command of his guard and led them against the Turks, who remembered the lesson of Varna, where Louis' predecessor lost the battle for the Hungarians by his suicidal charge. The Turks concentrated on Louis' bodyguard, which was wiped out, and the wounded King escaped with great difficulty. The attacking Hungarian cavalry was then cleverly lured into the murderous fire of the Turkish cannons and the musket fire of the elite Janissaries. Tomory and the other leaders died fighting. In little more than two hours the battle was over. About 16,000 Hungarians died and two thousand taken prisoner were killed after the battle. The rest escaped under the cover of a sudden rainstorm. Two archbishops, five bishops (including the young prophet, Perényi), and most of the high dignitaries were among the dead.

The wounded king was on the run, escorted by two of his bodyguards. As he crossed a flooded creek, he fell off his horse and his heavy armour dragged him down. He drowned and his body was only found days later. The last Jagiello king of Hungary has joined the "twenty thousand Magyar Martyrs."

Two kings

The loss of life at Mohács was not irreparable. Hungary still had larger, undefeated armies. However, the fact that the King and most of the nation's leaders were lost had such a paralysing effect that Hungary never recovered from the effects of this disaster.

Many of the rich magnates and nobles, who had so criminally mismanaged the country's affairs, had atoned for their mistakes in full. They did not know how to live for their nation — but they certainly knew how to die for it magnificently. Unfortunately, while many brave young men died, some of the evil old men managed to survive to continue their destructive intrigues, such as the Palatin, Báthori and the enigmatic Zápolya. The lesser nobility of the counties had sulkingly stayed away from the battle — as did the peasants. They were all to pay later: the burden of the coming 160 years was to be borne by the poor nobleman and the peasant.

The battle of Mohács was a strictly aristocratic parade, the last, splendid, foolhardy charge of medieval knights led by a brave, young King. There was hardly an aristocratic family left without at least one fallen hero at Mohács. Some great families were completely wiped out at Mohács and in the years following it.

Suleiman could not believe that this small, suicidal army was all that powerful Hungary could muster against him, so he waited at Mohács for a few days before moving cautiously against *Buda*. The young queen had already fled with her German courtiers to her brother, Ferdinand of Austria (without even waiting to find out whether the king was dead or alive).

Buda was undefended; only the French and Venetian ambassadors waited for the Sultan to congratulate him on his great victory. The Turks ransacked Buda and returned to the south with 200,000 slaves — the first of the millions who were to pay for the sins of their ancestors. Zápolya and his army — almost twice the size of the King's — stood at Szeged, practically watching the Turks move home with their booty.

Zápolya had always wanted to be King. Now with Louis II dead, he had no difficulty in convincing the few remaining magnates that he was the right choice for a King. He was crowned by one of the surviving bishops as *JOHN I* (1526-1540). He was the last of the Hungarian-born Kings — and probably the least. That foolhardy Polish boy at Mohács was much more of a Hungarian than the cruel, cunning, cowardly John could ever hope to be.

Queen Mary's brother, Ferdinand of Habsburg, promptly claimed the Hungarian throne by virtue of his double relationship to the deceased King. His sister, Mary, was Louis' queen and Louis' sister, Anne had married Ferdinand. Thus Anne was the only "Hungarian-born" queen in the nation's history. The fact that she had lived in Vienna since her childhood, that she could not speak a word of Hungarian and that she hated Hungarians made the irony even deeper: the daughter of a "Hungarian" king (Wladislas II), she was the pretext for the Habsburgs to gain their 400 years' rule over Hungary.

Ferdinand managed to gain the support of a large segment of the aristocracy (many of whom had promptly deserted the cowardly John) and soon he, too, was crowned as *FERDINAND I* (1526-1564).

Thus the country had two kings — a divided and confused leadership. The barons continued their self-destructive policy of squabbles and quarrels while the Turks stood in the south, probably wondering what could have happened to Matthias' great nation. This tragic division, more fatally than Mohács, ended five centuries of Hungarian independence. The entire Carpathian basin became a power-vacuum, the open freeway of external aggressions.

Thus Mohács, the "tomb of our national greatness" (as the Hungarian poet put it), also marked the end of a peaceful, independent Central Europe.

10. THE SPLENDOUR, THAT WAS...

(Hungarian art before the sixteenth century)

The ornamental articles of metal, horn and leather found in the graves of the *Magyars' ancestors* show a remarkable degree of artistic interest and talent. One can detect a strong Caucasian (Alanian)-Iranian-Mesopotamian influence upon the basic Turkic-Ugrian motifs.

The richest collection of such articles is the so-called "Nagy-szentmiklós treasure". These articles are believed to have belonged to one of the pre-settlement Princes. They show the Magyars' highly developed artistic taste, an interesting synthesis of cultural influences of the migration period. This characteristically Magyar style is different from that of the Central European neighbouring peoples.

The graves of the Avar-Magyars of the VIIth-IXth centuries in the present Hungarian settlement area also show a high degree of decorative artistry, akin to the famous Scythian metal ornaments with Mesopotamian-Iranian inspired figure symbolism.

The earliest Hungarian settlements in the Carpathian area were often built on the sites of Roman towns. The settlers frequently used stones, carved capitals of columns and other material taken from the impressive remnants of Roman buildings.

The influence of the western Christian art style, called *ROMANESQUE,* dominated the architecture of the first churches and castles, built in the Xth century, such as the Arch-abbey of Pannonhalma and the royal castles of Esztergom and Székes-fehérvár. The *Byzantian* influence was also considerable in orna-mentation, but sometimes also in style, as was the case of the first Gyulafehérvár cathedral in Transylvania. The best

Gothic fragment (Buda castle, XIIIth-XIVth century).

surviving examples of the later Romanesque style are the churches of Ják, Zsámbok and Lébény (of the XIIIth century).

Some fragments of Romanesque and early Gothic fresco painting are found in the ruins of the Esztergom castle and in the undercrofts of some village churches.

Early French-Burgundian *GOTHIC* reached Hungary during the reign of Béla III (1172-1192), who married a French princess.

Gothic *SCULPTURE* survived in some places after the Mongol devastation (1241) mainly as a decorative element and relief-carving. The first sculptors in the modern sense were the

Kolozsvári Brothers, who made the first free-standing bronze statues around 1370. Only one of the monumental statues has survived, the equestrian statue of Saint George (in Prague). They were probably the creators of the silver "herma" of Saint Ladislas (in Györ). The large number of pre-Renaissance stone sculptures found recently during excavations in Buda castle show a remarkably high degree of artistic taste and workmanship. They prove that Hungarian artists of the time of Louis the Great (1342-1382) possessed consummate technical mastery and originality of expression in creating true portrait-sculpture; and this in an era (long before Donatello) when sculpture was still little more than an ornamental extension of architecture.

The characteristic gothic art of *miniature-painting* left fine examples in the "Illuminated Chronicle" of Miklós Medgyesi (1370).

Some beautiful examples of the High Gothic period have survived in the areas not devastated by the Turks, such as the cathedrals of Kassa, (1395), Kolozsvár and Brassó. The royal castles of Visegrád and Diósgyör and later Buda were built in late gothic-early Renaissance style during the reign of the Anjou kings (XIVth century). Late gothic painting flourished under Sigismund (early XVth century). Well-known Hungarian painters of this period were Thomas Kolozsvári, Jakab Kassai, Pál Löcsei and the greatest master-painter and wood carver, who only signed his work with "M.S." Beautiful examples of decorative gothic sculpture can be seen in the Bártfa and Kassa churches together with some remarkable wood-carving by some of the above mentioned artists. While most gothic structures show French influence, some churches in the west of the country were influenced by the Austrian-German gothic style.

Wood-carvings and panel painting, forms particularly suited to the Hungarian taste, have survived in many village churches, often the work of anonymous folk-artists. Hungarian *goldsmiths* developed the "filigree enamel" technique, creating a singular style of their own which they used on chalices, hermae and book-covers (Suky-chalice, XVth century).

King Matthias (1458-1490) was a lavish and knowledgeable patron of the arts. Hungary experienced the full impact of the *RENAISSANCE* under his reign, especially after his marriage to the Italian princess Beatrice. Many Renaissance artists worked

73

The Abbey of Ják.
(Built between 1230-1256)

Saint Elizabeth cathedral, Kassa.
(Built between 1385-1402)

in Matthias' court and directed the rebuilding of Buda castle in "flamboyant" French gothic style with Renaissance ornamentation; they also worked on the Cathedral of Our Lady (the "Coronation" or "Matthias" church). An increasing number of talented Hungarian artists worked under these Italian masters and gradually took over. At the same time, Hungarian artists went to Italy to develop their talent, for instance the well-known "Mihály of Pannonia".

At the height of the Renaissance, in Matthias' later years and during the period before Mohács (1526) both the aristocracy and the people used Renaissance inspiration in building, painting and wood-panelling. Examples are found in the carving of some Transylvanian churches, and in wood-carving in the so-called "Báthori Madonna". In industrial arts and crafts the synthesis of Italian and Hungarian inspiration became more and more evident.

The inspiration of Renaissance art — so close to the pomp-loving artistic soul of the people — spread well beyond the "flamboyant" gates of Buda castle. It soon conquered the imagination of the peasant, for whom it seemed to revive the reflection of a long-forgotten eastern exuberance of colours and shapes. In its many facets, folk-art still preserves this Renaissance inspiration to the present day.

During the Turkish wars, artistic activity existed only in the non-occupied areas. In the western frontier area Italian influence prevailed (Siklós), while in the north German-inspired gothic coexisted with Italian Renaissance until the arrival of the Catholic-Austrian inspired Baroque.

In Transylvania, under the independent Princes, a late Hungarian Renaissance style developed, the *"TRANSYLVANIAN RENAISSANCE"*'s a colourful synthesis of western and Hungarian urban and folk artistry. In the large cities of Transylvania, and in the country castles and even in village architecture, the copious use of flower-motifs gave this style later the name of the "Flowery Transylvanian" style. The Renaissance ornamentation was enriched even more by Turkish motifs, blending with Magyar folk-motifs into a distinctive Magyar-Transylvanian folk art.

Renaissance art, born in princely castles, reached the poor villages and has lived since in the Magyar peasants' royal hearts.

The Virgin Mary and Elizabeth.
(By M.S., around 1500).

Most of the great creations of these periods were destroyed by the Mongols and the Turks. By a cruel turn of fate, the areas left untouched by these destroyers were allotted to the succession states in 1920 under the Treaty of Trianon. Thus Hungary today possesses but a few pathetic relics of the splendour that was Hungarian art during the first seven centuries of the country's existence.

II. WHERE EAST IS WEST

(The people, customs and folk art of the Transdanubian region)

Settlement, towns

Transdanubia — the region "Beyond the Danube" (in Hungarian: "Dunántúl") is the area enclosed by the Danube and Drava rivers and the foothills of the Alps. It was once a province of the Roman Empire called Pannonia. The ruins of the Roman cities still attracted the Magyars who settled there after the VIIth century: they often built their towns on the sites of Roman centres and used stones from Roman temples when building their cathedrals. The ornate sarcophagus of Saint Stephen was, for instance, made from an ancient Roman tombstone. This treatment compares interestingly with the Turks' use of the sarcophagus. They threw the King's body out of it and used it as a horse-trough.

Transdanubia had the only "open frontier" of the former Hungarian Kingdom, which was enclosed by the Carpathians and the large rivers in the south. This geographic factor has brought about a stratification of regional characteristics among the Magyars born and educated in Transdanubia. They have always represented the search for western culture, Christianity (Catholicism), love of art, science and western technology. In politics they usually sought the ways of peaceful co-operation and understanding as opposed to the fighting spirit of the Great Plains Magyars or to the astute and proudly independent spirit of the Transylvanians.

We shall mention some towns and regions of particular historic or cultural interest.

PÉCS, in the south of the region, the largest and probably the oldest town in Transdanubia. It had been a Celtic settlement before the Romans, who named it "Sopianae". Saint Stephen founded one of the first bishoprics here and the cathedral was built on the ruins of an earlier Christian basilica. The first Hungarian university was founded here in 1367. Near Pécs lies the old castle of *Siklós* with its gothic chapel and Renaissance ornaments. The castle-fort of *Szigetvár* bears witness to the heroic battle in 1566 when 1000 defenders held up Sultan Suleiman's immense army for weeks. *Mohács* on the Danube was the scene of the great military disaster in 1526.

Further to the north lies *SZÉKESFEHÉRVÁR* the old royal city. Saint Stephen called it Alba Regia and established his royal capital here. This city and its magnificent basilica remained the coronation and burial place for some 36 kings. Parliaments met here until the XIVth century. At the end of the 160 years of Turkish occupation nothing remained except the ruins of the old basilica, blown up by the Turks. They had ransacked the royal tombs and thrown out the bodies. To the north is the small town of *Zsámbék* with its beautiful XIIIth century Romanesque abbey.

ESZTERGOM lies on gently rolling hills on the south bank of the Danube. In Charlemagne's time it was the easternmost outpost of the Empire, called "Oster Ringum". This name was later magyarised in its present form. After the settlement of the country this city became the seat of the ruling chieftains and remained the Árpád kings' administrative capital during the Middle Ages. The hill is crowned by the massive basilica, Hungary's largest church, built in the XIXth century. The left aisle incorporates the so-called "Bakócz chapel", the only intact Renaissance structure in the country. The town itself contains the Christian Museum in the Primate's Palace, rich in early works of Hungarian and Italian masters.

GYÖR is situated on the banks of the Danube at the confluence of two smaller tributaries. Built on the site of Roman Arrabona, it became one of Saint Stephen's early bishoprics. Among the few remaining treasures of the city is Saint Ladislas' silver herma, an invaluable example of XIVth century Hungarian Gothic art. South of Györ lies *Pannonhalma,* the Benedictine Arch-abbey, founded in the Xth century.

In the north-west of the region, near the historic fortress-town Komarom, lies the small township *KOCS*. During the XVth century, the wheelwrights of the town began to build a horse-drawn vehicle with steel spring-suspension. This "cart of Kocs" (pron. "coach") as the Hungarians called it ("kocsi szekér") soon became popular all over Europe. Practically all western languages borrowed the Hungarian town's name to describe this new type of vehicle: "coach" ("Kutsche", "coche" etc.)

On the western border lies *SOPRON,* built on the site on an ancient Celtic centre. This is probably the only city in Hungary never destroyed by an invader. Near Sopron lies the town of Fertöd-Eszterháza with the sumptuous castle built by the Eszter-házy princes in the XVIIIth century. The great composer Haydn spent many years there as court musician. Around *Kapuvár* a characteristic folk-art style has remained in some villages. The Lébény Benedictine abbey was built in Romanesque style in the XIIIth century.

In the south-west area lies the city of *SZOMBATHELY,* the Roman Sabaria. It had been an important Christian centre before the Hungarian settlement. Nearby, at *Ják,* stands the largest remaining Romanesque building in Hungary, the twin-towered abbey built in 1256. North of Szombathely, near the border lies the town and castle of *Köszeg* where the Turks' huge army was held up for a month by a small garrison of defenders who thus frustrated the entire Turkish campaign and saved Vienna. (1532).

The *Bakony* mountains lie north of the lake Balaton. The dense forests once used to serve as hiding places for the "betyár", the outlaws who play an eminent part in the folklore of this area. *Zirc,* in the heart of the region, is a Cistercian abbey, founded in 1182.

Veszprém, the picturesque (cultural and religious) centre of the Bakony region, was one of the first bishoprics founded by Saint Stephen.

In the *Balaton* lake area one finds many places of cultural and folkloric interest. The Benedictine abbey of Tihany has preserved, in a Latin document (1055), the oldest recorded Magyar language words. The tomb of Endre I has remained intact in the crypt of the abbey. Keszthely, on the western shore of the lake, is the site of Europe's first agricultural college.

81

Population, folk-culture regions

The population of Transdanubia is predominantly Magyar. After the settlement this region was inhabited by the most important tribes. The few remnants of autochthonous pre-settlement population were soon assimilated (some of them had already been related to the Magyars anyhow). The German settlers invited by the Árpád kings formed the only exception in this otherwise homogeneous population. The eastern half of the area suffered from the 150 years of Turkish occupation but the western part remained more or less undamaged.

Within the area, we can distinguish certain *folk-culture regions,* small districts with characteristic folk traditions. They are the results of certain geographical, social and historical conditions which imposed isolation or a certain type of occupation on the population.

South of Szombathely, near the Austrian border, is the area of about a hundred villages called *GÖCSEJ.* This region, formerly isolated by swamps, has kept many old customs, songs, dances and artifacts connected with their mainly pastoral occupations, and a characteristic dialect.

A smaller group of villages near the western border is inhabited by the descendants of frontier guards, possibly Pechenegs (Besenyö: a race related to the Magyar), settled here in the IXth century as frontier guards. This occupation is remembered by the name of the area: *"ÖRSÉG"* ("Guards"). A watchtower-like superstructure on some houses is a reminder of the inhabitants' original occupation.

The *SÁRKÖZ* district, near the Danube in the south-east, is a fertile area, inhabited by prosperous peasants who spend their surplus revenue on colourful costumes and artifacts — they could do worse with their money. We shall look at the Sárköz folk art later in this chapter.

One region merits our closer attention: the *"ORMÁNSÁG",* consisting of about forty villages situated on the plain stretching along the northern banks of the Drava river. The floods of the unruly river had created large marshy areas around the slightly elevated hills on which the villages were built. The peasants have developed a unique method of protection against the floods. From the earliest times they have built their houses on flat, heavy oak-beams placed on the surface instead of foundations dug into the ground. The house itself had solid timber walls with an adobe cover, held together by crossbeams parallel to the foundation beams. The outbuildings were built the same way. When the floods began to threaten the village, they placed rollers under the foundation beams, harnessed teams of oxen before the house and moved it to higher ground.

The most important — and tragic — social development began at the end of the XIXth century: the size of the arable land which formed the property of the former serfs (liberated in 1848) was limited and there was no way of enlarging it. As the young peasants were unwilling to leave their village and marry elsewhere, the heads of the families began to impose the disastrous policy of "egyke" ("only child") upon the community, and this soon became the accepted social rule. It became customary to have only one child per family and to prevent the birth of the others by abortion. When this single child grew up, he or she was married to another single child and the two family properties were united. Sometimes the "egyke" died before marriage. As a result, whole families died out and their properties were then bought up by new settlers, mainly Germans.

There is a moral in this somewhere for the advocates of "zero population growth"!

Another — happier — result of the villagers' long isolation was the creation of a characteristic folk-culture. The families' preoccupation with the happiness of their few children resulted in the encouragement of playful and artistic occupations for them. The village often rented a house (there was no shortage of vacant houses . . .) as a "playing house", a sort of "youth centre" where the children could play and the young adults could meet. Thus there was no need to go to another village to look for a spouse. Adolescents' entertainments included such tempting games as "falling into a well": a lass or lad had to be "pulled out of the well" by the means of giving a kiss to the "rescuer" for each fathom given as the depth of the well. Consequently, Ormánság seemed to have the deepest wells in Hungary — and the least number of young people leaving their villages to marry elsewhere. There may be a lesson here too. . .

The period of isolation also created a treasure of folklore. Stories about the "betyárs" are still popular, especially the ones about Patkó Pista, who disappeared without trace, leaving behind a number of lovers and legends. At carnival times young lads in humorous disguises invade the villages and play practical jokes on people (such as taking a coach to pieces and re-assembling it in some inaccessible place). At New Year's Eve girls play guessing games, hoping to foretell the future, especially their future husband's name. (They need not bother: their parents probably know it already . . .)

Many customs are connected with death and funerals: a sadly symbolic trait among these dying people. Professional mourners are engaged at funerals, old women who praise the dead in long, wailing songs. The relatives themselves are not supposed to show grief. After the funeral a lavish wake is held. The folk attire is characterised by white: older women and the mourners often wear white. These customs seem to be evocative of ancient Asiatic rituals, just as the custom of the movable house seems to be reminiscent of nomadic times. The predominance of white in folkwear has resulted in exceptionally high standards of cleanliness.

Folk art

Transdanubia, Hungary's West, has produced folk art just as genuinely Magyar as the eastern regions, but this art shows a harmonious synthesis of the ancient, characteristic Magyar elements and of the effects of western influences: here Magyar East met Magyar West.

Western medieval (Gothic) art left its mark in geometrical patterns used in ornaments. The Renaissance left its deep impression here, too, as everywhere else among the Magyar people. The Italian-Renaissance flower clusters and colours are found on folk dresses everywhere. The arcaded porches of the farmhouses and the herdsmen's carvings both show Renaissance design. Because of the closeness of the Habsburg-Catholic influence, the effect of the Baroque is more marked than elsewhere and can be seen in ornamental furniture carvings in the south. Even some Turkish influence can be detected in folkwear orna-mentation, though the Turks were hardly their favourite people.

Some of the memorable forms of folk art are: *CARVING,* which used to be a herdsmen's art and flourished mainly in the Bakony region and in Göcsej. The materials were wood, horn and bone, and the objects were mostly those used by the shepherd: staffs, musical instruments, vessels.

The *POTTERY trade* in some western towns dates from the times of the settlement and has followed the medieval system of guild-towns: the entire population of each town practised a particular craft.

The *Sárköz* district is the richest centre of *DECORATIVE FOLKWEAR*. Their special type of weaving (pillow-slips, bed-spreads, tablecloths) covers the entire cloth with patterns showing birds, hearts, stars and geometrical patterns. The people are also accomplished embroiderers, their main colour scheme being white on black (the combination preferred by the equally aristocratic Matyós in Northern Hungary).

For their dresses the Sárköz peasants use expensive material: brocade, cambric, silk. The most characteristic part of their dress is the fourfold silk shawl. The colour scheme and shape of the head-dress indicate the age and status of women. The shift (of Renaissance design) is made of very fine material called "száda".

At *Kapuvár* (in the north-west) even some men wear traditional costumes. The girls wear blouses instead of shifts. A shawl tied to the shoulders is worn under a velvet or silk blouse. The skirt (brocade or velvet) is folded in large pleats. The apron is irridescent silk with lace trim. Three to four bead strings are worn around the neck.

The originally Slovak village *Buzsák* is famous for its fine embroidered pillow-slips.

Ornamental art is often used on festival occasions with a symbolic meaning. In the Sárköz, the "tree of life" — an artistic carving of a tree — is given to a young bride. This motif is of Mesopotamian origin. When a young woman dies, all her fine dresses are buried with her. At Csököly the shroud and the funeral pillow show the woman's age and status. When a young, unmarried girl dies, elements of the wedding ceremony are combined with the funeral customs and she is buried in a bridal dress. Some expensive articles are only used once a year, such as the "Christmas cloth" or the glazed dishes used at weddings.

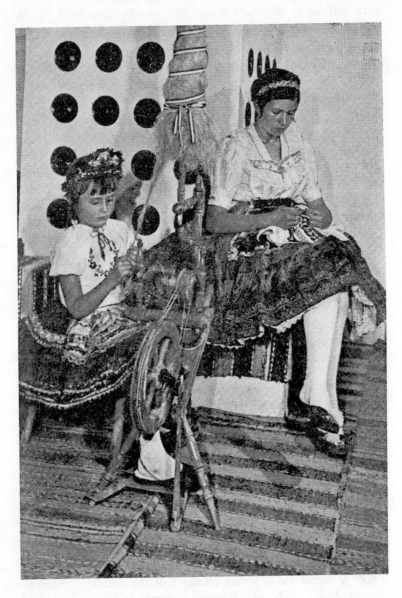

Sárköz folkwear

Folk customs

Transdanubia has preserved a rich folklore in spite of the western influence and the Turkish wars. This miraculous survival of old tradition, going back to pagan times, can be understood if we remember the particularly strong Magyar character of the population of this region. This ancient folk element resisted German influence and Turkish oppression with the help of the natural environment, which favoured the isolation and preservation of small settlements and cultural regions. We shall mention here some of the characteristic Transdanubian folk customs.

Minstrelsy ("regölés") still exists in the western counties. Around Christmas and New Year, boys or men form groups and go from house to house to sing their good wishes. (Cf. Chapter 6). The minstrels carry strange musical instruments: a stick with a chain and a pot covered with taut, thin skin with a long reed stuck in it. When drawn with a wet finger, this produces a strange, droning noise. Other instruments (bells etc.) are sometimes added. The "regös" often dress up as animals: bulls, stags and goats.

The charming custom of the *Whitsun-Queen* procession is undoubtedly of pagan origin. (Cf. Chapter 6). In some areas there is also a "Whitsun King" election or rather a competition among the lads for the title. The winner holds the title for two days with such privileges as free drinks and first dances at weddings and balls.

The Mohács *"buso"* procession claims to celebrate the anniversary of a Hungarian victory somewhat overlooked by orthodox historians. It is said that, shortly after the defeat at Mohács (1526), the population of the town hid in the swamps from the Turks. Eventually they came out of hiding wearing frightening masks of demons and monsters and chased the Turks out of their town. So today the people dress up at carnival time and parade in the streets wearing frightening masks.

There are many lighthearted customs at carnival time, such as the *"mock-wedding"* of Zala county, an elaborate comedy during which a boy and a girl, selected by their respective friends and wearing masks are "married" in a mock procession and ceremony. They remove their masks at the dance following the "wedding". Only then do they recognise each other. Though there is considerable verbal licence during these games, no rough play is allowed.

Vintage festivals are popular around lake Balaton, which is surrounded by world-famous vineyards. The process of gathering the grapes — "szüret" in Hungarian — became a word synonymous with good cheer and celebrations. Sumptuous meals, dancing and drinking conclude each day of the rather tiring work of grape-harvesting.

12. THE SONG IN HIS HEART

(Lyric folk poetry and folksong)

Hungarian folk poetry is almost always connected with singing and there is hardly any folk music without an accompanying text. This inter-relationship between poetry and music has imposed its mark upon the *structure* of the lyric folk poem. As a breath-unit could not easily extend over more than four syllables, the basic unit of the folk poem is the line made up of four syllables, often followed by another four-syllable or a shorter unit. The first verse of an ancient folksong (recorded in Transdanubia by Bartók) illustrates the point:

"Felszállott a páva　　　　*"Fly my haughty peacock,*
Vármegyeházára,　　　　　*Fly to yonder prison,*
Sok szegénylegénynek　　　*Where the captives languish,*
Szabadulására."　　　　　　*Set them free, o peacock. . ."*

The rhythmic division is greatly facilitated by the fact that in Hungarian stress falls on the first syllable.

The oldest and still frequent metre is the eight-syllable line, divided into two four-syllable units:

"Megérem még azt az idöt　*"I shall live to see you one day*
Sirva mégy el házam elött. . ."　*Pass my house bitter-weeping. . ."*

The strophe usually contains four lines. The rhyme is arranged in couplets but it is sometimes omitted when the rhythm alone is sufficient to carry the musical frame.[1]

The most frequent *theme* is, of course, love. Happy, contented love, however, rarely inspires the folk-poet. When it does, the poem is short, simple and usually made up of quick, short breath units.[2] The love of the mother and the mother's love for her child is also a source of inspiration — a rare occurrence in folk poetry.[3] The sorrow of hopeless love is more frequent. Often it is the peasants' rigid moral code or the parents' insistence on choosing their children's future spouses which causes the lovers' unhappiness.[4]

"You choose me and I choose you,
My flower, my darling. . ." (Folk song).

The sorrow of parting remains a recurring theme of many folk poems.[5] Compulsory military service in the army of the Austrian-Hungarian Monarchy, usually in some non-Magyar province of the Empire, had little appeal for the peasant boys.[6] Emotional patriotism is a frequent motif, mostly in the context of a farewell song or with melancholic references to the Magyar people's sufferings.[7] The two great freedom wars have created folk poetry of a more exuberant nature.[8]

The Magyar peasant loves *nature*, the soil which is rarely his, the animals which he seldom owns. He envies the freedom of the birds and the colour of the flowers satisfies his eternal longing for beauty. He feels that he is one with nature and

90

the animals; the billowing waves of corn and the forested hills can interpret his dreams, joys and sorrows.[9]

The recurring reference to the phenomena of nature leads us to the understanding of the deeper motivations of the Magyar lyric folk poem. The peasant observes nature's eternal logic and knows that the plants and animals obey the unchanging laws to love or to live. The devious tragedies of human destiny do not follow the simple ways of nature. So he asks: why? He becomes a philosopher and pours out the philosophy of his heart in a few moving words.

Thus his beloved river Tisza teaches him the melancholic lesson of the passing of time:

"Down went the Tisza — never shall it turn back — My Love went away — never shall she return. . ."

It is easier to bear his sorrow when he finds an image taken from his environment and uses it as a simile and a consolation. This is why many folk poems begin with a picture of nature, sometimes without any apparent connection with the theme. On a second look, this seemingly irrelevant image may present a surprisingly apt, symbolic parallel: *"There is no forest without boughs — my heart is never without sorrows. . ."*[10]

About 100,000 folk poems and songs have been recorded in Magyar-speaking areas of the Carpathian basin. This incredible treasure is, unfortunately, hardly accessible to those who cannot understand the language. Folk poetry, more than any other branch of literature, loses its flavour in translation. Fortunately, there is always the melody, which offers an eloquent interpretation.

The Appendix contains the complete English text of the poems mentioned in this chapter and added specimens offer a cross-section of Hungarian lyric folk poetry.[11] The reader is advised to listen to one of the many excellent recordings of these songs, comparing their musical content with the lyric theme indicated by the English translation.

"Snow-white my Rose is, snow-white she is wearing,
Turn to me, o turn to me, my bride, my darling."

(Wedding folk song)

13. "BETWIXT TWO HEATHENS. . ."

(The struggle against Turkish aggression and German oppression: the XVIth - XVIIth centuries)

Defeated, divided, doomed

John I (Zápolya) (1526-1540) and *Ferdinand I (Habsburg)* (1526-1564), the rival kings of Hungary began a long internecine warfare against each other. The Sultan, *Suleiman,* took the role of the amused spectator. He knew that Hungary was neither willing nor able to resist and therefore found it unnecessary to establish a permanent Turkish occupation. The Turks left Hungary unoccupied for fourteen years after Mohács, while the two kings performed their strange antics in their "fools' paradise", an "independent" Hungary.

Ferdinand, King of Hungary and Archduke of Austria, had already raised his eyes toward the crown of the Holy Roman (German) Empire. He regarded Hungary only as an expendable buffer-province. John I too was only interested in his own advancement.

Many details of the struggle of the two kings are unclear, unexplained or unimportant. The following events represent only the most grievous of the self-inflicted wounds which hastened the downfall of the once mighty state of Hungary.

After his coronation Ferdinand made a half-hearted attempt at taking Buda, the capital, from John. To Ferdinand's great surprise, John fled at once to his relatives in Poland. Once out of reach of his opponent, he collected what he thought were his wits and came to a disastrous resolution: he offered his fealty to the Sultan in exchange for help against Ferdinand! He was probably influenced by the Poles who had been paying

93

a tribute to the Sultan, and by the French, whose Francis I had been an ally of the Turks for years. John Zápolya failed to realise that Poland and France, both at safe distance from the Turk, could afford to "ride the tiger", while Hungary could not.

Suleiman magnanimously granted John's request, and accepted his hommage on the very field of Mohács, on the third anniversary of the battle . . .

He then chased Ferdinand out of Buda and handed the capital back to John. Later, in 1529 and 1532 Suleiman led his troops against Vienna, but had to call off both campaigns, defeated by the weather (Ferdinand's ablest general). On the second occasion, the small fortress of Köszeg defied his army for weeks during autumn until it became too cold and rainy to move on. It is not generally known that the Turks relied on camels to transport the heavy supplies of their army and European winters were too cold for these animals.

These abortive campaigns did, however, frighten Ferdinand into negotiations with the Sultan. The result was that the Habsburg king of Hungary agreed to pay the Sultan a yearly tribute in order to be left alone.

In order to save what was left of the independence of Hungary, John's able advisor, *"Frater" (Brother) George,* a Pauline monk, arranged a secret pact between the two kings in 1538. John was to "enjoy" the Hungarian throne alone, but after his death Ferdinand was to inherit the crown. (John was not married at the time). The ink was hardly dry on their signatures when both kings set about breaking the pact. Ferdinand hastened to report the secret agreement to Suleiman, in order to discredit his opponent. John promptly married the Polish princess, Isabella, who duly bore him a son. He then immediately repudiated the pact and appointed his infant son heir to the Hungarian throne. John died soon afterwards (1540), after having entrusted brother George with the unenviable task of enforcing his son's claim.

On hearing of John's death, the Sultan moved to Buda, occupied the royal castle (1541) and set up a permanent Turkish military occupation in the centre of Hungary, which he annexed to the Ottoman (Turkish) empire.

"Turkish marauders in Hungary" (A XVIth century German drawing)

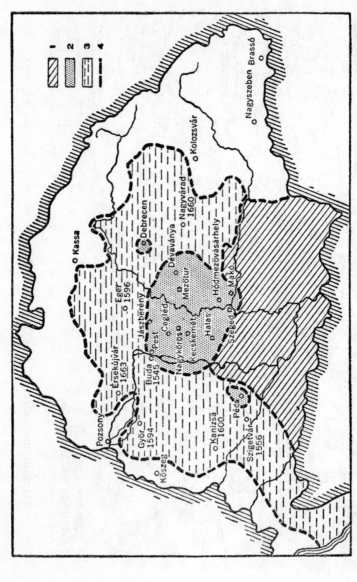

The three zones of Turkish devastation: 1. total (in the South), 2. heavy (in the centre),
3. erratic (in the fringe areas). 4. Farthest limit of Turkish occupation.

96

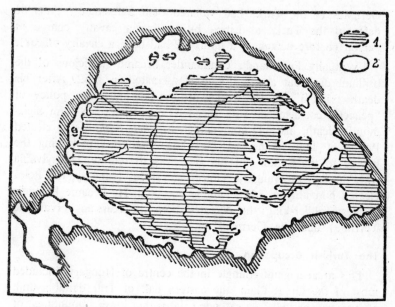

1. The shaded areas show the predominantly Magyar inhabited area of Hungary in 1500.
2. Uninhabited or sparsely settled by nationalities.

Transylvania

Brother George, the only able Hungarian statesman of the period, arranged with the Sultan to set up a semi-independent principality in the eastern regions of Hungary. This state consisted of the area generally known as Transylvania with some adjoining districts and towns. The infant *John Sigismund* (1540-1571), John's son, was accepted as Prince ("Fejedelem") at the first Diet of the three Transylvanian nations (the Magyars, Székelys and Saxons). Another Diet in Torda, in 1570 granted complete freedom to all religions in the principality. This was incredibly progressive legislation in the Europe of the XVIth century, then in the throes of the bloody "religious wars."

Brother George, the Regent, managed to keep the small country more or less independent by paying tribute to the Sultan (without becoming his vassal) and by remaining on friendly terms with the Habsburg king. He used this fact as a deterrent whenever the Turks became too aggressive. He did not hesitate to take up arms when he found that either the

97

Germans or the Turks had violated their agreements. Thus he defeated the Turks at Lippa by leading a cavalry charge in person (before becoming a monk he had been a cavalry officer).

Eventually Ferdinand's commander became suspicious of the brilliant diplomat and had him assassinated in 1552. After his death Isabella and the young Prince continued the policy of "peaceful coexistence" with the Turks. After Prince John Sigismund's death, his able commander, *Stephen Báthori* was elected Prince of Transylvania (1571-1586). Báthori kept paying the tribute to the Sultan but his goal was to reunite Transylvania with the rest of Hungary. Unfortunately for Hungary, the Poles elected him king in 1575 and he accepted. He became Poland's greatest soldier-king: he defeated both the Russians (Ivan the Terrible) and the Germans.

The Turkish occupation area

This area, a giant triangle in the centre of Hungary, included most of the Great Plain, the eastern half of Transdanubia and, at various periods, it extended into the lower mountains of the north. The area was a conquered colony of the Ottoman Empire: the indigenous population (called "raya": i.e. "cattle") had hardly any human rights. All land was owned by the Sultan, who gave it to his officers in fief. As no Turk ever settled in an occupied country permanently, the colonists' only goal was the complete exploitation of the people and their produce. Some larger towns survived only because their citizens bribed the Turkish officers and paid exorbitant taxes to the Sultan. Smaller settlements and villages were at the mercy of the Turks and their Tartar and Balkan auxiliaries who looted and raped at will. They took the young people to the slave markets and slaughtered the others, while rich nobles were kept in prison for ransom and systematically tortured in order to hasten the payment of the ransom. During the 150 years of Turkish occupation at least 3 million Hungarians were killed or driven like cattle to the Turkish slave markets.

After Suleiman's unsuccessful attacks against Austria several years of "peace" followed: there were no large-scale campaigns, but the raids along the vaguely defined demarcation line continued. After 1550 the Sultan began to attack systematically the strong fortresses along the demarcation line Those defended by German troops fell easily, but some smaller forts defended

"The Women of Eger" by B. Székely (cf. Chapter 25)
(Defence of Eger in 1552)

by Magyar troops put up a better resistance. The large fort of Eger, defended by some 2000 Hungarian men and women and commanded by István Dobó, resisted successfully a six-week siege by more than 100,000 Turks in 1552. In 1566 Suleiman's army was again held up by the fort of Szigetvár (in Transdanubia), which was defended by Miklós Zrinyi with 1000 men. Suleiman died during the siege, but Zrinyi and his men could not hold the fort any longer. They stormed out in a heroic sally and died to the last man. The women and the wounded then blew themselves up in the ammunition tower. During the siege, the Emperor, Maximilian, was waiting nearby with his huge army ignoring Zrinyi's calls for help because it was the height of the duck season and he did not want to interrupt his hunt.

"Royal" Hungary

The western counties of Transdanubia, the northern region and some towns in the north-east belonged to the third of the country which became the share of the Habsburg king of Hungary. Ferdinand I died in 1564. His successor, *Maximilian* (1564-1576) did nothing to stop the Turks. In fact his predatory generals and marauding soldiers soon made the Hungarians realise that the Germans were hardly better than the Turks. The bitterness of the population found its expression in the saying: "between two heathens we bleed for one country." Maximilian's successor, *Rudolf I* (1576-1608), would have settled for peace but the Turks were in an aggressive mood and began the so-called "fifteen years' war." As the Turks were attacking mostly in the general direction of Vienna in western Hungary, Rudolf had to commit larger contingents of his precious troops.

Whether it was "peace" or "war", the fighting along the demarcation line was continuous. The burden of these battles was borne by the soldiers of the *"frontier posts"* manned by Hungarian garrisons ranging from 20 to 200. They fought with tenacious courage and ingenuity as they were very poorly equipped and in case of a major Turkish attack they could not count on help from the Emperor-king's generals. Many of these "frontiersmen" were volunteer nobles for whom fighting the Turk was the only life they knew.

The "golden age" of Transylvania

The unpredictable Prince, *Sigmund Báthori* (Stephen Báthori's successor) (1581-1596) joined the Emperor in the war against the Turks. His able commander, István Bocskai defeated the Turks in Wallachia with the help of the voyvod (Prince) of Wallachia, Michael. Then the Turks counter-attacked in Transylvania and Báthori and his German allies lost an important battle. Sigismund abdicated in favour of his cousin, Cardinal

Prince Gábor Bethlen of Transylvania (1613-1629)

Andrew Báthori. The wily voyvod Michael turned against Andrew and defeated him with the help of the rebellious Székelys, then proclaimed himself Prince of Transylvania (1600). The Emperor rejected his claim and had him and his Vlach troops chased out of Transylvania by the imperial commander, Basta. After a short interregnum, *István* (Stephen) *Bocskai* (1604-1606) was elected Prince of Transylvania and he chased the marauding Germans, Turks, Vlachs and Tartars out of Transylvania. This brilliant soldier decided to reunite Transylvania with Hungary and free the entire country from both Germans and Turks. He launched a successful campaign against the imperial (German) troops in northern Hungary. The Emperor-King (Rudolf I) concluded a peace treaty with Bocskai. He acknowledged the independence of Transylvania and granted religious and constitutional freedom to the Hungarians in his (Rudolf's) territory. Soon afterwards, Bocskai arranged a peace between the Sultan and the Emperor, giving a much needed respite to the exhausted Hungarian nation.

Unfortunately, the great soldier-statesman died after only two years of his reign as Prince.

Prince *Gábor Bethlen* (1613-1629) continued Bocskai's policy of "negotiating from strength." He joined the Thirty Years' War on the Protestant side (against the German Empire). Though not entirely successful, he obtained important concessions from the Emperor-King and maintained Transylvania's independence. Under his absolutist, but benevolent rule, Transylvania enjoyed complete religious freedom and a high cultural and social standard unusual in war-torn Europe.

"Royal Hungary" during the XVIIth century

By the end of the XVIth century almost all the Hungarian magnates had adopted Protestantism in protest against the Catholic Vienna regime. This fact only increased the antagonism of the Austrian-German regime against the Hungarians and they began to use forced "Counter-Reformation" as a political weapon. So now the horrors of a religious war were also threatening the nation.

A Hungarian prelate, Cardinal-Archbishop *Peter Pázmány,* and his Protestant friends in Transylvania deserve credit for keeping Hungary out of the bloodbath of the European religious wars.

Cardinal Pázmány, born of a Protestant family, joined the Jesuit order after his conversion to Catholicism and eventually became Hungary's Primate (1616). He convinced the Hungarians that Catholicism was not synonymous with Austrian oppression and that religious debates did not have to degenerate into bloody battles, as in Germany, France and England. His Catholic "Counter-Reformation" used only the weapon of the spoken and written word. He established excellent schools and the university of Nagyszombat. He was a true Hungarian patriot

Count Miklós Zrinyi (†1664)

and the fate of his nation was his foremost consideration. He approved of the independent policies of the Protestant Transylvanian Princes. Under his influence many aristocratic families returned to Catholicism.

The new Emperor-King, *Leopold I* (1657-1705), a pious and bigoted tyrant, was endeavouring to turn the remaining Magyars into Catholic-Germans but he was not interested in chasing the Moslem Turks out of Hungary. A few rich Catholic magnates were able to conduct limited, individual campaigns against the Turks. The most eminent of these was *Miklós Zrinyi,* great grandson of the hero of Szigetvár. He was the greatest Hungarian statesman and soldier of the century and a talented poet and military scientist. A pious Catholic and a loyal subject of the King he had some liberty to fight the Turks using his own troops — whenever this did not interfere with the imperial policy. Once, when Zrinyi practically forced the cowardly imperial commander into a battle and won it for him, the Emperor immediately concluded a humiliating peace, bribing the Turks with Hungarian territory to stay away from Vienna. Soon after this shameful "peace" treaty, Zrinyi died under very suspicious circumstances. (1664).

Such was the degree of dissatisfaction in Hungary that the (Catholic and Protestant) leaders of the nation began to contemplate the deposition of the Emperor-King, Leopold. These leaders were headed by the Palatine, (the king's representative in Hungary), *Ferenc Wesselényi,* and they were supported by the Transylvanian Prince and encouraged by France's Louis XIV. Their aim was to invoke the nations' constitutional right to "resist", as codified in the Golden Bull. They had legal and moral justification, as Leopold and his ministers had ignored the Hungarian Constitution. But their plans were betrayed and the leaders brought before a military court in Austria. Wesselényi died before the betrayal, but the others, including Peter Zrinyi, the great hero's brother, were executed.

Transylvania and the beginning of the "kuruc" uprisings

The military successes of Prince György *(George) Rákóczi I* (1630-1648), an ally of the Protestant powers in the Thirty Years' War were of a rather ephemeric nature. More beneficial were the cultural activities of his princess, *Zsuzsanna (Susanna) Lorántffy,* a lady of remarkable humanistic education and advanced social ideas, a great patron of Protestant education (Sárospatak College).

The Prince *George Rákóczi II* (1648-1660) continued the forceful policies of his predecessors, but with less success. During one of his futile campaigns, the Turks occupied Transylvania and placed a puppet of their own choice on the throne. This practically ended the independence of Transylvania (1660).

The persecution of Protestants and patriots involved in the "Wesselényi Plot" forced many Hungarians to flee from "royal" Hungary to Transylvania. *Imre Thököly,* an able soldier, organised them into troops of freedom-fighters against the Germans. They called themselves "Kuruc", the name Dózsa's crusaders used. With the tacit support of the Turks, Thököly launched lightning campaigns against Leopold's forces in northern Hungary (between 1678 and 1682) and won some victories and useful concessions from the Vienna regime. He had to stop his "kuruc" campaigns after the Turkish defeat at Vienna (1683) and eventually took refuge in Turkey.

The liberation of Hungary

The ambitious Turkish Vezir (Commander-in-Chief), Kara Mustafa launched an offensive campaign against Vienna in 1683. Emperor Leopold was paralysed with fear, but the Pope, Innocent XI, managed to organise a veritable crusade against the Turks. Vienna was saved by its able defender and by the Polish and western armies. After Vienna's relief, the Pope kept urging Leopold and the crusaders to free Hungary. Thus an international army, commanded by the able Prince Charles of Lorraine, continued the counter-attack against the Turks. In 1686 they freed Buda where a large contingent of Hungarian troops (many of them Thököly's former "Kuruc") fought as their spearhead. By 1697 the southern Hungarian frontier was reached: the Turkish rule ended after 156 years.

Through this international victory, the Christian West paid some of its old debts to Hungary. But it was 300 years and 3 million victims too late. Moreover, the Vienna regime regarded its success as a purely Austrian-German victory and treated Hungary as a reannexed province of the empire. It resettled the depopulated areas with Balkan Slav, Vlach and German settlers and allotted the former Magyar estates to Austrian barons. A ruthless process of Germanification began under which Magyar properties were confiscated and resisting nobles arrested or executed on trumped-up charges.

It was not the first and not the last time in history that a country was "liberated" by a great power only to change masters. Hungary was out of the frying pan . . .

"Buda recaptured." (1686) by Gy. Benczur (cf. Chapter 25)

14. THE OTHER HUNGARY

(Transylvania: its settlement, people, customs
and folk art)

Settlement and history

This region of some 25,000 square miles is bounded by the rugged Carpathian mountains in the north-east and south. In the west a thickly forested group of mountains and hills (Bihar) separate it from the Great Plain, to which however several great river valleys provide easy access.

The Latin name, Transylvania, which appeared in the old Hungarian (Latin-language) documents, means "Beyond the Forests" — beyond the Bihar forests as seen from Hungary proper. The Hungarian name, "Erdély", means "The Land at the Foot of the Forests", referring to the Carpathians. The Rumanian language has no word for the land; their name "Ardeal" is a distortion of the Hungarian name.

The region is first mentioned in Roman sources. The rather nebulous "Dacian" empire was defeated by emperor Trajanus (105 A.D.) and held by the Romans until the end of the third century when they evacuated it completely. After them, nomadic tribes (Goths, Gepidae, Huns, Avars and Slavs) settled in the area. At the time of the Hungarian settlement in the IXth century, the remnants of these tribes and the Székelys (of Hunnic or Avar-Magyar origin) populated the area which was, nominally at least, part of the crumbling Bulgarian empire.

In the Xth century, the area was allotted to two Hungarian tribes. The chiefs of these two tribes bore hereditary offices in the Hungarian tribal federation: the head of the southern tribe (probably "Keszi") was the second highest dignitary

("Gyula") of the nation. The Székelys settled in the easternmost part and were given self-government as a tribe of frontier guards.

The powerful "Gyulas" of the southern tribe wished to emulate the head of the largest tribe, "Magyar" (the paramount chief of the Federation) and maintained independent cultural, political and religious contacts with Byzantium. The last "Gyula" actually rose against Saint Stephen's centralising attempts but he was defeated and the King broke the power of the tribal chief.

During the Middle Ages, Transylvania remained an integral part of the Hungarian Kingdom, but because of its relative isolation and strategic position it usually had a "governor" ("vajda") who co-ordinated the territory's administration and defence. During the XIIth century, Germans were settled in the remote areas and granted special privileges ("Saxons").

After the Turkish occupation of the centre of Hungary (1540) the region became separated from the rest of the state and gained a varying degree of independence. King John's son, John Sigismund, was the first Prince of Transylvania. This independence, forced upon the small country, maintained it as the bastion of the Hungarian nation during the 170 years of Turkish and German oppression.

After the failure of Prince Rákóczi's fight for freedom, the Habsburg regime ruled the region as a separate "grand-duchy" from Vienna. It did so against the protests of the Hungarians, who demanded the area's return to the mother-country. The compromise of 1867 reunited Transylvania with the rest of Hungary.

The Trianon Peace Treaty (1920) gave the territory and adjoining districts to Rumania. Of the total population of 5.2 million, 2.8 million were Rumanians (Vlachs), the rest Hungarians, Székelys and Germans. During the Second World War, the Second Vienna Award (handed down by Germany and Italy at Rumania's request), returned about 40% of the area to Hungary in 1940. During the rest of the War, the Soviet Union promised Transylvania to the country which changed sides first (both Hungary and Rumania were fighting on the German side). Rumania changed sides in 1944 and received Transylvania as her reward.

The Rumanian claim to Transylvania

Some Rumanian politicians claim that the Vlachs of Transylvania are the descendants of the original Dacian and Roman population and thus claim Transylvania as their ancestral homeland.

The racial characteristics of the Dacians are unknown, but we know that the Romans evacuated Dacia in 271 A.D. when the Emperor (Aurelius) ordered the entire Roman garrison to withdraw from the untenable and distant province. Contemporary Roman historians report that *all* the Romans left Dacia[1], that no Roman settler remained and that no Roman had mingled with the local population. There is no mention of Dacian or Latin-speaking descendants of the Romans in Transylvania until 1224 when a Hungarian document first mentions Vlach shepherds who began to move into the mountains and spoke a Latin-type language. As a matter of fact, the Rumanian language is partly Latin and partly Slavonic. German historians (not known for their Hungarian sympathies) place the Vlachs' original homeland in the centre of the Balkan peninsula[2] where they lived under Roman rule and probably spoke a mixed Latin-Slavonic language. From there they gradually moved away, a large contingent reaching the Wallachian plain in the XIth century and then Transylvania in the XIIIth century. Under Turkish pressure (XVth-XVIth centuries) many more found refuge in Transylvania. Although the Vlachs were not numerous enough in the XVIth century to become one of the "three nations" of Transylvania (Magyars, Székelys and Saxons), they received complete religious and cultural freedom under the tolerant rule of the Princes during Turkish times. They were, for instance, given the opportunity to print books in Rumanian. In fact, during the Turkish occupation of their home country (Wallachia), the only Rumanian-language books were printed in Transylvania.

During the XVIIIth and XIXth centuries the Hungarophobe Viennese administration encouraged Vlach immigration and at the same time oppressed the Magyars and Székelys in Transylvania. After the Compromise of 1867, Transylvania was reunited with the rest of Hungary, but the neglect and complacency of the Hungarian administration resulted in the decrease of the Magyar and Székely population as a result of their massive emigration to America. Thus by 1920 the area had a Vlach population slightly in excess of the Hungarians.

Towns and districts with historic or cultural interest

Kolozsvár (Rumanian: "Cluj", a distortion of the Hungarian name). This old city on the Szamos river used to be the capital during independence. It is the birthplace of King Matthias. The city still has many houses built in the typical "Transylvanian Flowery Renaissance" style. The Saint Michael Church is one of the few remaining Gothic cathedrals in the area. The city is the see of the Unitarian bishop of Transylvania. The Unitarian Church was founded by a Transylvanian Protestant preacher and is known only in the United States outside its country of origin.

Szamosujvár, north of Kolozsvár, is the centre of the Armenian community. They were given asylum from the Turkish persecutions in the XVIIth century.

The *Mezöség* region around Kolozsvár is an interesting Hungarian folklore region with characteristic art and customs. So is the larger *Kalotaszeg* district between Kolozsvár and the Bihar mountains, which consists of about 40 villages. The Magyar population of this region has preserved its customs, folk art and architecture, as well as magnificent folkwear to the present day.

At Keresd, south-east of Kolozsvár, the first books were printed in Transylvania in 1473. The town of *Torda* was often host to the Transylvanian Diet.

Torockó, near Torda, possesses the most sumptuous of all Magyar folk costumes, including some elements of Rhineland folk art borrowed from the neighbouring German settlers. Nearby, the gold-mining region in the Aranyos river valley used to be the centre of the gold and silversmith industry.

Gyulafehérvár on the Maros river, a former Roman centre, used to be the capital of the Magyar tribe of the "Gyula". Its first cathedral was built in the Xth century in Byzantian style. The crypt was the Hunyadis' burial place and the cathedral the scene of the coronation of many Princes.

The easternmost districts are the traditional homeland of the *Székelys*. The largest city is Marosvásárhely with its fascinating "Székely Museum" and Library. Csiksomlyó is the pilgrimage centre of the Catholics among the Székelys. The "Csángós" who live in seven villages in Rumanian Moldavia and Bukovina are Székelys who migrated there in the XVIIIth century. There are today about one million Székelys and Csángós.

Folk art and crafts

Transylvania is the only area where Magyar folk *architecture* is still found in its original form. Larger structures (churches) often combine stone foundations and walls with timber-roof superstructures. Separate timber bell-towers were added to the castles and churches. The timber constructions had to be renewed every two to three centuries but the renovators retained the original style (usually Gothic) of the building. The interior of many churches, especially in the Kalotaszeg area, presents elaborately carved, wood-inlay ceilings, pulpits and pews. The interior ornamentation is usually "Flowery Transylvanian" (Renaissance).

The entrance to the Kalotaszeg or Székely house is usually through an ornamental wooden gate, shingle-capped, carved, coloured or painted, with high side posts. These are called the *"székelykapu"* (Székely gate). In Székely regions the gates are more elaborate; the carved columns are ornamented with flower motifs, allegorical, mythical figures and runic writing. Among the flower-motifs the tulip and rose are the most frequent. They are reminiscent of old pagan symbolism: the tulip represents the male principle, the rose the feminine symbol. Another unique custom in Székelyland is the use of the carved wooden headboards in cemeteries: these are called *"kopjafa"* (lance-tip). The inscriptions are often humorous.

We find some special types of *weaving* in the Kalotaszeg region. The Székelys weave frieze-cloth for their trousers and coats. Their best-known product is the "Székely-rug", made of goat's or sheep's wool, richly patterned. Kalotaszeg is the home of the richest *embroidery;* some of it has free designs and patterns traced by skilled "writing women" (designers). Torockó produces a most elegant embroidery, finished in satin stitch. The Székely embroidery uses gothic geometrical patterns or free design.

In the Kalotaszeg and Székely areas even *men wear folk-costumes* on solemn occasions. They usually wear tight breeches of home made frieze and in winter sheepskin vests or jackets (called "ködmön") and boots. The colour scheme is grey and black-white.

Women's costumes are, of course, more colourful. Young girls wear colourful headgear ("párta") and the dresses are em-

"Kalotaszeg" folkwear and the "Székely gate."

bellished with embroidery and woven ornamentation. The shirts, skirts and aprons are long. The skirt, called "muszuly" — often has one or two corners tucked in at the waist, displaying the colourful lining of the shift. The skirt is always covered with an embroidered silk or satin apron. Torockó girls wear strings of beads around the neck to complement their lavish costumes. The Székelys, the poorest and most practical of these groups, wear simpler, more sombre dresses, with the red and white colours dominating.

Some folk customs

The old customs connected with the collective spinning of the flax-yarns in the *spinneries* have survived in the mountainous areas until the present day.

In the Székely villages, the families rent a house where the women and girls perform the tedious task of spinning during the long winter evenings. There, with the aid of the village lads, they enliven their work with songs, story-telling, games and occasional dances. This arrangement has made the spinnery into a pleasant centre of village social life where work and play find their desirable combination. It provides the young with an opportunity to meet socially under the watchful (but understanding) eyes of their elders. The quality of the hemp-yarn may suffer but the romantic yarns spun may have a more lasting effect.

The girls arrive first and they begin their spinning at once as each of them is expected to spin a certain quantity before the games may begin. Eventually the lads arrive, settle down near their respective "girl-friends" (a relationship taken rather seriously) and try to distract the girls with singing and story-telling. If a girl drops her spindle, she has to ransom it in the "customary" way, with a kiss. On completion of the quota (of spinning, not of kissing), the games may begin. Some of these are pantomime-like ballets by which the boys show off before the girls. One such pantomime is the imitation of the usual farming tasks. The boys sing in choir and mime the actions of sowing, reaping, thrashing and selling their corn. Then they end by mimicking how the wives spend on drink the hard-earned price of the corn[3].

The boys may sing then the "Bachelor's Song"[4] in order to tease the girls, though boys entertaining the ideas of eternal bachelorhood (which the song advocates) would hardly entertain girls in the spinnery. This may be followed by games, such as the "selling of the girls", during which each girl is driven to a boy by two lads holding a knotted handkerchief. The songs sung on these occasions retain echoes of pagan love-chants used

113

to "charm" couples together. The mildly erotic games of the spinnery follow certain strict rules, guaranteed by the presence of the parents. They have learned to tolerate these games and thus make it unnecessary for young people to seek secret meetings out of the sight of their elders (or so the parents hope, anyhow).

The ancient custom of *kaláka* is unique among the Székelys. It consists of mutual, collective help with hard, tedious tasks, to be rendered by each member of the community to each other member. House-building, well-drilling, ploughing and harvesting may be expedited by this system — invented by the Székelys a thousand years before the birth of socialism. Widows and elderly people receive these services without the obligation of reciprocation; the others are expected to pay with equivalent work. Winter tasks, such as corn-husking and spinning are always performed this way.

The Székelys thousand-year-old role as frontier guards has made them into a proud race of battlers. Today they fight the elements of their rugged country, poverty and constant pressure on their national identity from the Rumanian state. Their history has turned them into expert "survivors": a self-reliant people with a devastating sense of humour, unlimited faith in their ability, a deeply emotional love of their language and sincere Christianity. Their rough pastoral occupations have made them into excellent handymen, skilled tradesmen and good businessmen (this last quality separates them from the "ordinary Magyars"). Their wives are resourceful and they rule their families with firmness and faith. Their exuberant husbands need a good measure of discipline, which they accept from their wives — but from no one else on earth.

15. "BEYOND THE BEYOND..."

(Folk ballads, tales and legends)

As the plots and themes of most *ballads* are based on events, situations or conflicts brought about by the most common human emotions, love and hate, their origins can rarely be traced to any particular folk-culture. Thus the Magyar ballad owes its peculiar charm to its characterisation, ornamentation, dramatic structure and poetic technique, not to the originality of its subject. Whilst these characteristics draw a clear dividing line between Hungarian and neighbouring Slav and Rumanian folklores, there are some surprising similarities of structure and technique between the Székely ballads, (the majority of the Magyar ballads), and those of the Scots. As no historic or racial ties exist between these two nations, the similarity must be the result of parallel historic circumstances and environment effects of similar nature.

The well-known ballad *"Ilona Görög"* tells of a not very original ruse employed by the mother of a lad in order to gain his girl's love. On his mother's advice, the lad pretends to "die" and then miraculously "comes to life" when the girl appears among the mourners. The rapid a colourful dialogue maintains the suspense to the very end.[1]

"Clement Mason" treats a legend popular among the Balkan story-tellers. Twelve masons are commissioned to build the castle of Déva (Southern Transylvania) but they can make no progress. They decide to perform a ritual sacrifice by killing the first wife who arrives. Her blood mixed with the mortar would then assure success. It is Clement's wife who arrives first and is killed.

The tune is of the old Magyar pentatonic type, but the subject is not of Hungarian origin. Genuine Magyar tales do not favour black magic. Special Magyar ornamentation is the repetition of the wife's premonitions, her folk-tale like misinterpretation of the dream which eventually leads her to her doom and her child's pilgrimage to the walls in search of his mother.[2]

"Kate Kádár" is based on a real historic episode: the ballad is the re-creation, in peasant setting, of the story of Agnes Bernauer, the beautiful commoner who married the Prince of Bavaria and was, subsequently killed by her jealous in-laws. In the Magyar ballad, the husband is a nobleman and the wife a poor peasant girl. The girl is killed by her snobbish mother-in-law. On learning this, the young husband commits suicide. The two lovers are united in death and the flowers growing on their graves put a curse on their murderer.[3]

The *"Wicked Wife"* is a short ballad with a measure of macabre humour. The wife is gaily dancing while her husband is dying. Her daughter calls several times but the wife goes on dancing. When finally the poor husband dies, the wife suddenly begins to grieve — for having lost her breadwinner[4]. This is a Székely ballad. As we said before, the Székelys have a devastating humour.

The *"Fair Maid Julia"* is one of the few ballads in world folklore to use a Christian mystic theme. It is also that rare exception: unique to one folk culture, the Székely. Its deep religious emotion, subtle symbolism and rustic simplicity rank this poem among the greatest ballads of the world. The theme is inspired by the Catholic doctrine of the Holy Virgin's mystic elevation and heavenly union with God. Christian and pagan elements blend in a strange harmony: the reference to a "white, curly lamb" ("Jesus, Lamb of God") is followed by the pagan image: "carrying the sun and the moon between its horns. . ." (a typical "regös" song imagery). The miraculous picture of the gates that "open and shut by themselves" reminds us of the candles in the "regös" song that "light themselves" (cf. Chapter 6). The heavenly "wedding" invitation resembles the traditional ritual of the Székely wedding ceremony.[5]

"The Clever Prince" is a charming, gay poetic fantasy, a transition between ballads and folk tales, known in many variants in the Great Plain region. This "Cinderella in reverse" story tells of the search of a disguised Prince for his true love. He

eventually marries the modest daughter of the poor basket-maker and teaches the haughty judge's daughter a lesson. The easy-flowing, short metres and musical rhymes carry the song-tale to its natural happy conclusion. The gay ballad is suited to romantic, pantomime-accompanied presentation to singing or to reciting.[6]

*   *   *

The tales, myths, legends, religious parables, anecdotes, animal fables and other prose creations of the people are too numerous to be adequately treated here. We can only look at some selected features.

Folk-tales are characterised by certain recurring patterns and ornamental motifs. The beginning usually places the event some-where "beyond the beyond. . .", "beyond the Glass mountain" or "beyond the Operencian Sea" . . . This last name is a mispronunciation of the name of the Austrian district "Ober Enns" — the westernmost frontier of King Matthias' Hungary. The ending — usually a happy one — describes a wedding, often followed by the wry statement: "And if they are not dead, they are still alive today . . . " Some story-tellers add a touch of personal involvement: "I was there myself. . ."

A specially Magyar character of the tale is the "Táltos", a person (or a horse) possessing magic powers. He reminds us of the "shaman", the medicine-man priest of the ancient Asian religions. The "Táltos" may have been born with his special talents, in which case he is a "Garabonciás", but more often he acquires these gifts by performing certain difficult tasks. The (good) hero may also receive help from a "Táltos horse" which gives him sound advice or practical help, when needed. The "Tündér" (Fairy) appears in many shapes, pleasant or unpleasant. One of the latter is the "Lidérc", a haunting, ghost-like creature. The extracts from a very popular and specially Hungarian tale in the Appendix illustrate some of these features.[7]

Needless to say that the gothic horror tales of "Dracula", vampires, werewolves and zombies are but the figments of Holly-wood's fertile imagination and have nothing to do with the earthly folklore of the Magyar people (in Transylvania or elsewhere).

Legends and myths are probably the most ancient type of folklore. Historic legends claim to retell some important event

117

in the nation's past. Nebulous as they may be, these popular sagas are usually based on historic facts remembered for generations. Many historic events concerning the ancestors of the Magyars were recorded by the pagan priests in runic writing. During the XIth century, these "pagan" writings were destroyed by the Christian priests. Only in the remote areas (Székely region) do we find some ancient runic writing today. After the destruction of the runic records, the ancient legend lived by word of mouth among the people. The legend of the "Blood Treaty", for instance, as told by the peasants of the Great Plain, is based on a historic fact (Cf. Chapter 4).[8]

Among the historic anecdotes the ones connected with King Matthias are frequent. His wise judgments protected the poor and restrained the overbearing rich.[9]

The religious legends are, of course, anthropomorphic: Jesus and Saint Peter visit the Hungarian "puszta" and give lessons in common-sense Christianity to the shepherds.[10]

16. THE LOST CENTURY

(Hungary's history in the XVIIIth century)

The first European generation of this century lived under the rule of the absolutistic kings, such as France's Louis XIV, Russia's Peter I and Germany's Leopold I. The second generation saw the gradual weakening of these absolutistic empires. The third generation witnessed the rising of the oppressed in Europe and in America and the birth of new social structures and new, independent nations.

The Hungarians, with their "timeless" contempt for the logic of history, went through these three phases — in the reversed order. They rose against the monolithic German-Austrian Empire at the beginning of the century. They did the right thing — at the wrong time. The Empire had just defeated the Turks and now stood at the zenith of its power under its most Olympian monarch, Leopold.

Defeated, the Hungarians of the second generation watched at first stoically as their once mighty foe began to disintegrate for a rather ironic reason: the Habsburgs, who had established their rule over half of Europe through their clever marriage strategy, had suddenly run out of male heirs. Then, taken in by a clever, pretty queen, the Hungarians rushed to the rescue of the tottering Empire and offered their "Life and blood" to the same monarch whose grandfather had done his worst to wipe the Hungarian nation off the face of the earth. Having saved the Habsburg dynasty — the wrong thing for a Hungarian to do at any time — the third generation of Hungarians decided to do nothing — and they did it at the wrong time. While the rest of the world was busy creating new social, economic and state structures, the Hungarians turned their back to the world and went into a national hibernation of smug conservatism.

*   *   *

"Cum Deo- Pro Patria et Libertate"

FERENC (FRANCIS) RÁKÓCZI II (1676-1735) was a descendant of some of the greatest freedom fighters of Hungary. His mother, Ilona Zrinyi, the wife of Transylvanian Prince Ferenc Rákóczi I, was the finest example of patriotic Hungarian womanhood. She held the family fortress of Munkács for three years against the Austrian-German imperial troops after the defeat of her second husband, Imre Thököly, a great "Kuruc" leader. After the fall of Munkács, Ferenc was taken to Vienna with his mother. There they were separated, never to meet again. The young Prince was left to the care of the Magyar-hating Archbishop Kollonich, who had him educated in a Catholic Austrian school. On completion of his studies, Rákóczi returned to Vienna, married a German princess and remained under the watchful eyes of the Emperor Leopold, his godfather.

The handsome, mild-mannered Prince of the Holy Roman (German) Empire, a loyal subject and a devout Catholic who could not even speak Hungarian, seemed unlikely to stir up a Magyar rebellion, so the Emperor allowed him to visit his estates in Hungary.

It may well be that, on his arrival in Hungary, Rákóczi sincerely wished to reconcile his rebellious compatriots with their pious Emperor. Soon, however, the impact of the conditions he saw in Hungary and information gained from his Hungarian friends began to change his views about his "pious" godfather, the Emperor, and his "rebellious" Magyar subjects. He found the peasants and common people burdened with exorbitant taxes, the nobility intimidated and silenced and the imperial soldiers treating the country as their booty by right of conquest. His friends, especially Count Miklós Bercsényi, urged him to lead an armed revolt but Rákóczi agreed only to begin negotiations with the dynasty. In his naive manner he wrote a letter to France's Louis XIV, seeking his sympathy and moral support for Hungary's demands for her constitutional rights.

The correspondence was betrayed and the angry Emperor had Rákóczi arrested and held in the same prison in which his grandfather, Peter Zrinyi had been executed for treason. Rákóczi

Prince Ferenc Rákóczi II (1676-1735)
(By A. Mányoki)
(Cf. Ch. 17)

"Our weeping is more bitter,
More piercing torments try us.
A thousandfold Messiahs
Are Hungary's Messiahs."

(Ady)

managed to escape, however, and took refuge in Poland. The Poles offered the crown of their country to him, but he did not accept it.

In 1703 the insurgent peasants of Northern Hungary called upon Rákóczi in Poland to lead their uprising against Leopold. This time, the Prince responded to their appeals and to his friends' urging and returned to Hungary to direct his nation's armed fight for freedom. In his moving manifesto, "Recrudescunt . . .", he recounted his nation's grievances and stated that he wished to fight for the freedom of the entire nation, including the serfs and national minorities. It speaks well for the Hungarian aristocracy of the time that most of them joined Rákóczi's "Kuruc" troops. The nobles and the urban middle class joined them without reservation and so did the Slovak, Ruthene and Vlach peasants, and even the northern Hungarian Saxons. Catholics and Protestants swore allegiance to flags bearing the image of the Holy Virgin, Patron of Hungary and the motto "Cum Deo – Pro Patria et Libertate" (With God for Country and Freedom).

Only some prelates and magnates failed to join the uprising, either because they owed everything to the Emperor, or because they thought that the war was ill-timed and wasteful for a nation which had almost bled to death during the preceding three hundred years. Thus some honest and patriotic Hungarians remained in the imperial camp and their loyalty to both the Emperor and their nation was to alleviate later the sufferings caused by the war.

The bulk of the Kuruc troops consisted of light cavalry led by gallant, able but sometimes undisciplined commanders. They scored some spectacular successes at the beginning of the war but could not hold the occupied territory. More successful was the old general Bottyán in Transdanubia. In Transylvania and on the Great Plain, the imperials held most of the fortified cities but the Kuruc freed the countryside. In the north, the main theatre of operations, the Kuruc scored several victories but could not win decisive battles against the well-trained and better equipped imperials. In 1707 and again in 1710 the main Kuruc army was badly defeated, in both cases because the Kuruc commanders ignored Rákóczi's orders.

The lack of equipment, the general shortage of food and the lack of financial resources contributed to the final defeat of the Kuruc cause. Rákóczi did not tax the people. He tried to finance the war from his own income and the revenues of mines and excise — a woefully inadequate financial basis for a war lasting eight years. In 1710 a final, fatal blow struck the Kuruc army: the plague broke out in the Kuruc-held territory and killed half a million people, a fifth of Hungary's population.

Development in *international politics* also contributed greatly to Rákóczi's defeat. It had suited Louis XIV to have a rebel army in the east of the Habsburg empire but he never seriously considered concluding a formal alliance with Rákóczi. He kept encouraging him with vague promises and occasional financial support. It was on Louis' instigation that Rákóczi agreed to the dethronement of the Habsburg dynasty at the Diet of Ónod (1707). This assembly created Rákóczi "Ruling Prince" of the country. The timing of this fateful step could not have been more unfortunate: the Austrian-English victory over the French and Bavarians at Blenheim (1704) had already ruled out the chances of a military co-operation between the French and the Hungarians.

Rákóczi tried to find new alliances and hoped to negotiate with Peter I of Russia, who was even less reliable than Louis XIV. Still, the Prince went to Poland in 1711 hoping to meet Peter there. During his absence, his commander, Sándor Károlyi, correctly assessing the situation as hopeless for the Kuruc, concluded an armistice with the commander of the imperials, Count John Pálffy, an honest Hungarian soldier and statesman. Both commanders overstepped their authority but they were motivated by the best of intentions: the dying nation had to be saved.

"Vitam et Sanguinem . . ."

The armistice and capitulation of the Kuruc army was followed by the Peace Treaty of Szatmár (1711). Leopold had died in 1705: his successors, *Joseph I* (1705-1711) and *Charles III* (1711-1740), showed a little more understanding of the grievances of the Hungarians. The Peace Treaty granted amnesty to all participants and promised religious freedom and a constitutional government for Hungary.

Rákóczi and his closest friends did not accept the amnesty and left for Poland, then France. Eventually they were given refuge in Turkey, at Rodosto. The Prince died there in 1735 and his two sons, both unmarried, died soon after him. They were the last scions of the Rákóczi, Zrinyi and Báthori families.

Rákóczi's outstanding intellectual and moral qualities would have made him the nation's greatest king. It was his and the nation's tragedy that this charismatic leader was drawn into the unsuitable role of a rebel. Still, his struggle was not entirely in vain: with immense sacrifices, the Hungarians again proved that they would not tolerate tyranny. Rákóczi's revered memory has since lived as his nation's inspiration in victory and con- solation in defeat.

The wars of the preceding three hundred years had taken a frightful toll: the country which in Matthias' time (1460) had a population of over 4 million (85% Magyar) had now about 2½ million inhabitants, only about half of them Magyars. The war-weary nobles were now only concerned with their "privileges", such as their tax-exemptions. The survivors of the Magyar peasantry were expected to bear the crushing burden of taxation and to carry out the agricultural reconstruction of the country.

The Diet of 1722 accepted the decree called "Pragmatica Sanctio", which assured the right of succession of the Emperor- King's daughter, Maria Theresa. In return, the sovereign, Charles III, accepted the principle of "dual monarchy": an independent Hungary united with Austria under one sovereign. This "inde- pendence" was, however, little more than "home rule" as the important portfolios of Foreign Affairs, Defence and Finance remained under Austrian control. Neither was the territorial integrity of Hungary restored: Transylvania remained a "grand- duchy" administered from Vienna and the southern districts were made into a "military zone", (against the Turks) similarly under direct Viennese control.

When *MARIA THERESA* (1740-1780) ascended the throne, the Hungarians accepted her as their Queen but some provinces refused to do so. This eventually led to a war of succession between Austria and France-Prussia-Bavaria. Maria Theresa, whom someone once called the "only man of the Habsburg dynasty", began to show some remarkable qualities — mostly feminine ones. She had the Hungarian Diet recalled and appeared before the assembled nobles in mourning. With her infant child in her arms and tears in her eyes, she looked very much like the image of the Holy Virgin, Patron of Hungary — a familiar picture, indeed, as only a generation before this emblem had decorated Rákóczi's Kuruc flags . . . Now the beautiful, young Queen appealed to her "beloved, noble and chivalrous" Magyars for help against her enemies. Her "noble, chivalrous" (and forgetful) Hungarians stood up and cheered, promising her their "Vitam et Sanguinem . . ." ("Life and blood . . .")

Whatever the historians may say about her, Maria Theresa was quite a woman . . .

So Hungary, not long before a subdued colony, a defeated rebel, came to the rescue of her oppressor, Austria. Hungarian hussars, commanded by Hungarian generals, fought gallantly to defend their "Queen in distress". Thanks to their help, the war, which began disastrously for the Austrians, ended in a compromise; so did the following Seven Years' War (1756-1763).

The Queen rewarded the Hungarians by respecting their constitution and by guaranteeing the privileges of the landed nobility. Unfortunately, these privileges seemed to encourage agriculture and discourage urbanisation and industrialisation — in the age of the Industrial Revolution. Thus Hungary remained the backward agricultural provider of rapidly progressing Austria and Bohemia. It seems that, in addition to her other qualities, Maria Theresa was quite an economist too.

Her education policy was the product of "enlightened absolutism": a central, state-controlled system. *Latin* had been the language of government legislation and education in Hungary since the XVIIth century. Some historians have called this a "tactful" arrangement, as the use of Hungarian would have offended the nationalities. We have seen that, apart from the autochthonous Slovaks, all nationalities were immigrants settled with or without the Hungarians' permission in the territory of Hungarian sovereignty. Thus this "tactful" arrangement is comparable to the suggestion that the United States or Australia should replace English by, say, Esperanto in order to spare the susceptibilities of its migrants.

Unfortunately, *Transylvania* was still an Austrian colony and the drastic resettlement and military recruiting methods used by the Austrian commanders led to many clashes, such as the tragic incident at Mádéfalva where Székely families were massacred for refusing to allow their lads to be recruited for the Austrian army. As a result of this "Siculicidium" ("Székely massacre") (1763) whole Székely villages left their homeland and settled in Moldavia and Bukovina, then under Russian and Turkish occupation. The Austrian military authorities encouraged the mass immigration of Vlachs and Serbs to the eastern and southern depopulated areas.

Among the nobles of Hungary, unaware of all this, Maria Theresa's benevolent repression created an atmosphere of complacent, self-deluding euphoria.

Joseph II (1780-1790) brought the principle of "enlightened absolutism" to its logical conclusion: he decided to make his subjects happy, whether they liked it or not. He refused to be crowned and ruled by decrees, ordering reforms for which his multinational empire was neither ready nor grateful. He abolished the religious orders and granted freedom to all religions. Then he abolished the 700 year-old Hungarian county-system and replaced it with a German language central administration. He eased the burden of the Serfs and prepared plans for universal taxation. Some of these reforms shocked the Hungarians and the other nationalities. Disappointed, Joseph withdrew his edicts before his death.

His successor, Leopold II, had little trouble pacifying the nobles — they saw the unpleasant things happening in France to nobles who insisted on their privileges.

At the beginning of his long, dull reign, *Francis I* (1792-1835) hastened to reiterate the standard Habsburg procedure of reassuring the nobles that their privileges will remain untouched — as long as they kept producing food for the Empire and stayed out of mischief. He had no cause to worry: the world-shaking events in France found very little echo in Hungary. Only a small group of amateurish intellectuals attempted to organise some sort of a "Jacobin" plot. This was promptly discovered and quickly and ruthlessly suppressed by the most efficient branch of the Viennese government, the police.

Thus Hungary's "lost century" ended with the nation still licking its well-healed wounds and looking with full confidence into its glorious past . . .

17. "IN THE MIDST OF ARMS. . . "

(Hungarian literature and the arts in the XVIth - XVIIIth centuries)

Literature and music during the Turkish wars

Threatened with destruction, the Magyars found strength, hope and consolation in their literature and music during these turbulent centuries.

The wandering minstrels of the war, the "lute players", were the soldier-poets and musicians of the XVIth century. The best-known of these, *Sebestyén Tinódi* (called "Lantos": lute player), who died in 1556, sang the praises of the frontier soldiers to the accompaniment of lute-music, composed by himself. His epic accounts of heroic deeds (e.g. "The Siege of Eger"), exhortations or humorous sketches ("Of the Many Drunkards")[1] cheered the tired soldiers of the border fortresses and spread the news of the glorious battles. His music, noted down and printed in his lifetime with his poetry, had a characteristically Magyar richness.

The greatest poet of the XVIth century was BALINT (VALENTIN) BALASSA (1554-1594), an aristocrat who led a very eventful life, fighting as a volunteer among the frontier soldiers and getting into all sorts of amorous and financial troubles. His poetry reflects all facets of emotional expression: erotic passion and lusty love alternate with deeply religious sincerity and patriotic devotion. His poetic technique was quite remarkable, his language rich and colourful, unmatched by anything written in Hungarian until the XIXth century.

His "Soldier's song"[2] is a youthful, glowing praise of the frontier-soldiers: their sorrows, joys, sacrifices and rewards during a short life in the service of the nation. The poem "Forgive me" is a moving credo of his deep Christian faith[3]. Balassa was one of the Magyar millions who died with the name of "Jesus" on their lips. Mortally wounded, his last words were: "Jesus died for me — why should I have any doubts — I have been your soldier, my Lord, I have fought in your army . . ." His farewell songs[4] and love poems[5] show a fresh, natural inspiration, akin to that of folk poetry.

The ideas of the Reformation reached Hungary during the XVIth century. The need for Magyar-language hymns in the Protestant service helped the development of religious literature: original works and translations were required. The best-known *poet-preachers* were the Transylvanian Protestant pastors, Gáspár Heltay, also known for his fables, and Gáspár Károlyi the first Hungarian translator of the Bible. Their writings present many examples of a blend of patriotic and religious inspiration.

The rich magnates of the territories not occupied by the Turks had replaced the royal court as patrons of the arts. Their composers and orchestras provided relaxation and emotional comfort in the short periods of rest during the almost continuous fighting. Many of these composers' melodies have survived in foreign collections bearing such titles as "Ungaresca", "Ungarische Tänze", etc. The best-known Hungarian composer of the period was Bálint Bakfark of Transylvania. ("Lute Fantasia").

The XVIIth century presents a picture of spiritual and cultural consolidation. The Catholic "Counter-Reformation" produced some great writers, such as Cardinal *Péter Pázmány* (1570-1637), Archbishop of Esztergom. His many Magyar-language sermons, polemic writings, prayers and translations have greatly enriched the Hungarian language.[6] His contemporary, Albert Szenczi Molnár, a Protestant preacher, scholar and humanist translated psalms and set them to music of his own composition.

Count Miklós Zrinyi (1620-1664), the great general and statesman was also a remarkable poet. His long epic poem, the "Peril of Sziget",[7] describes the heroic defence of Szigetvár by his ancestor. Zrinyi dedicates his work not to the Muses, but to Hungary's Patron, the Blessed Virgin. His numerous prose works are political and military studies concerning the war against the Turks and written in racy, colourful Hungarian.

The two regions free from Turkish occupation had, by this time, developed a relatively secure and civilised form of living.

Dance and entertainment melodies, many inspired by folk music, have been preserved in notation in various manuscripts, such as the "Kájoni", "Vietorisz" and "Virginalis" "codices". The collection of Prince *Pál Eszterházy's* (1635-1713) Catholic hymns ("Harmonia Caelestis") contains many fine compositions by the great statesmen, including some inspired by Magyar religious folk melodies.

The "Kuruc" literature and music

The freedom wars, led by Bocskai, Bethlen, Thököly and Rákóczi, have created a rich treasure of poetry and music. These poems and melodies have survived by oral tradition only: it was treasonable to write them down during the decades following the Kuruc wars. For the same reason the authors preferred to remain unknown.

An early Kuruc poem: "Between the fire and the water" from around 1670 describes the bitter dilemma of the Hungarians of that period: between the Turkish aggression and German tyranny only their trust in God gives them consolation. The author may have been a Protestant pastor. Another song — obviously created by a common soldier — expresses the same idea, using the phrase which has since become the motto of those troubled times: *"Betwixt two heathens — fighting for one country — "* the Kuruc soldier, always hungry, always in battle, sheds his blood for one nation fighting the Turks and Germans.

The songs of the early Rákóczi period are more exuberant: they praise the bravery of the gallant hussars and their leaders who raided Austria. They ridicule the imperials (called "Labanc": from the German word "Lanze"), comparing the Kuruc' colourful, fine uniforms with the shabby looks of the "Labanc".

Toward the end of Rákóczi's struggle the songs again become melancholic. They are full of bitterness, recriminations and fear for the nation's future. The most moving of these poems is the so-called "Rákóczi Song" known in many variations, including folk song versions.[8] From these elements an unknown poet composed the final version around 1730.

Ferenc Rákóczi himself was not only an inspiration to poets but also a forceful and emotional orator, the author of manifestos, memoirs and history in Hungarian, Latin and French.

129

His faithful chamberlain, Count *Kelemen Mikes* (1690-1761), who followed him into exile and died there, wrote a number of letters to a fictitious aunt in Transylvania. These "Letters from Rodosto" are a deeply moving record of the lives of the exiles, a fine example of Transylvanian-Hungarian style.

Literature during the period of repression and stagnation

After Rákóczi's defeat a period of constant "benevolent repressions" followed: the various Habsburg regimes tried to Germanise the nation. At the beginning, the Hungarians, exhausted, offered little or no resistance. In a gesture of defiance, the Catholic schools turned to Latin and the study of classics, while the Protestant colleges maintained the use of the Magyar language. Some writers, during the second half of the century, began to discover the inspiration of folk poetry.

Some young members of Maria Theresa's Noble Guard in Vienna became interested in French literature and philosophy. The leader of this circle was *György Bessenyei* who, influenced by Voltaire, wrote several dramas as well as epic and lyric poetry of a philosophical nature with more enthusiasm than success. His most memorable work is the political-satirical novel: "The Travels of Tarimenes."

The repression and Germanisation increased under Joseph II. Even the complacent country nobility began to show some mild resistance. József Gvadányi, for instance, ridiculed the propagation of German and other foreign customs in his "Travels of a Village Notary". *Mihály Fazekas'* comic epic, "Ludas Matyi" ("Matthias and the Geese"), satirised the archaic social conditions of the late XVIIIth century in the form of a witty folktale in verse.

Music during the period of stagnation

The aristocracy of the XVIIIth century — especially in the western regions — welcomed and promoted Austrian and German music in Hungary. In the East, especially in the Protestant colleges, Magyar music became one of the means of maintaining and protecting the Magyar culture. The Hungarian songs of these schools — including those from some Catholic schools — show the mixed influence of western and Magyar folk melodic elements.

Hungara. quid trepidas, Tellus? accede Patronam.
Non patitur vacuas Illa perire preces.
Sint sua Scuta aliis, sua sint munimina, et Arces
Virginis, Hungariæ præbet Asyla, Thronus.

"Patrona Hungariae"
(The Virgin Mary with the Hungarian Saints.
Altar painting at Kolozsvár, XVIIIth century).

131

The army of the Empire was being organised as a permanent force. Recruiting for this army used the methods of the "press gangs" of the British Navy, as the peasant boys showed little inclination to leave their families for 7 or 12 years. The Viennese government knew what effect music had on the emotional Hungarians and sent recruiting teams with bands of gypsy musicians to the villages and towns. The band then played fiery music while the members of the team performed the *"toborzó"* ("recruiting dance" also called: "verbunk"). The impressionable young men, tempted by their favourite tunes, often joined in the dance — only to find that they had signed up by this symbolic act as recruits. This clever method seems to bear the trademark of a certain Lady in Vienna who must have been an expert in the psychology of Hungarian men . . .

The gypsies collected and ornamented many contemporary folk melodies. The richer, new-style folk songs were particularly suitable for this type of orchestration. From this "toborzó" or "verbunk"-type music evolved, during the XIXth century, the well-known "Magyar song".

Fine arts and architecture

The *Baroque* style reached Hungary through Austria during the XVIIth century. The Catholic inspiration of this style found its main expression in *church architecture,* religious painting and decorative sculpture. The church of the Minorites in Eger is the best example of this style in Hungary. The simpler, one-tower type of Baroque church became the prototype of the numerous village churches built during the XVIIIth century which constitute today the architectural image of the Catholic villages in Hungary.

Secular architecture consisted mainly of palaces, such as the sumptuous Eszterházy residence at Fertöd.

Baroque *sculpture* served mostly as a decorative element in ecclesiastical architecture. One of the few Hungarian sculptors was Sebestyén Stulhoff, a Benedictine monk.

While Austrian artists were commissioned to decorate the churches and palaces with their *paintings,* Magyar artists were often obliged to leave the country for political or religious reasons. To these belonged *János Kupeczky* who spent most of his life in Germany, except during Rákóczi's freedom war. His "Kuruc Soldier" was painted during that period.

Ádám Mányoki (1673-1756) the greatest Magyar painter of the XVIIIth century, worked in Rákóczi's court during the war. After the armistice he followed his Prince into exile. He painted his masterpiece, Rákóczi's portrait during their exile. He captured the true personality of the great man in this fine portrait (P. 121).

Unknown, probably Hungarian craftsmen left fine examples of woodcarving in many churches. Goldsmith János Szilassy of Löcse used the Renaissance "filigree enamel" technique of painted enamel work — a Hungarian innovation.

It seems that the Baroque, a form of artistic expression imposed upon the Magyar people by a regime which had remained foreign for centuries, had little appeal for the peasants. Their folk art rarely uses Baroque motifs — a surprising fact if we remember what a deep impact Matthias' short-lived Renaissance had on folk art.

*   *   *

The damage caused by the Turkish and German devastations to the nation's spiritual and artistic potential was not as obvious as the appalling loss of life and material but the result, Hungary's cultural retardation, has taken much longer to remedy. This is why the foreign observers of the XIXth and early XXth centuries were struck by the "conservative" or even "retrograde" aspects of Hungarian art and way of life. Yet before the XVIth century Hungary was in the forefront of European social and cultural progress. Even during the XVIIth century embattled Transylvania managed to remain the easternmost bastion of Christian humanism and culture.

Then, after the collapse of the last great struggle for freedom in 1711, the nation reached the point of physical and spiritual exhaustion. The Magyar soul was empty, the one million survivors of this people had lost their wish to seek new horizons.

So began a long century of cultural convalescence. Apathy, passivity, retrospection and slow awakening marked the various stages of this period — from 1711 to the Vienna Congress, 1815 — while the rest of the world was making rapid industrial, social and cultural progress. When, at last, the Hungarians awoke from their long torpor, the West was a century ahead of them.

On the Great Plain

"Tinkling beneath a sky mirage-possessed,
Kis-Kúnság's fatted herds by hundreds stray"

(Petöfi)

18. "HERE YOU MUST LIVE AND DIE. . ."

(The life, customs and art of the people of the Great Plain)

Towns and settlement areas

The "Great Plain" is not large by Australian standards: only some 30,000 square miles, but for the land-locked Magyars, surrounded by foreign, often hostile nations, the uninterrupted vistas create the illusion of unimpeded freedom. *"My spirit soars, from chains released, when I behold the unhorizoned plain . . ."* said the poet Petöfi.

This area lies between the Danube river and the northern and eastern foothills of the Carpathians. It is cut into half by the Tisza river. The Treaty of Trianon has allotted the southern districts to Yugoslavia and the eastern fringes to Rumania.

Debrecen is the cultural and economic centre of the area east of the Tisza and the spiritual centre of Hungarian Protestantism. This town played an interesting role during the Turkish occupation. Situated on the crossroads of the three divided parts of Hungary, the town managed to retain some degree of independence by skilfully manoeuvring between the warring powers, paying taxes to all when this was necessary. The town fathers — peasants and burgesses with remarkable commonsense and will to survive — made their town a refuge for the population of the nearby smaller towns and villages plundered by the Germans and Turks. Their numbers were thus swelled and reached a size which had to be respected by the marauders.

The *Hortobágy* is a grassy plain between Debrecen and the Tisza. Until recently it was a semi-arid area, called the "puszta" (desert). For centuries, the "puszta" represented, for the foreigner, the genuine "Magyar" atmosphere and the primitive lifestyle of the semi-nomadic herdsmen ("csikós") and outlaws ("betyárs"), the proverbial "Magyar" way of life. This myth, born in the imagination of the XVIIIth century German travellers, was gleefully propagated by the Viennese rulers of Hungary and gullibly supported by the songwriters of Budapest (who sweetened it, of course, with romantic "gypsy" music).

A shepherd of the "puszta".

"It is time to go
And to get married.
The question is only
Whom should I marry?" (Folksong).

Irrigation and artificial fertilisation have now made this area fertile again and only a few "reservations" remain where the "csikós" perform remarkable feats of horsemanship for the benefit of tourists.

Kecskemét is a sprawling town between the Danube and the Tisza, situated in a region ideal for fruit-growing. During the Turkish occupation, this town — in the centre of the Turkish

136

occupation area — remained relatively unharmed because the astute town-leaders managed to make the town a "Sultan's fief". This assured its protection against plundering troops at the cost of enormous collective taxes paid to the Sultan. Other large towns (Szeged etc.) followed Kecskemét's example protecting a considerable number of refugees, mostly peasants.

The city is Zoltán Kodály's birthplace and the fine "Kodály Music School", the prototype of scores of music schools, preserves his memory.

Village with sweep-well

*"It gave thee life and in thy death
Its earth will cover thee . . ."*

(Vörösmarty)

Large areas around Kecskemét are settled by scattered farmsteads, called "tanya". The "Bugac" "puszta" is a grazing area among barren dunes with some relics of primitive agriculture of the past (sweep-wells with their tall upright and cross-beams). It has a "romantic" reputation similar to that of Hortobágy.

Szeged, on the banks of the Tisza in the south, is well-known for its "Votive Church" (in memory of the 1879 flood), which forms a majestic background to an open-air theatre with 7,000 seats. The rich alluvial soil around the town produces the famous "paprika" (red pepper or capsicum) rich in Vitamin C (the study of which earned professor Szentgyörgyi his Nobel Prize).

Kalocsa, near the Danube, was one of the original arch-bishoprics founded by Saint Stephen. Two of the archbishops died on the battlefield commanding Hungarian armies. The peasants of the neighbouring villages have enjoyed great prosperity since the draining of the swamps at the beginning of the last century. They have used their affluence to develop luxurious folkwear and decorative artifacts.

Certain *regions* were already settled by non-Magyar ethnic groups before the Turkish occupation. Such a region is the *Kúnság* (Cumania) in the north. The ancestors of the Cumanians were eastern nomads (related to the Magyars), when they fled to Hungary in the XIIIth century before the Mongol onslaught. They were given refuge and have since completely assimilated into the Hungarian population.

The *Jászság* is a neighbouring area populated by the descendants of the "Jász" (Yazygs), a people of Caucasian (possibly Iranian) origin. They came to Hungary at the same time as the Cumanians and integrated the same way.

The *Hajdúság* around Debrecen is named after the "Hajdús", who were Magyar cattle drovers, then, during the Turkish wars, foot-soldiers. In recognition of their gallant service, Prince István Bocskai of Transylvania gave them special privileges and resettled them in this area.

The people and their art

The Great Plain is the most typically Magyar region of the Carpathian basin. Árpád's Magyars settled here first and in Transdanubia. Their descendants constitute the hardy peasant stock which has survived a thousand years of floods, droughts, wars, pillage and destruction. Their destiny is best described by the words of one of the Hungarian national anthems: "Here you must live and die . . ."

The peasant culture of the Plain is remarkably uniform as the development of large market towns and easy communication have prevented the formation of specific regional cultures.

Timber belltower (Northern Great Plain).

History left its mark on the *art* of the people here. The inheritance of pre-Christian art still lives in certain ornamental patterns on carved objects. Asian motifs are sometimes found in folk-costume decorations, such as the patterns of Iranian inspiration in the Jász region. The Renaissance culture left its mark on costume decoration. Turkish influence was also rather strong: gaudy ornamental patterns were introduced by Turkish craftsmen.

In this treeless area the main *building* material used to be reinforced adobe. Timber structures are found in the northeastern wooded areas only, around the town of *Nyiregyháza* where several villages have fine timber belltowers with steeples topped by four little turrets. Woodcarving has been an ancient art in the Nyiregyháza district, the best example being the Calvinist church at Nyirbátor. Furniture carvings often preserve the religious medieval inspiration on the hewn (bridal) chests. Around Kalocsa women paint the furniture and walls with improvised, gay flower designs.

Leatherwork and horn-carving had been the favourite craft of the nomadic horsemen before their settlement in Hungary. Shepherds and others connected with animal husbandry have kept this ancient art alive till the present times.

The Plain is a thirsty country — drinking vessels of various shapes, mugs, pitchers and jugs are popular artifacts. During the Middle Ages *potters* settled in special towns and specialised in certain types of pottery.

The cold winters of the continental climate suggest the use of hides and sheepskin as the basic material of the shepherds' outer *clothing*. Short jackets, called "ködmön" or "bekecs", are worn by men as well as women. The shepherd's thick coat, called "suba", is made of the skins of long-woolled sheep. The wool is left in its natural state whilst the skin side is often ornamented with applique embroidery made by the men. It protects the wearer against the extremes of the Plain climate: in summer, with the wool outside, it protects him from the heat; in winter the wool is inside to keep him warm. The "szür" is more elaborate: it is a frieze mantle or felt-coat with applied embroidery.

Women's dresses are, of course, much brighter and more varied. The *Kalocsa* region is world famous for its brightly

140

Kalocsa folkwear

coloured, embroidered dresses. The colour schemes are gay (22 shades are used), as befits the sunny climate, and the decorative patterns are mostly stylized flowers (roses and tulips): their choice of colouring shows the effects of Renaissance taste. The white apron is trimmed with lace, the full skirt pleated and many petticoats are worn under it. Coloured stockings and (red) slippers complete the dress. Unmarried girls wear a bright-coloured headdress ("párta") which they exchange for a bright-coloured kerchief after marriage. As they grow older the colours become sombre. Blue is the colour of the widows.

Embroidery in all shades is frequently applied not only to dresses but also to pillow slips, tablecloths and bedcovers. The designs often contain imaginative flower patterns or shapes resembling peacock-tails. In the Cumanian region homespun linen is decorated with applique homespun wool — a special art, the Cumanians' eastern inheritance.

Folk customs

Unlike folk music and poetry, customs do not change with the times. They perpetuate the original gestures and actions connected with some long-forgotten myth or rite of pagan times or some mystic, superstitious belief which is no longer respected. The pantomime-like movements add colour and mystery to festival occasions of the peasants' life without any religious or moral relevance.

The folk customs mentioned in this chapter are common to most regions in Hungary. The central and open location of the Plain did not favour the development of characteristic regional folklore.

Easter is the first festival of spring and spring is the herald of love. Thus on Easter Monday the boys sprinkle water on the girls in a poetic well-wishing gesture. Usually scented water is used, except when things get out of hand with a few bucketfuls of fresh well-water "thrown in". The girls thank the boys for the gesture by offering them colourful painted eggs — an old pagan symbol of spring. This old custom has survived everywhere in Hungary and even among Hungarians settled in foreign countries.

Setting up *maypoles* on the first of May used to be a popular custom. The lad set up a tall pole with a large bunch of lilac (a native Hungarian flower) at the top in front of the house

142

of his sweetheart. She indicated her acceptance by adding colourful ribbons to the decoration of the pole.

Each region has its characteristic *wedding customs* with local songs, dances, well-wishing and farewelling addresses in verse. The most moving scene is the bride's farewell to her parents and their reply, often tinged with nostalgic childhood reminiscences and good peasant moral philosophy.[1] Peasant weddings are elaborate and expensive affairs and it is no wonder that divorce is unknown among peasants: obviously no one can afford two weddings in a lifetime.

Harvest and vintage festivals are still popular in a country where so much depends on the year's harvest. At these festivals, a variety of slow and fast dances and songs expresses the various moods of the harvesters: the dignified ritual of thanksgiving alternates with the more temperamental celebration and tasting of the results of their toil: the fresh bread and the new wine.

The long continental *winter* is the period of light work around the house, rest and relaxation for the peasant. The winter calendar has many festival days connected with some ancient customs which have lost their original significance. The period before Christmas is also the right time to kill the fattened pigs which provide many items of the farmers' winter diet. The killing and preparing are usually done in a co-operative fashion with the help of the neighbours, who stay for the tasting of the fresh products.

The Christmas and Epiphany customs with their Christian religious character are discussed in Chapter 21.

On New Year's Eve and on New Year's Day the usual revelries are often seasoned with certain customs of pagan origin. Such a custom is the "kongó" (sounding), a noisy procession. The noise is supposed to "frighten the darkness away": a relic of pagan Winter Solstice rites.

Name-days are welcome opportunities for family celebrations, especially in winter. Hungarians do not celebrate their birthdays, but they celebrate the Church feast day of their patron saint, whether they are Catholics or Protestants. On this day, especially if it is a parent's name-day, the family and friends gather and often sing one of the beautiful well-wishing folksongs and include the name of the person celebrated.[2] By the same token,

Catholic villages hold their annual fair ("búcsú") on the feast-day of the patron saint of their local church.

Constant *social changes* characterise the peasants' life today. Young men and girls flock to nearby towns or big cities to find employment, abandoning their ancient, peasant way of life. Thus much of the folk art, music and customs have ceased to be the spontaneous manifestation of the peasant soul. Instead it has become a carefully preserved and treasured cultural heritage. Folklore and folk art have, by their originality, inspired urban art, music and literature and by their very decline have helped to create a revival of folk-inspired art and music in Hungary.

19. REFORMS, REVOLUTION, REACTION

(Hungary's history from 1800 to the Freedom War
of 1848-49)

The awakening

When Napoleon reached the Hungarian frontier during his Austrian campaign (1809) he called on the Hungarians to rise against Austria. Remembering Louis XIV and his promises to Rákóczi, the Hungarians did nothing — and for once that was the right thing to do. They even fulfilled their obligations by supplying troops to the Emperor, *Francis I* (1792-1832) against Napoleon, though with considerably less enthusiasm than their ancestors did to help Maria Theresa — but then Francis lacked the remarkable attributes of his grandmother.

After Napoleon's fall the Vienna Congress (1815) set up the Holy Alliance of the victorious powers with the aim of re-establishing the rule of absolutism in Europe. In Austria, which had become an Empire after the demise of the unlamented Holy Roman (German) Empire in 1804, Chancellor Metternich, the most forceful statesman of the time, ruled with an iron will on behalf of the feeble-minded Francis I.

It was during the years of this despotic government that, at long last, a number of young Hungarian nobles began to assess the condition of their nation. Slowly awakening after her "lost century", Hungary was a century behind the West and in need of urgent social, economic and constitutional reforms. The problems awaiting solution were immense:

(a) The language of the government, legislation and education was still either German or Latin.

145

(b) As a result of the Austrian resettlement policies the proportion of the non-Magyar nationalities rose to 50% of the total population of 12 million by 1820.

(c) Agricultural production — Hungary's allotted role in the Empire — suffered from old-fashioned methods, fluctuation of prices, inflation caused by the wars and neglect by absentee landlords.

(d) There were hardly any Magyar middle classes. The Austrian policy discouraged the creation of industry in Hungary and the rudimentary trade and commerce were almost exclusively in the hands of German-Austrian burghers and recent Jewish immigrants.

When the Diet was finally convoked in 1825, the rapidly increasing group of reformers was ready to suggest measures to solve these problems, but the Viennese Imperial Council, headed by Metternich and Count Kolowrat, an avowed enemy of the Hungarians, refused to respond to their demands.

The first of these reformers was Count ISTVÁN (STEPHEN) SZÉCHENYI (1791-1860), son of one of the few progressive Catholic aristocrats of Transdanubia. After a distinguished service with the imperial cavalry, young Széchenyi visited the western countries, (especially Great Britain), studying their democratic institutions, industry, economy, finances and agriculture. Returning to Hungary, he attended the 1825 Diet where he offered a large endowment toward the foundation of a National Academy of Sciences. Soon afterwards he summed up his suggestions in a book entitled "Hitel" (Credit) (1830). He advocated equality of opportunity for all members of the nation, including serfs and nationalities, and blamed the complacent and reactionary nobility for the nation's backwardness. He also advocated the solution of the social and economic problems before attacking the constitutional ones. A surprisingly large number of aristocrats and nobles welcomed his suggestions, however unpalatable they seemed to the conservatives.

At the Diet of 1832 another leading figure appeared, LAJOS (LOUIS) KOSSUTH (1802-1894). Scion of an old Protestant noble family of Upper Hungary, he was a lawyer by profession and possessed exceptional talents as an orator, writer and statesman. He immediately joined Széchenyi's reform circle. Though they eventually became political opponents,

Count István Széchenyi (1791-1860)

> *"Either the Magyar words*
> *Shall have new senses,*
> *Or Magyar life will stay sad,*
> *Ever changeless . . . "*

(Ady)

Kossuth always maintained great respect for Széchenyi, whom he called "the greatest of Hungarians." Kossuth considered the nation's political freedom and the constitutional reform as his prime target, while Széchenyi insisted that the nation must maintain its traditional ties with the dynasty and Austria and should carry out internal social and economic reforms first. During the subsequent Diets this difference in priorities separated Kossuth's "Liberals" from Széchenyi's "Moderates". The Vienna Council looked at Kossuth's activities with increased suspicion and had him imprisoned for a while for breaches of the censorship laws (for having published a handwritten record of the Parliamentary proceedings).

After his release from prison, Kossuth became the political leader of the reformers while Széchenyi concentrated on promoting in a practical and unspectacular way the *economic and cultural reforms* he had suggested. He spent most of his considerable income in financing or initiating such projects as the development of steamship navigation, river regulation and flood mitigation schemes, the building the the first suspension bridge between Pest and Buda over the Danube river and the publication of further works expounding his ideas.

The new Emperor-King, *Ferdinand V* (1835-1848) was an imbecile and had no say in the affairs of the Empire. The incessant demands of the Diet had finally some effect upon the Imperial Council and so the 1842 Diet was able to codify the use of Hungarian as the official language of the country. After 300 years the nation was allowed to use its own language in its own country . . .

The peaceful "Revolution"

The Diet of 1847-48 was opened by the Emperor-King — in Hungarian. The first Habsburg in 300 years to use the language of his "loyal subjects" caused immense enthusiasm (and some merriment) among the assembled deputies. The Liberals, led by Kossuth in the Lower House and by Count Lajos Batthányi in the Upper House, had practically unanimous support in both Houses. The Viennese Council began to show a more lenient attitude, especially after the fall of the French monarchy which was followed by uprisings in several cities of the Empire — though not in Hungary (February 1848). Metternich resigned and a deputation of the Hungarian Parliament was received in Vienna by the Emperor (or rather by the Imperial Council, nicknamed "The Kamarilla"). The deputation submitted the demands of the nation and these demands were accepted by a much mellowed Council. A *responsible government* was ap-

The first Hungarian Government of 1848
and the Parliament (built in 1885).

pointed with Count Lajos Batthányi as its Prime Minister and the other leaders, such as Kossuth and Széchenyi, as Ministers.

Dissatisfied with the progress of the Diet (which was meeting in Pozsony, on the Austrian border) and not knowing of the Vienna development, the youth of Pest and Buda decided to go into action on the *15th March, 1848*. The poet Petöfi wrote a stirring poem "Rise Hungarians" and read it to the assembled demonstrators. A crowd moved in a disciplined procession to the Buda Chancellery (the Office of the Governor-General) and presented their demands — the famous "12 Points" — printed, for the first time, without the censor's permission. These points were almost word for word identical with the Liberal platform which had just been accepted in Vienna. The military watched the demonstration with sympathy — not a shot was fired on this day.

Thus the people of the nation's capital expressed, without bloodshed, its unanimous decision to abolish serfdom and accept sweeping reforms — an achievement which had cost the French nation hundreds of thousands of lives half a century before.

March the fifteenth, with its symbolic gesture has since remained the Hungarians' greatest national day, the one day of the year when Hungarians all over the world forget their differences and discover what unites them: their love of freedom.

In April 1848 royal sanction was given to Hungary's *new constitution*. The main innovations of this constitution were:

1. Establishment of a responsible government. The King's decrees were only valid when countersigned by the government.

2. Re-establishment of the union with Transylvania.

3. Abolition of serfdom and equality for all before the law and equality of tax burdens.

4. Freedom of religion and of the press.

5. The establishment of a national guard (the "Honvéd" army).

6. Parliamentary elections by popular vote.

The relations with Austria remained unchanged: Hungary became an "independent kingdom" within the framework of the dual monarchy under the Habsburg ruler.

Though the feudal privileges were abolished overnight and no compensation was ever paid to the landlords for the loss of their serfs, there was no hostile reaction from the Hungarian nobility. It was obvious that the nobility's much criticised "feudal attitude" had been motivated by lassitude and passivity rather than anti-social ideology.

Austrian intervention

The new Austrian Chancellor, Kolowrat, decided to neutralise the effects of the new constitution, "extorted, under revolutionary threats, from the feeble-minded Emperor" (as he put it). The Council roused the nationalities against the Magyars. The Magyar-hating Governor of Croatia, Colonel Jellasich, claimed that the new constitution endangered the traditional Croat freedom. So he demanded the restoration of centralised Viennese administration. The Serbs began to demand an independent Serbian state in the southern districts of Hungary. The Rumanians of Transylvania became the most willing weapons of the Viennese interference. They and the Serbs set out on a cruel and senseless campaign of pillage and murder against the defenceless Magyar population (which had no Magyar defence forces yet), while the Austrian garrisons stood by passively. In the north the Slovaks and the Ruthenes did not follow the example of the southern minorities. In fact thousands of them later joined the Hungarian "Honvéds" in fighting the Austrians.

In June 1848 the murderous rampage of the Rumanians and Serbs moved the Hungarian Parliament to set up the National Defence Force. A National Defence Committee was formed with Kossuth as its chairman to co-ordinate the defence of the nation. By the end of September, the Imperial Council had practically repudiated the April constitution and ordered the Austrian and Croat troops to crush the Hungarian "rebellion". As a result of an unfortunate misunderstanding, the Austrian general Lamberg was killed in Pest. This inexcusable violence had far-reaching consequences: Prime Minister Batthányi resigned and so did Széchenyi. This great man, horrified by the vision of a civil war, suffered a nervous breakdown and was taken to a Vienna asylum where he died by his own hand in 1860.

Kossuth, as head of the *National Defence Committee,* became virtually the Prime Minister. He remained, in fact, the actual leader of the nation during the ensuing struggle. In October the Emperor-King was made to sign a decree dissolving the Parliament and dismissing the government. As this decree was not countersigned by the government, it was not legal, of course.

Austrian and Croat troops crossed into Transdanubia under Jellasich in September but this well-equipped regular army was defeated by a small force of hastily mobilised national guards under two young officers, Arthur Görgey and Mór Perczel. The news of the defeat caused a short-lived uprising in Vienna (during which the hated war-minister, Latour, was lynched by the Austrian rebels). So, in retaliation, the imperial commander, Windischgrätz, launched a full-scale campaign against Hungary.

In December the Council forced the old Emperor, Ferdinand, to resign and his 18 year-old nephew *Francis Joseph* was declared Emperor. He was not even next in line of succession, the Hungarian government was not consulted and Francis Joseph was not crowned King of Hungary,

Thus Hungary was facing what amounted to external aggression by a nominal ruler imposed illegally by a coup d'etat.

The war of self-defence

The subsequent war has been called "War of Independence" or "Freedom War", even "Revolutionary War". At this stage it was none of these. Hungary did have her independence, guaranteed in the April constitution, similarly the freedom of a modern democratic society. No Hungarian leader wanted more in December 1848. Thus the subsequent armed conflict can be termed nothing but the defensive war of an attacked nation and its legal government against an external aggressor and its internal allies, the insurgent nationalities. For the same reason, many imperial officers — Austrians and Germans — joined the newly organised "Honvéd" army.

The Diet, on Kossuth's advice, appointed *Arthur Görgey* commander-in-chief of the National Army. Görgey, a former guards officer, a man with a cool scientific approach to military strategy, but also with great personal courage, was an excellent choice. On learning of Windischgrätz' attack he withdrew his untrained troops to the northern mountains. In Transylvania Kossuth appointed the brilliant Polish general, *Joseph Bem,* to restore order, which this admirable old man did, against overwhelming forces (Austrians and Rumanian irregulars). He was equipped with little more than the admiration of his soldiers, a strategic intuition and determination.

The northern army of Görgey, trained, hardened and rested, launched the victorious *"Spring campaign"* in March 1849 and soon reached the Danube-bend, north of Budapest. It then turned to the north, defeating and outmanoeuving Windischgrätz' well-equipped regulars repeatedly. At the end of this whirlwind campaign, the imperials held only the fort of Buda and the frontier city of Pozsony. Windischgrätz was dismissed in disgrace. In the meantime, the south of Hungary was pacified by Mór Perczel, a gifted civilian-general and the Serbian-born John Damjanich who, disgusted with the atrocities committed by his fellow nationals, joined the Hungarians and became one of their most successful generals. Bem was holding Transylvania: Hungary seemed to have defended herself successfully.

Independence, Russian intervention, defeat

On the 4th of March, 1849, Francis Joseph proclaimed the abolition of Hungary's self-government. Kossuth decided to end Hungary's constitutional vacuum and convened the Diet in Debrecen. On the 14th of April, 1849, the Diet declared Hungary's *complete independence,* dethroned the Habsburg dynasty and elected Kossuth Regent. A new ministry was formed with Bertalan Szemere as the Prime Minister.

Whilst legally justified, this action came at the wrong time. The revolutions and uprisings of Europe had by then been defeated, except in Hungary. Moreover, unknown to the Hungarians, Austria had already asked for the Russians' help to crush the Hungarian "rebellion". The Tsar obliged and dispatched 200,000 elite troops against Hungary.

On the government's instructions Görgey undertook the wasteful siege of Buda and took the strong fort in May. By that time, however, a newly organised Austrian army and fresh Russian troops were preparing for a new assault — a total force of 450,000 with 1,700 cannon, against the exhausted, under-equipped Honvéd army of 170,000 (with 450 cannon). Görgey made several bold attempts at defeating the Austrians before the arrival of the Russians, once he led a cavalry charge himself and was gravely wounded. Eventually he had to withdraw before the joint Russian-Austrian forces. In August Kossuth realised that the war was lost and transferred all his powers to Görgey, then left the country.

On the 13th of August, 1849 Görgey, at the head of the remaining Honvéd troops, *capitulated* before the Russian commander. The fortress of Komárom under the brilliant young general Klapka, held out for another six weeks.

The sadistic Austrian general Haynau (nicknamed "the Hyena" for his cruelty in Italy), was made Hungary's military dictator to vent his wrath upon a defenceless people. He had 160 soldiers and civilians executed, among them 13 generals and ex-Prime Minister Batthányi, and sentenced thousands to long prison terms. At the Tsar's special request Görgey was pardoned and interned in Austria.

20. ROMANTIC RENAISSANCE

(Literature, art and music in the first half of the XIXth century)

Classical literature and culture have always had their attraction for the Hungarians. Thus, at the end of the XVIIIth century, the first writers attempting to arouse the somnolent nation used the inspiration of the great Greek and Roman poets.

The "Horatian" odes of *Daniel Berzsenyi* (1176-1836) expressed his thoughts in rhythmic, classic metre and rather old-fashioned Hungarian language. He was a pessimist — but then he had so much to be pessimistic about: the attitudes of the Hungarian nobles at the turn of the century gave him little hope for national revival. So he found consolation in the memories of the glorious past and, eventually, in the placid haven of stoicism in the true Roman fashion.[1]

MIHALY CSOKONAI-VITÉZ (1773-1805), the restless minstrel of Debrecen, a lyricist with a pleasant blend of classic-humanistic and Magyar folk inspiration, wrote love poetry in fresh, folkish language with just a touch of melancholy and eroticism. This, and his volatile way of life, made him unpopular with his hypocritical contemporaries. The lyric cycle "Lilla's Songs" (published, like most of his work, after his death) is a collection of sincere, often sensuous love songs, sometimes under the disguise of the fashionable flower imagery of his age ("To the Rosebud")[2]. His comic epic, "Dorothy", a satire of the "high society" of his time, with its gently erotic fantasies became one of the most popular works young ladies were not supposed to read. He also wrote lyrics for many songs of contemporary Hungarian composers. These, being intended for use in "good society", limit themselves to romantic meditations of the type young ladies were allowed to swoon about. ("To Hope")[3].

Though his classic-humanistic education was coloured by considerable French influence, *Sándor (Alexander) Kisfaludy* (1772-1844), deserves mention here for his pleasant lyric cycle, "Himfy's Loves", divided into two parts. The first, "Lamenting Love", was written after his return from French captivity, which seemed to have been made more than bearable by the charitable attentions of the French ladies. No wonder that the young hussar, none the worse for his "French leave", received a rather cool reception from the lady of his heart (the Hungarian one, that is). In the rhythmic, rhyming stanzas (a verse form of his own creation), Kisfaludy used a smooth, pleasant flow of rather old-fashioned but rich and colourful phrases to describe mankind's oldest sentiment. His colourful nature descriptions show the inspiration of French Romanticism (the result of his extended study-tour in France), without any of the popular German sentimentality of the period.[4] His obvious sincerity and veiled threats to take up military service again caused his Rosa to forget and forgive. She married him and Sándor wrote the second part of his cycle, "Happy Love", which turned out to be considerably shorter than the first part. Then they lived happily ever after — for forty more years — without the help of poetry.

The Renewal of the Language

The Magyar language which had already demonstrated its suitability for literature during the XVIth and XVIIth centuries, became practically obsolete during the XVIIIth century with its German and Latin culture. Reading Hungarian books was just "not the thing to do". Thus the young intellectuals of the "Reform generation" at the beginning of the XIXth century realised that the Magyar language needed rejuvenation. The leader of the "language renewal" was *Ferenc (Francis) Kazinczy*, a great linguist, man of letters and poet. He and his circle of language reformers enriched the language with many new words made up by linguistic methods of derivation.

Kazinczy's disciple, *Ferenc Kölcsey* (1790-1838) is remembered as the author of Hungary's national anthem, the "Himnusz"[5], a great but rather melancholic patriotic elegy. His calm stoicism tended to turn into despondent pessimism toward the end of his life. His last poem, "Zrinyi's Second Song", the saddest voice in Magyar literature, conjures up the harrowing vision of the self-destruction of the Hungarian nation, its place *"taken by another nation on the banks of the four rivers. . ."*

The independent Romantic poet, KÁROLY (CHARLES) KISFALUDY (1788-1830), Sándor's brother, broke with the conservative traditions of his family and began his artistic career as an itinerant painter. His first literary creations were romantic tragedies, followed by more successful comedies. The basic concept in both was the conflict between conservatism and progress, often presented as the "generation gap". In his search for fresh vocabulary, he turned to the people and adopted many folk poetry phrases and even wrote folkish song texts, some of which are still popular Magyar songs. His patriotic poetry ("Mohács") expresses hope in the future instead of lamenting over the past as was the fashion in his days.

The humorous ballad "The Sorrowing Husband"[6] gave the Magyar language a proverb — the last line of the poem.

Kisfaludy's literary review "Aurora" became the rallying point of critics and poets.

The Romantic Drama and Prose

József (Joseph) Katona (1791-1830), author of the great drama "Bánk Bán", remained practically unknown during his lifetime. The drama, written in 1815, is a historical tragedy in five acts in blank verse. The plot is based on a doubtful historic incident of the XIIIth century: the Palatin, Bánk, in the absence of the King is drawn into a violent clash with the Queen and her foreign advisors and eventually kills her. Katona's characterisation is excellent. Following the example of the French drama, he uses several strong personalities whose violent confrontation causes almost unbearable tension. The drama was later made into a great opera by the composer, Ferenc Erkel.

The historical novel "Abafi", written by the Transylvanian Baron *Miklós Jósika* in 1836, was the first successful Hungarian novel.

Baron József Eötvös (1813-1871), a man with many talents, was a well-known political figure, a moderate reformer, before and after the War of 1848-49, a pioneer of the social novel, a lyric and epic poet and an important and respected literary critic. His first novel, "The Carthusian", was a typical product of the epidemic melancholy called "mal du siecle" which became the fad of the mid-XIXth century. "The Village Notary" is an excellent satire of backward country nobility.

Mihaly (Michael) Vorosmarty

Born in 1800 of a poor, Catholic noble family of Transdanubia, and educated in Pest, Vörösmarty spent most of his life in the Hungarian capital as Director of the Academy of Sciences and leading literary critic. During the War of 1848-49 he was a member of the Parliament and had to hide after the capitulation. Amnestied, he spent the last years of his life in Pest. He died in 1855.

He established his poetic fame in 1825 with the *epic* "Zalan's Flight", based on the legends of the conquest of Hungary in the IXth century. This work revived the art of the epic, silent in Hungary since the XVIIth century but very popular in western Europe during the Romantic period. The colourful style and the imaginative beauty of the descriptive passages lend an almost lyric character to this youthful work. The smoothly flowing classical hexametres blend remarkably with the flexible Magyar language of which Vörösmarty became the accomplished master.

In addition to several heroic epics, he also wrote pleasant *narrative poems* of a lighter nature, of which "Fair Helen" is the best example. The romantic love story of King Matthias and the beautiful Ilonka comes to the inevitable melancholic ending so dear to the hearts of the readers of the age.[7]

Vörösmarty established his fame with his epic poems but he really excelled in an original type of contemplative *lyric poetry,* of which he was the greatest master in Hungarian literature. The most characteristic of these philosophical poems is his wedding gift to his bride: "To the Daydreamer"[8]. A few years later, Petöfi wrote his most beautiful poem to his wife. Being inspired by their own wives, a rare occurrence in world literature, seems to be another of those "Hungarian inventions".

Many lyric poems are elegies or odes with ballad-like elements in a meditative mood, often ending in melancholic messages. Stoic reflections on the futility of human progress inspire Vörös-

Mihály Vörösmarty (1800-1855).

marty's deep "Thoughts in a Library"[9], a pessimistic vision of the value of human knowledge. His great patriotic hymn, "Appeal" ("Szózat"), though pessimistic in its tone, became the nation's second anthem.[10] His greeting to Ferenc Liszt received a gratifying echo from the great composer in the form of the symphonic poem "Hungaria".

Vörösmarty's last poem; "The Old Gypsy", conjures an apocalyptic vision of the nation's destruction but ends in a glimmer of hope.[11] It was written at the height of Austrian oppression after the Independence War.

His most durable *drama* is the fairy-tale fantasy "Csongor and Tünde", based on a medieval romance with some Magyar folk-tale elements.

Vörösmarty's poetry is romantic and objective — classical — at the same time. It expresses the temperament of a typical Magyar of Transdanubia, the "western Magyar", like his great ideal, Széchenyi. His deep Catholicism is devoid of dry puritanism, his sincere emotions lack the fiery passion of the "eastern Magyar" poets (Csokonai), his rich vocabulary describes his themes with classical precision and clarity, his wit is anodyne and his patriotism, though melancholic, is never despondent.

*   *   *

The search for a national art form

By the turn of the century, the Hungarian writers had found their Romantic-Classical-Magyar style but the artists had grave problems. There were no art schools in Hungary; they had to go to the West in order to study. Many did — and some never returned to Hungary. Those who did return found it hard to receive commissions from the Hungarian magnates, who preferred foreign artists.

The pressing need for new churches, public buildings and ornate homes called for increasing activity in the field of *architecture*. The Hungarian-born architects chose neo-classicism as their favourite style in silent protest against Vienna's Rococo and Baroque. Neo-classicism, congenial to the Magyar taste, gained special national characteristics by the addition of certain provincial elements, especially in the smaller country buildings.

The first monumental building of the neo-classic style was the Debrecen Reformed Church built by M. Péchy, who also

"Portrait of Mrs. Bittó" by M. Barabás.

built the Reformed College in the same town. The most eminent neo-classic architect was *Mihály Pollack,* who worked in Pest. His chief achievement is the Hungarian National Museum (1837). József Hild took part in the building of the Esztergom cathedral (the largest in Hungary) and built the Eger cathedral.

The first noteworthy Hungarian *sculptor* of the era was *István Ferenczy* (1792-1856), who received no support from the rich magnates and prelates who preferred foreign sculptors. His first

161

success, a bust of the poet Csokonai, was his gift to the town of Debrecen. His masterpiece, "The Shepherdess", is the best example of Hungarian sculpture since the Renaissance. He was acclaimed — but remained poor. In his later years he conducted an art school which eventually produced the greatest Hungarian sculptor of the century, M. Izsó.

The *painters* suffered less from lack of financial support as their art did not need much capital. Still, many talented painters remained abroad as their country did not seem to need their talent.

Károly Markó, the romantic landscape painter, worked abroad most of the time, but on his short visits to Hungary he painted impressive landscapes ("Visegrád"). Károly Kisfaludy, the poet, was also an imaginative painter of stormy landscapes.

The eighteen-forties witnessed the beginning of the career of the greatest Hungarian romantic painter, *Miklós Barabás* (1810-1898). He lived and achieved success in Hungary. His specific style, a synthesis of Romantic and Classic elements and Magyar temperament appealed to the aristocracy as well as the middle classes. The great majority of his works were portraits with just a degree of romantic idealisation but without sentimentality or eccentricity ("Mrs. Bitto").

Károly Brocky studied and worked abroad. He acquired fame in London with his romantic mythological themes and portraits.

The *applied arts* suffered similarly from financial problems. The Herend porcelain factory was founded during this period and began to produce its world-famous figurines.

*   *   *

Romantic and patriotic music

Interest in the *music of the people* added impulse to the revival of Magyar music at the beginning of the XIXth century. Collections of folk songs began to appear. Poets and musicians began to discover the rich treasures of folk music and poetry.

When the Germanisation policies of Joseph II finally aroused the Magyars' national pride, the so-called "toborzó" ("verbunk") became the fiery symbol of Magyar spirit, especially through the interpretation of the gypsy bands.

The popular composers of the early XIXth century found inspiration in the "toborzó"-folkmusic type melodies; they included János Lavotta, the famous violin virtuoso, Antal Csermák, the first Hungarian composer of chamber music, and Mark Rózsavölgyi, composer of ballroom music and opera.

The folk and "toborzó" melodies served as inspiration for the melodic themes of the emerging new music form, the *opera*. József Ruzicska's "Béla's Flight" was the first noteworthy Hungarian opera.

Ferenc Erkel (1810-1893) was the real creator of Hungarian opera and its greatest master. A native of the Great Plain, he went to the capital where he became the conductor of the National Theatre and later the Director of the Academy of Music (under its president, Ferenc Liszt). Erkel found the harmonious synthesis of western operatic structures, techniques and styles and genuine national themes, taking his inspiration from the popular music of his time. His romantic interpretation of the spirit of Hungarian history suited the mood of the national revival.

His first opera was performed in 1840. His first great success was "László Hunyadi" (1844), a true expression of the romantic-patriotic mood of the forties projected into the XVth century atmosphere of the plot: the tragic story of János Hunyadi's elder son, László, destroyed by the king's perfidious counsellors. The music and the plot presented a strikingly accurate picture of the nation's emotions in the forties: the impatience and frustration caused by the Viennese king's counsellors' delaying and repressive tactics.

Erkel's greatest opera, "Bánk Bán", was performed long after the failure of the struggle for independence, a few years before the "Compromise". Based on Katona's drama with a slightly modified libretto, the story and the melodies expressed the nation's will to survive in spite of the Austrian oppression.

In his later years Erkel composed several operas which came increasingly under Wagnerian inspiration and lost some of their characteristically Hungarian flavour.

Mihály Mosonyi, Erkel's contemporary, aimed to find a national music form in the field of instrumental music. His more memorable works were composed for single instruments or orchestra and choir. The best known of these is his "Funeral

Music", commemorating the death of István Széchenyi. His romantic-mythological oratorio, "Feast of Purification", deserves to be better known.

Some performing artists of the period became world famous. Apart from Ferenc Liszt and János Lavotta, Ede Reményi and Jozsef Joachim violin virtuosos made Hungarian popular music known all over the world.

Imre Madách (1823-1864)
(Cf. Ch. 23)

21. "SHEPHERDS AND KINGS. . ."

(The Christian inspiration of Hungarian folk poetry)

The old religion of the pre-Settlement Magyars presented remarkable similarities to Christianity. Its moral and theological structure was basically that of a monotheistic, animistic faith, based on the adoration of one God ("Isten") and respect and veneration for many spirits, such as the spirits of their departed ancestors and angel-like super-beings. These were respected in much the same way that Christianity respects its saints, angels and the memory of departed souls. Thus *the ancient Magyar religion* cannot be called "paganism" in the polytheistic sense of the Greco-Roman or Assyrian-Babylonian religions.

Christianity has often accepted and used the framework of certain pagan myths and festivals, replacing them with its own liturgic content. Thus the Magyars found it congenial to celebrate the mysteries of Christianity, such as Christmas, Easter, Whitsun and the feasts of some saints (especially those of the Blessed Virgin), by providing them with the colour and warmth of their own millenia-old poetic myths and rites. Folk poems, ballads, legends, anecdotes and dramatic presentations connected with Christian festivals abound among the Magyar people of all denominations. This folk poetry of Christian inspiration offers a fascinating field of folklore study, hitherto not sufficiently explored.

The *language* of Christian liturgy has provided the people with a rich store of religious phraseology. The colourful imagery of Christian liturgy has always appealed to the anonymous poets of the people who adopted this inspiration with their characteristic emotional-religious nationalism.

165

The richest treasure of religious folk poetry is found in plays and songs connected with *Christmas*. Many *Christmas carols* are sung in connection with the Church service, others form part of the Bethlehem plays.

This time of the year, the winter solstice — the resurrection of the sun after the shortest day of the year December 22 — used to herald the increase of life-giving sunshine in pagan liturgy. Thus from time immemorial this has been the season of festivities. The pagans used to celebrate the Sun-God, the Christians the birth of Christ, their "Life-giving Sun". Ancient rites have been Christianised, but memories of old festivities of the Sun still linger in Hungarian folk hymns, such as the refrain of a popular carol: *"Oh life, oh sunshine — Oh dear little Jesus . . ."*

The role of the humble herdsmen in the Bethlehem story has always appealed to the Magyar peasant. Some carols present a cheerful, dance rhythm, such as the "Shepherds' Dance" from Central Hungary.[1] Some carols of a more solemn nature begin with the Latin words of the Catholic liturgy[2]. The angels' call to the herdsmen of Bethlehem on Christmas night inspired many folk carols. The best-known of these: "Herdsmen . . ."[3], first recorded in a XVIIth century hymn book, is found in many varieties in all Magyar-speaking areas.

One of the most popular carols, known in Transylvania and the Great Plain, begins with the Greek words of the Catholic liturgy (slightly Magyarised): "Kirje, kirje . . ."[4]. The naive charm of the text and the purity of the ancient tune leave no doubt that we hear one of the genuine creations of the people, probably the Székelys of eastern Transylvania from where it must have spread to the other regions. Here the majestic Christ of the liturgy becomes a sweet little baby surrounded by His mother and simple shepherds, worried about the cold and wishing they could give the Divine Child the comfort which, according to the gospel, had been denied to Him in Bethlehem.

Another shepherd-carol, "Shepherds . . ."[5] is known in many regions. Both the text and the melody are folk creations and show no scholarly influence. This simple folk hymn has become a standard part of the Christmas Midnight Masses in Hungary.

The commemoration of Jesus Christ's birth in Bethlehem has been the subject of festival plays and puppet-shows presented

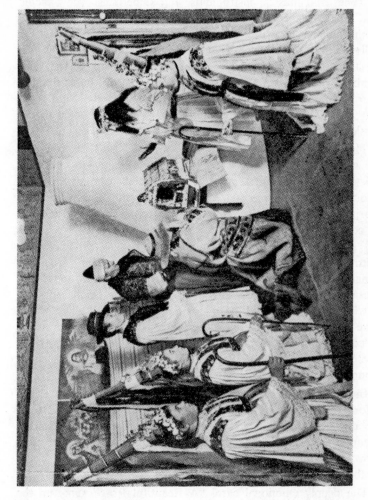

A "Bethlehem" play.

at Christmas time in all Christian countries since the Middle Ages. These *Bethlehem-plays,* impromptu dramatic performances, have become part of the Hungarian peasants' Christmas celebrations too. Performed by troupes of children or adults, these plays are often combined with presentations of puppets, accompanied by songs and musical instruments, and sometimes even dancing. The scene is usually the stable with Mary and Joseph standing at the manger in which the child Jesus — a doll or sometimes a live baby — is lying. The herdsmen arrive during the play or stand at the manger when the play starts. Angels and other symbolic characters — representing the good and bad principles — often take part in the play. In some regions the child-actors may even take the manger to church and perform there a shorter version of the play.

The songs and texts have many variations and the costumes are sometimes quite elaborate. In the Catholic regions the texts are serious and conform more or less with the church texts and traditions. In the Protestant regions (where the Bethlehem plays are just as popular), the actors often improvise and add a touch of comedy to the play. Their principal actor may be a sleepy old shepherd on whom the younger boys play various tricks. Throughout the play improvisations — humorous or earnest — mingle with beautiful old folk hymns. In many songs the peasants' naive, nostalgic devotion is presented in the form of a wish: "If Jesus had been born in Hungary, things would have been different. He would certainly have received a warmer welcome from his Magyar shepherds"[6]. In the Appendix we quote extracts from a Bethlehem play recorded in western Hungary[7].

In some Bethlehem plays, *marionettes* are made to dance before the manger. They represent symbolic characters: Death, the devil, angels, shepherds, peasants, Herod, soldiers. Candles decorate the elaborate puppet stage and they flicker in the cold, snowy night of the village as the children move from one house to the next.

The deeply emotional carol "A Beautiful Rose" sums up the spirit of these Bethlehem plays as it paints a picture of the Holy Virgin bending over the manger where her Son, the "Beautiful Flower" sleeps: Jesus, who brought sunshine and life to the Earth. Thus Christian and ancient thoughts meet in harmony in the humble, rustic image of the candle-lit scene of Bethlehem.

On the *6th of January (Epiphany),* the Three Wise Men (the Magi or Three Kings) are remembered by the re-enactment of the scene described in the gospels. Three children — often girls — dressed in white robes with mitres, and holding long stocks (sceptres), represent the three Kings. They are often preceded by an "angel" holding a "star" on a pole. They enter each house, calling on the people to "seek the Star over Bethlehem . . ." Their play is connected with the Bethlehem plays and contains carols of a similar nature.

"If I were your cradle I would rock you gently,
I would serve you, Little Jesus." (Folksong)

The customs connected with Easter show, curiously enough, little Christian inspiration. The same is the case with Saint Ivan's Day (Midsummer Day, June 22), as mentioned in the previous chapters. The Whitsun customs, such as the Whitsun-Queen procession, mingle Christian and pagan elements. (cf. Chapter 11).

Of the saints, Saint Stephen, the first king of Hungary, is often remembered in songs. As is the case with the other saints' days, the people who bear the saint's name celebrate their "name's day" and are congratulated, often in flowery verse.

The Magyars accepted Christianity during the XIth century with some reluctance, directed not against the faith but against the foreigners brought to Hungary to propagate it. Once, however, the Christian faith, and with it western civilisation, had been accepted, it became the nation's own heritage, jealously defended through centuries of wars. The new faith became a Hungarian religion, and Christian devotion and Magyar patriotism became synonymous notions. The Magyars began to regard themselves as soldier-knights of Christ and of the *Holy Virgin, the "Patron of Hungary"*. They have an almost romantic veneration for the Virgin Mary, the "Great Queen of Hungary". (By a strange turn of fate, Hungary never had a Hungarian-born queen). Since the XVIIIth century, Catholics have often referred to Hungary as "Regnum Marianum" (Mary's Kingdom").

This emotional cult of Christianity's loveliest saint found deep echoes in the hearts of the Magyars. There are many hymns devoted to the Holy Virgin, some folk creations, others written and composed by unknown artists. The best-known of these is the rather melancholic hymn "Our Mother, Lady of Hungary"[8], probably composed by an unknown scholar of the XVIIth century.

22. GLORY WITHOUT POWER

(Hungarian history from 1849 to 1914)

Passive resistance and compromise

Though Hungary's dictator, general Haynau, was dismissed in 1850, after a year of his reign of terror, the Viennese administration proceeded with its plans for a total absorption of Hungary into the Austrian empire. The entire country was divided into districts administered directly from Vienna. This arrangement, aimed at the forced assimilation of the Magyars, angered the nationalities as well, as they lost even the limited cultural freedom they had enjoyed under Hungarian rule, against which they had so enthusiastically helped the Austrians.

Only a few of the 1848-49 political leaders dared to remain active in Hungary. The most eminent of these was the moderate and wise *Francis Deák,* minister in the first 1848 government. Helped by the leading writers and intellectuals of the nation, Deák urged the Magyars to fight for their freedom by peaceful, passive resistance.

Thus the Viennese regime had to face the mounting dissatisfaction of the nationalities, the passive resistance of the Magyars and soon also the impact of disastrous military and political events in other parts of the empire. The successful uprising led by Garibaldi lost Italy for the Habsburgs. In order to appease the Hungarians, Vienna offered some concessions, but Deák and the other leaders insisted on complete acceptance of the 1848 April constitution (cf. chapter 20). When the short Austrian-Prussian war ended in disaster for Austria (1866), Vienna realised that the empire could not survive without the Hungarians' co-operation. In 1867 the Emperor, Francis Joseph, accepted the entire 1848 April constitution and appointed a second responsible ministry under count Gyula Andrássy. Francis Joseph I and the Empress, Elizabeth were then solemnly crowned in Buda as King and Queen of Hungary.

The 1867 agreement of reconciliation between Austria and Hungary, called *Compromise* ("Kiegyezés"), re-established the dual state structure (cf. chapter 20). The sovereign states, Austria and Hungary, ruled by one hereditary Habsburg monarch, were to share three "common" departments: Foreign Affairs, Finance and Defence, but both states had their own defence forces (national guard) as well as a "common" army.

Lajos Kossuth and the emigration

After the collapse of the freedom struggle, Kossuth sought refuge abroad, accompanied by several political and military leaders. After a short stay in Turkey, he was invited to the United States by the government of that country. An American warship brought Kossuth and his fellow-refugees first to Britain, where he captivated his listeners with his English oratory. (He had learnt English in his Austrian prison). After a triumphal welcome in New York, the Hungarian statesman was invited to address a session of the U.S. House of Representatives (an honour only granted to one other foreign statesman, Winston Churchill). During his stay in America as the "nation's guest" he delivered several hundred speeches in English. Thus he managed to make the fate of his nation known to the western world.[1]

Returning from the U.S., Kossuth lived in England, watching the European political scene and hoping that an opportunity would arise to launch another campaign for his country's freedom. During these years he managed to gain world-wide sympathy for the oppressed Hungarian nation. General Klapka organised "Hungarian Legions" in Italy and during the Prussian-Austrian war a Hungarian legion was actively engaged against the Austrians. Though there were no real prospects of a revolution in Hungary or of an armed intervention, the constant pressure of European and American public opinion maintained against Austrian oppression, and fomented by Kossuth's activities, remained a real threat to Francis Joseph's shaky empire and became a deciding factor in hastening the Austrian acquiescence.

After the Compromise — which he refused to accept — Kossuth withdrew from international politics. He objected to the Compromise because he believed that Hungary, tied to a doomed Austria which was led by ultra-conservative politicians, would eventually suffer the same fate: annihilation. This prophecy turned out to be tragically true. It was Austria's bumbling diplomacy which brought forth the War of 1914, causing Austria's — and with it Hungary's — downfall.

Kossuth in America.

The elderly Kossuth retired in Torino, Italy. In his writings he advocated the formation of a *"Danubian Federation"*, a confederation of Central European nations from Poland to Greece, forming a block of united states between Russia and Germany. These suggestions of the great political philosopher are wishfully remembered today as the only solution that could have prevented the horrors of two world wars.

Kossuth died in Torino, Italy, in 1894. Only then was he allowed to return to the country of his birth. His remains were brought to Budapest and laid to rest there.

The Liberal governments

Prime Minister Andrássy resigned in 1871 to become the Monarchy's Foreign Minister. Eventually, count *Kálmán Tisza* formed the so-called "Liberal Party" which was to govern Hungary for the next 40 years. Tisza himself remained Prime Minister from 1875 to 1890.

The shortcomings of the Compromise all but nullified the concept of equality between Austria and Hungary. The important "common" portfolios of Foreign Affairs, Finance and Defence were managed almost entirely by the Emperor's Austrian advisors and the ministers were Austrians most of the time. Soon, under Kossuth's influence a number of Hungarian politicians began to feel dissatisfied with the 1867 Compromise. The representatives opposed to the spirit of 1867 called their group the "Independence Party". The members of this Parliamentary opposition presented a more or less emotional attitude toward the Compromise but their views on social and cultural matters differed little from those of the government. There was no party with a radical social program in the Hungarian Parliament during the last decades of the XIXth century.

The subsequent Liberal governments were headed by such Prime Ministers as the able economist *Sándor Wekerle* (1892-1895), the efficient administrator *Kálmán Széll* (1899-1903) and the energetic count *István Tisza* (1903-1905).

It was during this period, in 1896, that the nation celebrated the millenary of the occupation of the Carpathian basin by the Magyars of Árpád. The Hungarians celebrated their *"Millenium"* with great pomp and flourish, contemplating their glorious history, cultural, artistic and technical achievements with justifiable pride, but in their complacent euphoria they ignored the signs of the gathering storm which was to destroy their thousand-year-old kingdom in little more than two decades.

The problems of the "millenary" era

Three factors had contributed to the *social problems* of these decades in Hungary: the general European social atmosphere which caused upheavals in almost every country, the conservatism and complacency of the Hungarian ruling classes and the deficiencies of the Compromise.

The Compromise had allotted to Hungary the role of agricultural provider, while Austria, with her industries (well established during Hungary's "lost" XVIIIth century), was to be the prosperous, industrial partner. As there were no tariff frontiers between the two states, Austrian industry had first claim on the cheap Hungarian produce, including Hungary's considerable mineral wealth. The fledgling Hungarian secondary industry had the unenviable task of competing against the efficient Austrian factories. The ineptly managed, often foreign owned, unprofitable Hungarian industries could not assure decent living standards to their workers and soon created discontent among the urban proletariat. Besides, the raw materials and power sources were situated in the mountainous areas of Hungary, which were inhabited mainly by the national minorities. Thus the modest benefits of mining and industrial exploitation affected mostly the non-Magyar population. The Hungarian landed aristocracy made matters worse by preferring the gentlemanly comforts of their old-fashioned estates to the challenges of modern industrial ventures. Similarly, the poor Magyar peasants preferred the poverty of their ancestral villages to the uncertain prospects offered by the slowly developing urban industrial centres. The small landowners — the former lower nobility — were practically ruined by the cheap food prices and their inefficient production methods. So they flocked to the cities to increase the rapidly growing army of public servants — the only occupation worthy of a gentleman. Trade, commerce and the free professions were left to the Germans and Jews.

The ruined peasants and the urban workers dissatisfied with their conditions found the solution for their problems in emigration. Between 1890 and 1914 more than a million Magyars and other nationalities left Hungary for the haven of America.

Like these social problems, the problems of the *national minorities* were largely ignored by the governments and leaders of the "millenary era". At the 1910 census, Hungary proper

175

(without Croatia) had a population of about 18 million. 60% of these — about 11 million — were Magyars, the rest — 7 million — "minorities": Slovaks, Serbs, Rumanians, Germans and others. The *"Nationalities Law" of 1868* granted equal rights to all citizens of Hungary, irrespective of nationality or religion. The official language of the central administration was Hungarian but the lower echelons (counties, municipalities, shires) accepted the use of the language of the national minorities of that area. Denominational schools were allowed to use the language of the supporting nationality. This meant practically unlimited primary and secondary education in the minority languages as in 1868 almost all such schools were denominational.

No European country gave more rights to its minorities at that time. Neither were the social conditions of the minorities harsher than those of the Magyars. In fact the number of landless Hungarian peasants was equal to the *total* number of the Rumanian and Serbian minorities.

Thus the disagreements between Hungarians and the nationalities were not caused by legal, social or economic discrimination but solely by external political interference. After gaining their independence from the Turkish empire, Serbia (independent since 1844) and Rumania (independent since 1866) embarked upon an imperialistic policy of their own: both states made every effort to acquire the territories of Hungary inhabited (partly) by their fellow nationals who had migrated there in the previous centuries. To promote their aspirations, both states incited their brothers in Hungary to fight for their independence. On external instigation, the Serbs and Rumanians of Hungary protested against the dual Austrian-Magyar state-structure, demanded equal participation, rejected the equitable 1868 Nationalities Law and refused to co-operate with the Hungarian government in every way. Soon the Czechs — who were then still Austrian subjects without territorial autonomy — began to instigate the Slovaks of Northern Hungary in preparation of their planned "Czecho-Slovak" state.

The Hungarian leadership failed to see the master design behind this discontent and attributed it to the impetuosity of individual extremists. Sporadic emotional reactions by Magyar politicians were of no help: they only provided more ammunition for the well-planned Rumanian-Serb-Czech campaigns.

The road to World War I

The heir to the Habsburg throne, Archduke Francis Ferdinand (successor to Crown Prince Rudolf, who died in 1889) took an active part in internal and external politics. He disapproved of the Hungarians' "equal" role in the Monarchy and planned to re-establish a XVIIth century type of absolutistic, centralistic empire. In order to neutralise the Magyar influence he favoured the Slavs, especially the Czechs.

When in 1905 the Hungarian opposition, led by Kossuth's son, Ferenc, toppled the Budapest government, Francis Joseph refused to appoint a Kossuth government. After a period of internal wrangling a coalition government was eventually formed under the former Liberal Premier, Sándor Wekerle. This coalition government was unable to carry out the promised reforms in the face of stiff Viennese resistance, inspired by the Magyar-hating Crown Prince. The government resigned and at the 1910 election the Liberal Party regained its absolute majority and formed a new government. At this election smaller opposition parties with radical social and cultural programmes began to appear on the Hungarian political scene. Some of these were the Catholic People's Party (Christian Democrats), the Social Democrats, the Peasant Party and the Radical Party.

The foreign policy of the Monarchy was influenced by heavy-handed Austrian politicians and generals who ignored the signs of the Monarchy's decline and kept dreaming about a great Austrian Empire. In 1908 they decided to annex the provinces of Bosnia and Herczegovina, freed from the Turks. The Budapest Parliament protested against the annexation of the entirely Slav-populated territories.

The Balkan wars of 1912-1913 seemed to foreshadow the end of the long period of peace in the area, but only count *István Tisza,* Prime Minister (for the second time) since 1913, heeded the warning. He wrested from the Parliament a much-needed defence-appropriation and used stern methods to end the sterile obstruction of the opposition in order to introduce progressive legislation. It was too late: the modernisation of the antiquated Hungarian defence forces and of the archaic electoral laws had hardly begun when the storm broke . . .

On June 28, 1914, the Crown Prince, Francis Ferdinand and his wife were assassinated in the capital of recently annexed Bosnia by a member of a Serbian secret society.

177

The balance of the "millenary" era

The unsolved social and minority questions were the main items on the *debit side*. Austrian pressure and foreign agitation, though real, do not entirely excuse the Hungarian leaders' indifference to these problems. Their complacent self-deception made them avoid unpleasant questions — an attitude which, incidentally, complied entirely with the European code of behaviour in the Victorian era.

To this splendid indifference the Hungarians added their own brand of *"patriotic isolationism."* Not having any influence on the foreign policy of the Monarchy, the Magyars practically ceased to be interested in the important events outside their frontiers. The false adage: "Extra Hungarian non est vita. . ." ("Outside Hungary there is no life. . . ") became the motto of the conceited leadership of this apparently prosperous nation. No wonder that the rest of the world ignored the real Hungary. The image of the Magyar — a mixture of a Gypsy and a Hussar — with his fateful penchant for wine, women and song, was spread by globetrotting, free-spending aristocrats, operetta-composers and prodigal noblemen of the Budapest cafés.

Yet there was a *credit side* too: the cumulative achievements of the many talented, industrious and inconspicuous creators among the day-dreamers. In spite of the difficulties and indifference, national culture, economy and technology were enriched to an unbelievable extent even though the casual observer rarely noticed real progress behind the ostentatious glamour of Budapest.

The progressive Minister of Education, József Eötvös, introduced the *1868 Education Law* which made schooling compulsory for all children to the age of 12. Only several years later did England and France introduce similar laws. Five universities, many colleges and countless secondary and primary schools were established. Opera houses, theatres, great public buildings were built in cities and towns.

The first underground *railway* system on the Continent was opened in Budapest in 1896. The country's railway network was enlarged sixfold in fifty years, with several lines electrified.

By 1896 Budapest and the larger towns had complete sewerage, water, electricity, gas and public transport systems.

Around 1905 Austrian opposition to Hungarian *industry* weakened and secondary industries experienced a rather belated pros-

Our Lady's cathedral in Buda.
(The scene of the crowning of the last Hungarian Kings).

P. Szinyei-Merse: Lovers (Cf. p. 209)

perity. Electricity became the main power-source. Industries connected with agriculture (milling, sugar-refining etc.) developed by leaps and bounds.

Science and technology, though handicapped by the depressed conditions of manufacturing industry in the XVIIIth and XIXth centuries, produced such eminent scientists as the two *Bólyais: Farkas* (1775-1856) and his son, *János* (1802-1860), remembered for their contributions to the theory of integral calculus and absolute geometry respectively. Lorand Eötvös enriched Physics and Geology with several inventions, such as the torsion pendulum used in gravity measurements.

Technological inventions were more difficult to test, manufacture and market during these two centuries. Thus János Irinyi, a student of chemistry, made the first phosphorus match in 1836 but sold it to a manufacturer for a pittance. *Ányos Jedlik* constructed the world's first electro-magnetic motor in 1828 (long before Siemens) but he had neither the money nor the ambition to patent it (he was a Benedictine monk).

The obstetric physician, Ignac *Semmelweis* (1818-1865) discovered — years before Pasteur — bacterial infection, the cause of puerperal fever.

At the end of the century, the sudden upsurge in industry helped to create a number of useful inventions, such as the phase-alternating electric locomotive of Kálmán Kandó and the petrol carburettor invented by D. Bánki and J. Csonka. Tivadar Puskás developed the principle of telephone exchange and invented an interesting predecessor to radio broadcasting, called the telephonograph.

The "Jewish question"

This sudden economic growth caused certain intrinsic problems. The Magyar middle-classes were neither willing nor prepared to participate in industrial and commercial activities. Their place was taken, in many instances, by newcomers, mainly Jewish immigrants. Hungarian hospitality had welcomed refugee Jews ever since the Middle Ages. These early immigrants had adapted themselves to the Hungarian civilisation and way of life and had become well-integrated citizens of the country. Jews took an active and loyal part in Hungarian freedom struggles, especially during the 1848-49 war.

Now however, a large number of Jewish refugees began to flee from Russia through the Austrian province of Galicia to Hungary. In little more than a century their numbers in Hungary increased twelvefold: in 1910 Jews represented 5% of the total population (1 million). These recent arrivals, speaking a tongue foreign to everybody in Hungary (Jiddish), and preserving their primitive eastern mode of living, rituals and ghetto-born secretiveness, constituted a homogeneous ethnic group unwilling and unable to assimilate.

For the first time in history the Hungarians felt antagonistic to the Jews, especially when they noted that the newcomers were taking over finance, commerce and the free professions (medicine, journalism). The expressions of this antagonism — though only verbal — angered the young Jewish intelligentsia, which reacted by seeking satisfaction in radical and revolutionary activities, especially toward the end of the War years, while avoiding military service or finding secure employment behind the lines. The leaders of the Marxist-Communist movements at the end of the War (1919) were almost exclusively Jewish.

23. LOVE, LIFE AND LIBERTY

(Hungarian literature between 1848 and 1910)

Sandor Petofi

He was born in 1823 in a village of the Great Plain of peasant parents. A talented but restless student, he did not complete his studies. Instead he led a rather bohemian existence for a while. Finally he found his true vocation in writing and settled in Pest, working as the contributor and editor of various publications. On the 15th of March 1848 he became the leader of the bloodless uprising in Pest and his poem, "Arise Magyars!"[1] became the battle hymn of the freedom struggle. At the outbreak of the hostilities he joined the national army and became the aide of general Bem whom he worshipped. He married Julia Szendrey, the inspiration of his love poems. At the end of the freedom war, Petöfi died on the battlefield at the age of 26, in 1849.

His poem, *"At the End of September"*, written to his young bride on their honeymoon, quoted in chapter 7 and in the Appendix, illustrates Petöfi's art which, for lack of a better term, we call classical. His language is characterised by its beautiful simplicity and the ability to say the right word at the right place. He expresses his thoughts in meaningful, short sentences and pictures of nature without any romantic symbolism. He manages to maintain a disciplined harmony between his soaring, romantic imagination and strict, classic rhythm, rhyme and metre. The picture of the autumn landscape evokes thoughts about the passing of time, described in the first line of the second strophe in one of the most beautiful sentences in Hungarian literature. The poet's reflections on death and love in the second strophe are devoid of sentimentality and his own protestations of eternal love in the third strophe are not marred by unnecessary pathos.

His *love poetry,* inspired by his wife, reveals his sincere, almost puritanistic morality: deep sensitivity without needless sentimentality.[2]

A true son of the people, he speaks their simple language without affectation. He describes village and peasant life in his *idyllic poems* with their sad and humorous episodes in the manner of the folk poet. His smooth rhythm and language could easily be set to music and many of his poems became popular songs.[3]

He loves his Great Plain, his native soil, its unlimited horizons and thoughtful silences. His elegiac praises of the land are intertwined with thoughts of love and patriotism.[4]

His dominant emotion was his love of *freedom.* His moving credo has been translated into more than one hundred languages:

> "Liberty and love
> These two I must have.
> For my love I'll sacrifice
> My life.
> For liberty I'll sacrifice
> My love."

(transl. by G. F. Cushing)

He identifies his personal freedom with the nation's struggle for its freedom and beyond it he dreams of a romantic-humanistic freedom for all mankind. Love for his nation carries him to the extremes of exuberance and dejection. In one of his last poems he describes, in a sombre vision, his own manner of heroic death.[5]

Even his *narrative poetry* shows his lyric qualities. His descriptions of the fairy-tale adventures of "John the Hero", an epic folktale, have the quality of the popular tale told on winter evenings in the village spinnery.

It may be interesting to know that a word-count made of Petőfi's vocabulary shows that his most frequently used noun was "man" and that his favourite adjective was "good". This good, great humanist rightfully occupies a place of honour in the hearts of all Magyars.

Sándor Petöfi (1823-1849)

Janos Arany

The son of an impoverished noble, Arany was born in 1817 in a little town of the Great Plain. His father taught him Hungarian and Latin writing and the elements of their Protestant faith. Eventually, the talented boy completed his education at the Debrecen Reformed College and returned to his birthplace, where he worked as the village teacher until the 1848 war. He served in the national army (as a simple soldier) and had to hide for a while after 1849. Amnestied, he became a secondary teacher in another Great Plain town, then settled in Budapest where he became the Secretary of the Academy and the foremost man of letters of his time. He died in 1882.

He knew the soul, the language and the folklore of his peasant people. He collected folksongs and tales and even wrote poems in the vein of a folk song. He also studied foreign literature of folkish inspiration, reading and translating widely.

His inspiration stemmed from his understanding of the Magyar people and his epic style suggests the calm wisdom of the Plain and the millenia-old humanistic realism of its hardy people.

His first masterpiece, "Toldi" (1846), an epic of classical popular realism, earned him national recognition and Petöfi's friendship. This folk-tale in verse is based on local legends and medieval chronicles and tells the adventures of a popular Magyar hero in the XIVth century. Arany's hero is a typical Magyar with all the characteristics of the people. This work of great human value has never been translated: its rich Magyar language defies translation. The second and third parts of the epic ("Toldi's Love" and "Toldi's Eve") are reminiscent of a medieval romance and had less attraction for Arany's readers.

After 1849 Arany found the form of expression of which he eventually became the greatest representative in the Hungarian language: *the ballad*. He was first inspired by the Transylvanian and Scottish ballads — and he was the first to note the remarkable affinity between these two. Each ballad is a little drama written in concise style and with a deep understanding of the workings of the human mind. There is little background description, the action is told in a dialogue. Most of the ballads are tales of crime and punishment. The crime is instigated by the powerful human passions of hate or love, and the punishment is meted out by the criminal's own conscience: it is usually madness.

János Arany (1817-1882)

Of Arany's early ballads, the gothic horror-tale "Bor the Hero"[6] deserves closer attention. Its universal theme makes it fairly translatable. The allegoric ballad *"The Bards of Wales"*[7] was written in 1857. Francis Joseph, the Emperor, was visiting defeated Hungary and Hungarian poets were asked to write an ode in his praise. Arany answered with this symbolic ballad, based on a dubious historical event, the revenge of King Edward I against the bards of Wales who refused to sing his praise. In Arany's ballad the cruel king receives the usual punishment: the song of the martyred bards drives him to madness.

Arany's later ballads are based on themes from Magyar peasant and urban life, such as the "Corn-husking" and "Red Rébék", most of them untranslatable because of their compact, racy language. Many short descriptive poems share the fate of the ballads: the "Family Circle", an idyllic description of a peasant family evening has not yet found its translator.

Toward the end of the oppression period, Arany turned to Hungarian history for his own and his readers' inspiration. The *"Death of Buda"*, a magnificent epic, is the first part of a trilogy which was to contain a cycle of Magyar legends and myths.[8] In it, Arany tells the popular myth of the Hungarians' and Huns' common origin in the tone of a medieval minstrel. Unfortunately, he never completed the trilogy.

Whilst essentially an epic poet, Arany did create in his old age *meditative lyric poetry* of considerable charm. These poems are mostly reminiscences and melancholic reflections interspersed with wisdom, humour and often resignation, as in the elegy "I lay the Lute down"[9]. Arany was very reticent about his patriotism: his deep love of his people and country remained hidden in his allegories and tales most of the time.

Arany, still a favourite of Hungarians, deserves to be better known abroad.

Some poets of the oppression period

Imre Madách (1823-1864) found ample emotional inspiration for his great drama in his own, tragic life. Born and educated in northern Hungary, he suffered persecution and prison for his participation in the freedom struggle. During his imprisonment his wife became unfaithful to him. Madách divorced her, but never ceased to love her: she was the only woman in his life. He lived under tragic family circumstances and died soon after the completion of his great opus: the drama *"Tragedy of Man"* (1860).

In this Faustian tableau of the fate of mankind Adam and Eve are guided by Lucifer through various phases of human history. The Devil shows the successive frustrations of their descendants to the ancestors of mankind. The final scene, however, ends with a message of hope: God's last words to Adam are: *"Man — strive and have faith, unfaltering faith. . ."* The message of the drama is Madách's "pessimistic idealism": though often futile, human endeavours are rewarded by the very satisfaction of one's own courage and faith. Madách presents the main characters with perfect modern psychology. Adam is the naive idealist who is easily discouraged and Eve is the "eternal woman" who lifts his spirits with her inflexible faith and love.[10]

Mihály Tompa's poetry (1817-1868) is characterised by emotional melancholy and an interest in folk poetry. His elegies, written in his upper-Hungarian village (he was a Protestant pastor), reflect the pessimism and moral preoccupations of his times but they present some pleasing tableaus of rustic landscape and stoic philosophy.

János Vajda[11] (1827-1897), the lonely, sad poet of memories and forest tableaus, and *Gyula Reviczky* (1855-1889), the gentle bard of the lonely city-dwellers, illustrate the mood of the Hungarian poets after the Compromise. They did not share the optimism of the politicians and their dissonant melancholy made them unpopular in the prevailing atmosphere of self-deluding happiness.

Mor Jokai

The most popular novelist of the era, Jókai was a Transdanubian by birth (in 1825) and temperament. Though connected with Petöfi's circle in 1848, he became more moderate during 1849 and so received an amnesty after the failure of the freedom struggle. Soon he began to publish his novels and short stories and in 56 years of literary activity had over one-hundred volumes published. He died in 1904. He is still the most popular novelist in Hungary and is well-known abroad in many translations.

Jókai's first *historical novels,* written during the oppression, describe imaginary events in Hungary during the Turkish occupation. He disregards the historical truth and changes the Turks and Hungarians into heroes and villains (the villains are often Hungarians, the heroes often Turks), painting a fantasy world of "Goodies" and "Baddies" whose main concern is personal pride and honour, not the country's plight. After the Compromise he turned to the more recent period of the Freedom War with his "The Baron's Sons". One of the finest prose epics of Hungarian literature, this novel of romance and realism describes the great war through the fate of one aristocratic family. Jókai's historical-social novels of the Reform Age (early XIXth century) present well-documented and accurate pictures of the Magyar society of that era. The "New Landowner" is a thoughtful work describing, with surprisingly deep psychology, the assimilation of an Austrian estate owner settled in Hungary after 1849.

Jókai's most popular *social novel,* the "Dark Diamonds", suggests easy solutions to the social problems of the working class (miners) who are redeemed by the joint efforts of the patriotic scientist-hero (the owner of the mine) and the beautiful, chaste and brilliant daughter of a miner. The two transform a mining village into a Utopian community where everybody lives happily ever after — including the two heroes. A commendable solution to labour-management disputes.[12]

"The Man with the Golden Touch" is a more realistic picture of the cruel world of finance, which is conquered by a hero with the Midas touch and the Magyar peasant's common sense.

The hundreds of *short stories and novelettes* written by Jókai were the favourite intellectual diet of the Sunday-paper reading bourgeoisie, offering relaxing, uncomplicated, pleasant entertainment without any cumbersome messages.

Jókai's *topics* include the complete range of human experience (and a few inhuman ones), all possible periods of history (and some impossible ones), all known corners of the world (and a few known to Jókai only), but only two emotions: love and hate. He describes history not as it was but as it should have been, human relationships as they might have been and science as it could have been.

He has to be read with a grain of salt and a liking of the unlikely, a wish to get away from it all. . . He has tales to tell — hundreds of them — and he tells them with humour and a twinkle in his eye. He must have enjoyed writing them just as we enjoy reading them today. He does not preach, does not teach — he entertains.

They call him the "greatest Hungarian teller of tales." In a nation in which every second man is a politician, this is real praise.

Kalman Mikszath

In many respects Mikszáth was the opposite of Jókai. Born (in 1847) of a poor bourgeois family of northern Hungary, he moved in the circles of the lower middle-class country folk. Eventually he settled in Budapest as a writer (and part-time politician, like Jókai, but then who was not a politician in those days?) He died in 1910.

Mikszáth is a realist. His humour always has the touch of cynicism and his view of society is usually expressed in the form of a satire. His characters are not heroes, but complex personalities with virtues as well as vices. He began his literary career as a writer of *short stories,* such as the collections "Slovak Kinfolk" and the "Good Palóc", in which he describes the simple peasants of the North: Hungarians and Slovaks and their peaceful co-existence. Mikszáth also discovered the world of children — whom Jókai ignored. From his children's stories arose his popular novel "The Two Mendicant Students", one of the all-time favourites of Hungarian youngsters.

Mikszáth tackled the problems of simple people in his *novels and novelettes.* "Saint Peter's Umbrella" is a delightful mixture of legend, fairy tale and social satire: the story of a successful search for happiness. The short novel, "Magic Kaftan", describes with historical and psychological accuracy the life of a Magyar town under Turkish rule. "The Case of the Noszty Boy" is a social satire, a fine and instructive picture of early XXth century Hungarian society: it concerns the conflict of a conceited but penniless nobleman who wants to marry the daughter of a rich bourgeois. The historical-psychological novel, "The Black City", is based on a true incident of the XVIIth century: the tragic conflict between an aristocratic county sheriff and a bourgeois town mayor, ending in the death of the one and the unhappiness of the other. Both sides are represented by personalities who possess an equal number of virtues and weaknesses.

Mikszáth looks at his characters with compassion and understanding, though he criticises their actions, as in the short story "Gentry" in which he describes the hypocritical vanity of the impoverished country-nobility of northern Hungary.[13]

His narrow choices of local Hungarian themes and his witty, racy language, made it very hard to translate his works.

The novelist and playwright *Ferenc Herczeg* (1863-1954), a defender of aristocratic values, was the favourite author of the upper middle-class urban society of Hungary before and after World War I. He depicted the Hungarian "high society" in pleasant, flattering tableaus with just a touch of satirical humour without serious criticism.

His many *dramas and comedies* have pleased thousands of theatre-goers with their ingenious plots, humour and technical perfection. His historic dramas revolve around conflicts of well-defined personalities. ("Byzantium", "Ladislas the Orphan King" and "The Bridge"). His comedies do not analyse, criticise or satirise: their sole aim is to entertain (The "Gyurkovics Family" cycle). His *social novels* and short stories were the best-sellers of the "happy years" before the War and they brought back nostalgic memories to the readers of the difficult post-war years. His *historic novels* ("Pagans", "The Gate of Life") present clear, credible characterisations and colourful background tableaus, sometimes at the expense of the historic truth.

24. HUNGARIAN RHAPSODY

(Hungarian music from Liszt to Kodály)

Ferenc (Franz) Liszt

The life of this eccentric genius was as colourful as his music. Born in western Hungary (1811), he studied in Vienna and Paris. He became a concert pianist at the age of nine and in his teens became known in most European countries as an exceptional prodigy, the "Paganini of the piano". He then spent five years in Switzerland with his first mistress, a French countess, who bore him three children (one of them, Cosima, married Wagner).

During his frequent visits to the country of his birth Liszt became acquainted with the gypsy interpretation of Hungarian folk music. These popular melodies inspired his well-known "Hungarian Rhapsodies". He lived in the art-loving German principality, Weimar, for 15 years with his second mistress, a German princess. He became the official conductor of the court, the supreme musical authority, arbiter and critic, and the musical promoter of such young composers as Wagner, Berlioz and Weber.

In 1861 Liszt broke with his previous life style and had himself admitted to the Franciscan order. Ordained a Catholic priest, he gave up all worldly interests, except his music. Dividing his time between Budapest and Weimar, he helped to promote musical education in Hungary by founding the Academy of Music in Budapest of which he became the first president and professor. He died in 1886.

Liszt began his career as a *piano virtuoso*. His first compositions were little more than piano-arrangements of well-known works. He began to produce *original compositions* during his travels in the forties: his "Preludes" and "Symphonic Poems" (a musical form of his own creation) show romantic inspiration but he soon began to experiment with novel harmonies. His 15 "Hungarian Rhapsodies" also present a romantic interpretation of his country's music. Though he failed to separate the genuine folk-music elements from the gypsy and urban ornamentation, the technical perfection, vivacity and flexibility of these compositions made them the most popular expression of "folkish" Hungarian music (especially the "Second Rhapsody" — probably the best known Hungarian composition abroad).

The last period of his activity — his musical maturity — produced novel harmonic and thematic structures, free from romantic influence. Many creations of this period herald a musical approach akin to twentieth-century modern music (Bartók). Liszt's *Hungarian themes* — frequent in this period — discover the true folk-music interpretation, free from gypsy ornamentation or ballroom impressions. His great symphonic poem *"Hungaria"*, composed in 1856 expresses Liszt's own visionary interpretation of true Magyar music, his Magyar patriotism and European humanism. The cycles called "Years of Pilgrimage" (especially the "Faust" and "Dante" symphonies) represent harmonies and musical concepts far ahead of his period — they are probably his greatest creations.

Liszt composed his "Coronation Mass" for the coronation of Francis Joseph and Elizabeth in Buda in 1867. Its somewhat melancholic, modern Hungarian music was little appreciated by Liszt's contemporaries. His "Oratoria" show his *religious inspiration:* best known are the "Legend of Saint Elizabeth of Hungary" and the "Christus" oratorium. The "Csardas Macabre" — one of his last compositions — is a hauntingly beautiful mixture of Magyar tunes inspired by Liszt's preoccupation with death.

Romantic and popular music

The Hungarian composers of the period after the Compromise (1867) represented, with a few exceptions, neo-romantic, popular music trends, dominated by the demands of the unassuming middle-class tastes and Viennese bourgeois mediocrity. They did use Hungarian folkish melodic inspiration — the gypsy-ornamented operetta variety.

Károly Goldmark (1830-1915) who was of Jewish extraction, studied in Vienna. His first works show marked Wagnerian inspiration, such as the opera "Queen of Sheba." His orchestral compositions, such as the "Rustic Wedding Symphony" show the inspiration of Magyar folk music and remarkably modern orchestration.

Similarly, *Ede Poldini's* light opera, "Carnival Wedding", uses many Hungarian folk motifs in a rather Wagnerian frame.

The light-hearted *operetta* became the most popular form of musical entertainment of this era. Vienna, the "capital of the operetta", influenced the Hungarian composers of this genre at the beginning of their careers.

Imre Kálmán (1882-1953) composed in Vienna, Paris and then, at the end of his life, in the U.S. He always emphasised his Hungarian roots and wished to be known as Hungarian. The Magyar popular tunes are noticeable in his most popular operettas, such as the "Gypsy Princess", "Countess Marica" and the "Circus Princess".

Ferenc Lehár (1870-1948), the best known of the Hungarian operetta composers, freed himself from Vienese influence at an early stage and created an individual type of operetta of a rather philosophical style, often melancholic, with themes ranging well beyond that of the popular operetta of the period. Lehár placed the plot of each operetta in a different country and attempted — with success in most cases — to recreate the musical atmosphere of that country. "Gypsy Love" was a gift to his native Hungary. The action of "The Merry Widow", "the most successful operetta of all times", is placed in the tiny principality of Montenegro, "Frasquita" in Spain, "Paganini" in Italy, "Frederica" in Germany etc. The Hungarian public's favourite, "The Land of Smiles", places its romantic-melancholic plot in China.

Jenö Huszka (1875-1960), popular operetta and film-music composer, used many folk-inspired tunes in his compositions. His mellow, sweet, uncomplicated operettas, such as "Prince Bob" and "Baroness Lily", became very popular with the urban audiences in Hungary.

Pongrác Kacsóh (1873-1923) made his fame by composing the most popular operetta of Hungary: "John the Hero", based on Petöfi's folk-tale epic of the same title. Entirely unknown abroad, the operetta uses popular "Magyar song" inspiration in its pleasant, sentimentally-patriotic songs, the favourites of two generations.

Ákos Buttykay and *Pál Ábrahám* represent more international styles. Ábrahám's "Victoria and her Hussar" is better known in Germany than in Hungary.

The prosperous middle classes of Hungary at the turning of the century expected unpretentious, sentimental musical entertainment of a romantic-patriotic nature. This soothing, mellow music was presented to them by the popular operettas and by the so-called *"Magyar song"* of the period: gay or sad melodies usually presented by popular singers, accompanied by the ubiquitous gypsy orchestras. The combination of mellow song and gypsy music provided the urban audience with suitable moods to fall in or out of love, to forget or remember, to feel despondent or exuberant by. The moods created were flexible and the gypsy orchestras could easily be induced (for a slight consideration) to change the mood, rhythm and atmosphere at the whim of the audience. The melodies and texts of these popular "Magyar songs" were written and composed by urban song-writers (Pista Dankó, Lóránt Fráter, Árpád Balázs and many others).

The search for a true Hungarian musical expression

Some XXth century composers demonstrated a more genuine and critical approach to a new Hungarian musical style. Their understanding and interpretation of Magyar music was deeper and their contribution to the development of an independent, folk-music inspired Hungarian music complemented and supported Kodály's and Bartók's efforts.

Leo Weiner (1885-1960) presented Magyar folk music in its true nature ("Hungarian Folk Dances"). His not too numerous compositions bear witness to a refined musical culture and romantic charm ("Csongor and Tünde": inspired by Vörösmarty's epic).

Jenö Hubay (1858-1937) was a violin virtuoso who became a professor, then director, of the Budapest Academy of Music. He had a great impact on Hungarian musical education between the Wars. He was a prolific composer with a refined taste and the ability to interpret Hungarian folk music themes in a pleasing, unpretentious style ("Csarda Scenes", "Lavotta's Love"). Some of his operas and symphonies show Italian inspiration ("The Violin Maker of Cremona", "Dante").

Ernö Dohnányi (1877-1960), composer, piano virtuoso, professor and director of the Academy of Music, presents elegant, romantic themes in modern orchestration and melodic structures with a marked Magyar folk-music inspiration ("Ruralia Hungarica"). His ballet-pantomime, "Pierette's Veil", and his "Variations on a Nursery Song" are still popular concert pieces.

Bela Bartok

He was born in Transylvania in 1881. While studying at the Budapest Academy of Music, Bartók became acquainted with Zoltán Kodály and the two began studying and collecting Magyar folk music by travelling to remote Hungarian villages. Later Bartók extended his folk-music studies to other nations. For a while he was professor at the Academy, then gave up his chair in order to concentrate on composing and performing as a concert pianist. In the 1930s he and Kodály were commissioned to collect, transcribe and edit the nation's folk music. He went to the U.S. in 1940 and remained there during the war. He died in 1945 without returning to his homeland.

Bartók and Kodály published their first Magyar folk-song collection in 1906. Bartók's preoccupation in researching and evaluating his nation's folk music has left its mark on his compositions: Magyar inspiration remained at the root of his otherwise original and unique creations. He wrote many *arrangements,* transcriptions and variations of folk themes. In many cases he rearranged the original melody and extended it into an original art form, at times by projecting the new style folk song back into an original, old type (pentatonic) structure. He also created music which was both his original composition and indistinguishable from folk music: the result of complete assimilation of folk culture, similar to Petöfi's "folk poetry".

Béla Bartók (1881-1945)

This fusion of folk inspiration and his original genius created music which struck the audiences as harsh, even raw, ultramodern and certainly original. His simple basic themes were accompanied by disharmonic decoration. The result was a unique, hard-to-understand philosophical music.

His *compositions* include a great number of piano solos and duos ("Mikrokosmos", "Allegro Barbaro"), several piano concertos and piano sonatas. His string quartets are said to be "the most important contribution to chamber music since Beethoven" (Sir Malcolm Sargent). Orchestral compositions, such as "Music for Strings, Percussion and Celesta" and "Divertimento" are among his most often performed works.

Bartók's only opera, "Prince Bluebeard's Castle" is based practically on two solos and is therefore very difficult to perform. The two ballets, "The Wooden Prince" and "The Miraculous Mandarin", are more often seen.

Bartók was a true Hungarian humanist: his love for his nation blended with his love for all his fellow humans. He appreciated the art of people everywhere and he gained his inspiration from the folk music of the neighbouring Central European peoples as well as from folk cultures of other continents. His musical expression, built on themes of eastern inspiration used western harmonies in a classic synthesis of East and West.

Zoltan Kodaly

Kodály was born at Kecskemét, in the heart of the Great Plain (1882). During his student years at the Budapest Academy of Music he began studying and collecting Magyar folksongs with Béla Bartók. His career as a composer began in 1906 with a work of Hungarian folk inspiration. He was professor of the Academy for a long time but continued his folk-music research. After World War I he became interested in choral compositions and noticed the educational possibilities of vocal music. He found that choral singing was a practical and inexpensive vehicle of musical culture, capable of reaching even the poorest and remotest villages. In his role as the nation's foremost *musical educator,* Kodály realised the cultural importance of the study, identification and evaluation of true Magyar folk music. The Hungarian Academy of Sciences has co-ordinated and financed the task of folk-music collection since the 1930s. Thus

Zoltán Kodály (1882-1967)

today the "Folk Music Research Institute" of the Academy possesses the recordings of some 100,000 folk melodies.

Kodály expounded his educational principles and folk music evaluations in scores of articles and books. He died in Budapest in 1967.

His rich collection of choral works includes the "Székely Spinnery", a colourful operatic tableau of Székely songs and ballads (1932), the various collections of regional and children's songs and dances with or without orchestral accompaniment ("Mátra Pictures", "Kálló Double Dance" etc.) and the numerous religious folk songs, along with his original choral compositions to classic Hungarian poetry.

In his *orchestral compositions* Kodály retains the traditional melodic elements, such as the popular "toborzó" ("verbunk") type motifs. His "Dances" are collections of orchestral variations of regional dances ("Galánta", "Marosszék"). The "Peacock Variations" present an orchestral paraphrase of an old folk song.

Among his more original and individual creations, the "Psalmus Hungaricus" (1923), a choral oratorio based on a XVIth century Hungarian psalm, established his reputation in Hungary, while *"Háry János"*, a comic opera based on the tales of a village story-teller (1926), became the favourite of national and international concert programmes, especially the "Háry János Suite", with its pleasing, emotional rhythms and folk-music inspired melodies. The "Concerto for Orchestra" (1939) is, in its more abstract form, a modern symphonic treatment of Magyar folk tunes. Kodály's last orchestral creation, "Symphony" (1961) constitutes practically an apotheosis of the Magyar folk song.

Kodály treated many *religious themes,* often connected with Hungarian historical events, such as the "Budavár Te Deum" (1936) on the anniversary of Buda's liberation from the Turks and the "Missa Brevis", composed during the capital's siege by the Russians in 1944.

The so-called *Kodály method* (Kodály concept), is the basic philosophy of musical education which aims at the developing of the very young (pre-primary) child's musical ability by using singing as the first activity with solmization (solfege) as the vehicle of vocal music teaching. This musical "alphabet" (solfege) is impressed into the child's memory by hand signals and then by visual notation. The content of the first exercises is the

Magyar folksong (this "classical music par excellence", as Kodály put it). This awakens the child's musical imagination and enables him to distinguish the separate tones of the pentatonic and, later, the western scales.

Kodály's emphasis on early musical education reaches back to the classic Greek concept of the educational importance of music. Thus the "Kodály concept" becomes a universal, classic-humanistic educational principle, easily adapted to any national education system, as is the case in many advanced countries today.

25. "ECCE HOMO"

(The Fine Arts in Hungary after 1849)

Popular Romanticism

Architecture sought neo-gothic, oriental and exotic forms in protest against the Viennese Biedermeier-Baroque. The search for new Hungarian forms resulted in such interesting examples as the Budapest "Vigadó" (Casino and Concert Hall), designed by F. Feszl. This exotic mixture of Byzantine, Moorish and Magyar inspiration reminded an onlooker of a "csárdás carved in stone". The new building programme after the Compromise produced some fine examples of eclectic styles, such as the Parliament House (I. Steindl) with its neo-gothic exterior and strangely harmonious Baroque-Renaissance interior. The Opera House (M. Ybl) was built in a more uniform Italian neo-Renaissance style with interior decorations and murals by the best painters of the period. The "Fisherman's Bastion" (F. Schulek) is a historic recreation of the walls of Buda castle and one of the best-known landmarks of Budapest.

The *sculptors* turned to the inspiration and dynamism of folk art or to the symbolism of historic figures. *Miklós Izsó* (1831-1875) continued Ferenczy's search for a national style. Most of his work remained largely experimental. The symbolic "Sorrowing Shepherd" is a poignant expression of the Magyar people's sorrow. His source of inspiration, the art of the people, resulted in such fine genre figures as the "Dancing Shepherd".*János Fadrusz* created remarkable historical bronze statues (King Matthias at Kolozsvár).

The *painters* replaced the carefree serenity of French Romanticism with a rather sombre patriotic symbolism. Hungarian

"Dancing Shepherd" by M. Izsó

realism and folk-inspiration blend in the popular, spectacular historical compositions of the era. *Mihály Zichy* is known for his romantic-patriotic illustrations to great literary works of the era. *Victor Madarász* found his inspiration in the tragic-heroic events of Hungarian history. The compositions "Ilona Zrinyi Before her Judges", "Zrinyi and Frangepán", "Zrinyi's Last Sally" and his masterpiece, "The Mourning of László Hunyadi" clearly convey the spirit of defiance against Austrian oppression.

Bertalan Székely (1835-1910) had a remarkable sense of composition. He, too, expressed his strong feelings for his nation through historical tableaus with an intense message of defiance. His great composition, "The Finding of the Body of King Louis II", links symbolically the Mohács disaster with the defeat of the 1848-49 war. Romantic pathos and vivid use of colours characterise "Dobozi" and the "Women of Eger". Needless to say, neither Madarász nor Székely received official recognition, let alone support in Hungary under Austrian oppression. (p. 99)

Károly Lotz on the other hand soon became the favourite of the "official" critics with his pleasing, serene, allegoric (and unpolitical) scenes, murals, tableaus and neo-classic figures ("Girl in Bath", etc.). *Gyula Benczur* (1844-1920), Professor at the Academy of Munich, shows a belated Rubens influence in his academic compositions, such as the "Baptism of Vajk" and the "Recapture of Buda". His brilliant portraiture and harmonious, precise composition without any dangerous defiant message received official approval in Vienna and Budapest. (p. 106)

Mihaly (Michael) Munkacsy

Born in Munkács (eastern Hungary) in 1844, the son of a freedom fighter in the 1848-49 war, he was orphaned in childhood and placed in a joinery as an apprentice. He soon made himself independent and began painting without any formal education. His talent was soon discovered and he was sent to Vienna to an art school. Here he sold his first paintings: tableaus inspired by his childhood memories of the Freedom War and the landscapes of his country. Thus he was able to finance his further studies in Munich then in Düsseldorf, Germany. His genre paintings and Hungarian landscapes attracted considerable attention. The fine study "The Yawning Apprentice", inspired by memories of his childhood, shows early realist-naturalist influences.

The greatest creation of Munkácsy's Düsseldorf period *"Condemned Cell"* (1870), is a homage to a childhood idol, a "betyár" (highwayman-freedom-fighter). It represents the fierce spirit of defiance against the Austrian "establishment". The painting gained the coveted Gold Medal of the Paris Salon. This success encouraged Munkácsy to settle in Paris, where he was welcomed by the critics and patrons of the arts. After several successful genre compositions, he painted the striking "Woman carrying Faggots", capturing the contrasting impressions of the fresh vitality of the forest and the tiredness of the old peasant woman. There are many other examples of his dramatic and compassionate approach to poor and old people, such as the "Vagabonds of the Night", Woman Churning Butter" and "Parting".

Munkácsy's aristocratic French wife drove him to almost frantic activity. *"Milton Dictating his Paradise Lost"* became his most successful painting to that day. He painted the tragic genius, exiled, blind and deserted by his own family, creating his masterpiece in an atmosphere of loneliness and hate. Though successful, Munkácsy himself was an exile, a lonely man who received no real response from his selfish and snobbish wife; he was without children and without real friends: the French resented the fact that he refused to become a French citizen and the Hungarians disliked him for living in France. So — to some extent — he portrayed himself in Milton.

Munkácsy's gigantic masterpiece, *"Christ before Pilate"*, was completed in 1881. In it he expresses the contrast of Christ's dignified silence amid a shouting, hostile crowd with the pallid, hesitating Pilate in the background. After having tried many models for Christ, Munkácsy finally painted his own tormented, sad face. During intervals while working on the majestic tableau, he "relaxed" by painting still-lifes and portraits. Once in a sudden burst of bravado, he painted "Sitting Woman" using 572 shades of blue.

Three years later he completed the *"Golgotha"*: the moment after Christ's death on the cross and the crowd of spectators. The amazing range of colours includes several shades of white: the deathly pale of Christ's face, the living white of the

"Ecce Homo" by M. Munkácsy

mourning women, the pallor of fear on the soldier's face and many other shades.

Tortured by an old illness and certain of his approaching death, Munkácsy continued to work feverishly: he completed portraits of famous men (Liszt), a mural in Vienna (Mozart) and then a commission from the Hungarian Government to paint the "Conquest of Hungary" for the new Parliament House. His last great work was *"Ecce Homo"* ("Behold the Man": Pilate shows Christ scourged to the Jews). He painted it while mortally ill, concluding his "Christ Trilogy" — and his own life's work. He died in 1900.

Munkácsy, the toast of his time in Paris and the initiator of an entirely new style, is today hardly known abroad. His unpronounceable name and the fact that he insisted on remaining a "foreigner" in France have made the emotional French forget him quickly. He did not belong to any "school". Most of his masterpieces were snapped up by rich Americans and thus removed from Europe. His own countrymen failed to appreciate his talent. His delicate colours, shades of blue and brown especially, are very hard to reproduce, moreover, many of his original paintings have begun to fade.

Munkácsy's original style — we may call it *"compassionate realism"* — shows a deep insight into the suffering of the human soul (especially of the poor and old — his favourite models). His portraits and compositions are studies in human psychology: he always grasps a moment of eloquent silence: the principal character has just said something or is about to say something, whilst the secondary characters usually supply a disturbing background of sounds, shouts and abuse.

This great, lonely artist was another example of Hungarian Christian humanism.

Munkacsy's contemporaries

László Paál, Munkácsy's friend, spent his short, creative life in France (Barbizon) painting soft, melancholic landscapes. *Géza Mészöly* was basically a genre painter with a mixture of Munkácsy's realism and impressionist colouring ("Balaton Fishermen").

The members of the so-called "Szolnok Group" were influenced by Munkácsy's themes but added considerable originality to their tableaus. *Lajos Deák-Ebner* and *Sándor Bihari* show the precision and vitality of early realism in their peasant scenes.

Pál Szinyei-Merse (1845-1920) was independent from Munkácsy's realism and the Munich Romanticism. His masterpiece, *"Picnic in May"* ("Majális"), painted in 1872, used vivid colour schemes reminiscent of French Impressionism — with which he had never been in contact. In fact the great French Impressionists created their masterpieces after Szinyei's "Picnic". The perfection of his "open air" ("plein air") tonalities is amazing. He seems to have gone a little further than the Impressionists: the effect of air vibration on his colouring is a concept found only in post-Impressionist painting (Cézanne) long after Szinyei's time.

He painted a few more landscapes and portraits, including the "Woman in Mauve Dress" which has an almost pre-Rafaelite landscape background. Szinyei's subsequent creations ("The Swing", "Lovers", "The Lark") represent the work of only a few years. He received hostile reception from the critics for his vivid colours and so, discouraged, stopped painting. His "Picnic" was belatedly "discovered" and appreciated three decades after its creation, but by that time Szinyei had lost his interest and initiative. Thus Hungary lost a genius who could have heralded a modern, XXth century Hungarian art — but the country's artists and critics preferred the comfortable conservatism of the XIXth century.

The period of the Millenium and World Wars

Szinyei's "Picnic" inspired a small group of avant-garde painters, called the "Nagybánya Group", around the turn of the century. Their founder, *Simon Hollósy,* was interested in a wide range of themes, from humorous peasant topics ("Corn Husking") to historic tableaus ("Zrinyi's Last Sally") with breezy, hazy colours and impressionist experimentation. *Károly Ferenczy,* another "Nagybánya" painter, perfected his artistry of light and shade contrasts ("October"). *Oscar Glatz'* outdoor tableaus are characterised by his preoccupation with the sun, his indoor compositions are idyllic peasant scenes ("Mother and Child").

The *sculptor Fülöp O. Beck* (1873-1945) turned away from the "approved" neo-Baroque styles and pioneered a modern

"Lonely Cedar" by T. Csontváry-Kosztka

Hungarian art style which was little appreciated by his contemporaries ("Fountain of Youth"). He was also a skilled silversmith and medallist and his plaquettes were more appreciated than his sculptures.

The *architect Ôdön Lechner* applied the motifs of Magyar folk art to the decoration — and sometimes even to the forms — of such buildings as the Town Hall of Kecskemét and the Savings Bank of Budapest. He searched for new ways but rejected the reckless eclecticism of some of his contemporaries.

The independent painter, *László Mednyánszky* chose scenes of desolation and sadness for his landscapes and city tableaus.

Tivadar Csontváry Kosztka (1853-1919), the most original genius of Hungarian painting, travelled extensively and began to paint only after his 40th year: his actual artistic career lasted only a decade, and was characterised by a feverish search for his own style: he became the forerunner of surrealism (long before Dali) and symbolism. His landscapes ("Hortobágy", "Tarpatak") are realistic, but in his later compositions he succeeded in creating a hauntingly beautiful, melancholic dreamworld of his own, as in his masterpiece, *"Lonely Cedar"*, a defiant, tragic symbol of his own loneliness. The religious-pantheistic-mystic compositions inspired by his travels, "Pilgrimage", "Mary's Well", "Athens", are products of a visionary genius.

For a while, during the early decades of the XXth century, *French influence* characterised such popular painters as *József Rippl-Rónai,* the creator of serene, cheerful scenes and philosophical portraits ("Flox", "Memories", "My Father"). *István Csók* (1865-1961), the most successful painter between the wars, worked under the inspiration of French post-impressionism (Renoir). He sought the expression of beauty in children ("Zuzu") and in women fashionably dressed or undressed ("In the Studio", "Hony Soit").

The "Group of the Eight" sought a synthesis of German-inspired expressionism and French art-nouveau trends (Károly Kernstock). Other avant-garde representatives were the fresco-painter *Vilmos Aba-Novák* whose expressionist simple figure delineations were set off by glaring, contrasting colours, and the graphic artist *Pál C. Molnár. Jenö Paizs-Göbel* explored the

"Madonna" by P. Molnár C.

The Budapest Opera House (M. Ybl)

possibilities of surrealism. *Gyula Derkovics,* inspired by German expressionism, became interested in tableaus of the proletariat and brought Socialist tendencies into his expression.

Aurél Bernáth and *József Egry* used expressionist colouring in their landscapes. *István Szönyi* chose more robust realism in his powerful landscapes and group tableaus.

"Princess Elizabeth"
(the future Queen Elizabeth II)
by Zs. Kisfaludy-Strobl

The conservative *sculptor Zsigmond Kisfaludy-Strobl* made his name with academic-style figures. *Ferenc Medgyesy,* the most remarkable talent of modern Hungarian sculpture, found a harmonious synthesis of classical, modern and Hungarian folk inspiration in his allegorical and sepulchral figures.

26. AUSTRIA'S WAR — HUNGARY'S DEFEAT

(Hungary's history from 1914 to 1930)

The beginning of World War I

The Austrian government made it clear that it intended to take stern measures against Serbia for fomenting Francis Ferdinand's assassination. At the Crown Council, Tisza, the Hungarian Prime Minister, desperately protested against any measures which might lead to war, but the joint Foreign Minister and the Chief of Staff (both Austrians) insisted on armed retaliation. In vain did Tisza point to the danger of Russian intervention: the Austrian militarists managed to sway the old Emperor, Francis Joseph, who had, in the meantime, received reassurances from Germany's bellicose emperor, William II.

The ultimatum expired and, as expected, Serbia refused to comply. On July 28, 1914, Francis Joseph *declared war on Serbia*. The reader will be familiar with the chain of events set off by this declaration: by August 3 most of Europe was engaged in the War.

The Budapest Parliament took a typically Magyar attitude. Before the declaration of war the entire Parliament had supported Tisza's efforts to avoid the war. Now, all parties, including the Social Democrats and Mihály Károlyi's Liberal dissidents, agreed to a political truce to enable Tisza's government to support the war effort — which Tisza did, against his own convictions. The Hungarians' quixotic code of honour demands absolute loyalty to the nation's commitments, however unpalatable. Political realism and expediency are unknown words in the Magyar language. For four years the Magyar soldiers and their combat officers fought with dutiful courage on foreign soil mostly under foreign generals for an empire that was not theirs, in a senseless war to avenge the death of the man who had hated Hungarians. 3.8 million Hungarians served in the armed forces of the Monarchy. No Hungarian unit deserted, no factory sabotaged the war effort till the final collapse. Hungarian troops suffered very heavy losses : 660,000 dead and 750,000 wounded. The high command of the Monarchy was led by Austrian and Czech generals. There were no Hungarians in high positions on the General Staff and the highest position held by a Hungarian officer was that of a corps commander (General Szurmay, the able defender of the Eastern Carpathians). It is therefore pointless to revise the conduct of the war in which Hungarians had the subordinate role of providing the fighting troops. History books delight in listing examples of the muddled thinking and wasteful strategy of the archaic Austrian leadership.

The tragic role of the Magyar soldier is illustrated by the so-called "Limanova charge" in 1915. The Austrian commander sent Magyar hussars in an old-fashioned cavalry charge against the Russian trenches defended by barbed wire and machine-guns. The charge of this "light brigade" (ten times the size of the famous Balaclava brigade) must have been a magnificent sight: riding their splendid mounts, resplendent in their blue-red-white uniforms (ideal targets for the machine-guns), armed with nothing but sabres — they were a sight to gladden the heart of their proud general (who watched the charge from the proverbial hill). The charge was a success: the general was praised and the hussars received countless decorations — most of them posthumously . . .

Italy entered the war against the Monarchy in 1915. *Rumania,* promised Transylvania and adjoining regions by the Western Allies, attacked Hungary in August 1916. For a while the Rumanian armies made some progress in Transylvania, which was defended by village policemen and the autumn rains. A few weeks later the German general, Mackensen, with hastily collected German-Hungarian troops chased the Rumanians out of Transylvania, then, in two months captured Bucharest and annihilated the Rumanian army.

On November 21, 1916, emperor-king Francis Joseph died after a reign of 68 years.

The reign of Charles IV

On December 30, 1916, Hungary's last King and Queen were crowned in the historic cathedral of Our Lady in Buda. After the long, solemn ceremony (somewhat reminiscent of the ordination of a Catholic priest), the young king mounted his horse and rode up a man-made hillock built of the soil collected from the 73 counties of Hungary. There, with Saint Stephen's heavy crown swaying precariously on his head, Charles IV made four symbolic strokes with Saint Stephen's sword in the four wind directions, swearing to defend Hungary against all enemies.

At first glance, the position of the Monarchy seemed unassailable at the end of 1916: Rumania and Serbia were crushed, The Russian and Italian fronts securely held. But Charles IV was an intelligent man and he knew that the empire's war potential was exhausted. He also knew that the nationalities were preparing to destroy the Monarchy. On his initiative, the Central Powers (Germany, the Monarchy, Bulgaria and Turkey) sent the Allied (Entente) powers a detailed *peace offer* in December 1916, suggesting the restoration of the 1914 status quo. The Entente rejected the offer, insisting on the "liberation of the Slav and Rumanian minorities". This rejection (costing another two years of war and another ten million dead) was the result of the successful propaganda campaign conducted by Czech intellectuals (Masaryk, Benes) and their Rumanian, Serb and other emigré colleagues in France and Britain. They managed to convince the Western Allies that the creation of Slav and Rumanian national states would stop German and Russian expansion in Central Europe. Tisza pointed out to the U.S. Ambassador that the breaking up of the Monarchy would result in the creation of several weak, multi-national states unable to resist imperialist pressure. (We know today who was right. . .) After hearing Tisza's arguments, the British (on American advice) suggested new negotiations with Austria-Hungary but the joint foreign minister of the Monarchy (count Czernin — of Czech nationality) broke off the negotiations, claiming that it would be disloyal to negotiate without Germany.

The effects of the entry of the U.S. into the War against the Central Powers were temporarily offset by Russia's collapse and an offensive against Italy which was so successful that it took a considerable amount of bungling on the part of the Austrian generals to save the Italians.

In the *Hungarian Parliament,* count Mihály Károlyi, now leader of the opposition, harassed the government, demanding radical electoral and other reforms. In May 1917 Tisza resigned. His two successors, count M. Eszterházy and S. Wekerle, were unable to contain the opposition, the growing profiteering and increasing unrest at home. Still the frontline was holding everywhere, thanks mainly to the millions of hardy Magyar peasant soldiers. Russia and Rumania signed Peace Treaties in 1918 — but the impact of the American intervention was already felt and the total economic exhaustion of all the Central Powers had already decided the fate of the War. In September 1918 the Bulgarians collapsed and soon the Turks asked for an armistice.

In November 1918 the *Monarchy signed an armistice* with the Allied Powers in Padova, Italy. The terms of the agreement left the national frontiers untouched and directed the troops to return to their respective countries with their arms, under their officers.

The Monarchy soon ceased to be a federal structure: the various nationalities declared their autonomy and constituted National Councils. On Wekerle's resignation, Károlyi, emulating the nationalities, formed a Hungarian National Council (quite needlessly: Hungary had her own constitution and government) and on October 31, helped by the so-called "Military Councils" (composed mainly of deserters), took over the capital, Budapest. The coup was bloodless (and senseless) — but a commando of the "Military Council" assassinated Tisza, who lived in a Budapest suburb.

The King, after some hesitation, appointed Károlyi Prime Minister.

Karolyi and the Republic

On being appointed Prime Minister, Károlyi commenced a feverish activity as the virtual ruler of the country. As the troops were returning from the fronts — with their equipment and under their officers, as directed by the Padova armistice — Károlyi's government ordered the soldiers to lay down their arms and disperse: *"Never again do I want to see another soldier. . .",* said the Defence Minister, Béla Linder. Károlyi and his government naively believed that a "pacifist" Hungary would be regarded as the "friend of the Entente". Then Károlyi decided to "improve" on the Padova armistice and led a delegation to

Belgrade, the headquarters of the southern Allied Forces. (This fateful pilgrimage had been suggested to Károlyi by one of his Czech friends. . .) The French commander, general Franchet d'Espérey, treated Károlyi and his deputation with utter contempt.[1] On finding out why he came (uninvited) and on learning that Károlyi had dispersed the Hungarian armed forces, d'Espérey consulted his Rumanian and Serbian liaison officers and handed Károlyi extremely harsh instructions, including the immediate cession of large territories demanded by the Rumanians and Serbs. As it turned out later, the French commander had neither the desire, nor the authority to conclude an armistice with Károlyi and he made up his instructions on the spur of the moment.

Károlyi's first fateful decision, the *disarmement* of the returning Hungarian troops, had far-reaching consequences. In November, 1918, no enemy soldier stood on Hungarian soil. The Hungarian units on the various fronts were well-disciplined, armed and in reasonably good spirits. They were willing and able to defend the Hungarian frontiers against the invaders whom they had either recently defeated (Serbs, Rumanians) or who had only makeshift units made up of deserters and ex-prisoners of war (Czechs).

On November 13, King Charles IV "withdrew from the direction of the affairs of the State". Károlyi interpreted this as the King's resignation and had the *Republic of Hungary* declared by the Parliament. The nation was now facing the fifth winter of the war. Rumanian, Czech and Serb troops moved into the undefended land, hundreds of thousands of refugees fled towards the centre of the country, the food, accommodation and fuel situation was catastrophic and the (Spanish) influenza killed thousands. The Károlyi government limited itself to promises of radical electoral and land-reforms and free welfare services — without doing anything. Disappointed, his former middle-class and moderate supporters left Károlyi and in January only the Socialists and Radicals supported him.

For more than two months the country had been without a head of State. Then in January 1919 Károlyi was elected President of the Hungarian Republic. By that time however, a new force was ready to fill the political vacuum created by Károlyi's paralysed government.

Bela Kun's "Council Republic"

There had been no Communist Party in Hungary before November 1918. During the War some Hungarian prisoners of war had joined the Soviet (Bolshevik) Communist Party in Russia and were trained to prepare a Communist revolution in Central Europe. In November 1918 a group of these trained agitators, led by Béla Kun, were sent to Budapest and founded there the "Hungarian Communist Party".

The Social Democrats and the workers of the Trade Unions resented the Russian-financed activities of the Communists and bloody clashes soon occurred between the Budapest workers and Kun's terrorist detachments (such as the "Lenin Boys"). Eventually even Károlyi's meek government had to arrest some Communist agitators (including Kun).

In the meantime the Paris Peace Conference was in session, making decisions without consulting the defeated nations. In February, 1919, the Budapest Allied Commission demanded the evacuation of about three-fourths of Hungary in favour of Czechoslovakia, Rumania and Serbia. Károlyi, who now realised the folly of his "pro-Entente" and "pacifist" policies, resigned in March, 1919, handing over the supreme authority to the "Proletariat of the Nation".[2]

The left-wing Social Democrats (the only active political group) promptly handed over the power to Kun and his fellow Communists. On the 21st of March, 1919, the *Hungarian Council Republic* was formed, governed by the Communists and some Social Democrats. Misnamed "Dictatorship of the Proletariat", Béla Kun's regime lacked the support of most of the city proletariat and certainly of the entire agrarian proletariat: in fact it lacked the support of all classes or established parties. Its ideological basis, "Bolshevik Communism", manifested itself by little more than parrot-like repetitions of Russian-Bolshevik terminology in the service of the self-preservation of a group of unscrupulous adventurers. The organisers and supporters of the regime were people whose mentality was foreign to Hungary's political, social and cultural atmosphere. Of the 45 "Commissars" (Ministers) 32 were unassimilated Galicians (cf. Chapter 22). Most of the urban workers and Trade Unions refused to co-operate with them or seceded from the "coalition". The peasants (the largest, most oppressed class) were not represented in the government. Neither were the middle classes (let alone the upper classes) nor any politician with appreciable Parliamentary experience.

The regime was maintained by ruthless terror exercised by the "Soldiers' Councils" or other armed commandos, consisting of criminals, deserters, ex-prisoners of war and vagrants and led by sadists, such as the Commissar Tibor Szamuelly. This method of control was called the "Red Terror" by the Communists themselves.[3]

The administration of the country (or what was left of it) was left to the town and village "Councils" which held absolute legislative, executive and judiciary powers (including the power to impose capital punishment for "anti-revolutionary" activities). These Councils were staffed by "reliable" city Communists. The estates were nationalised, *not distributed to the peasants* but administered by "Farmers' Councils" (of reliable city Communists). Businesses and factories were similarly "socialised" (managed by reliable Communists). As a result, industrial and agricultural production practically ceased; the peasants refused to feed the "city scoundrels". Brutal requisitions evoked resistance, often in the form of sizable uprisings, which, in turn, were followed by the brutal retaliations of the terror gangs.

Kun recruited a "Red Army" to hold back the approaching Czech and Rumanian troops which threatened the existence of the Communist regime. The "Red Army", led by some able officers of the former Hungarian Army willing to defend their country under any circumstances, regained considerable territory from the Czechs in the north but was then ordered by the Allied Powers to withdraw. Thus the Rumanians could move toward Budapest practically unopposed. On learning this, Kun and his "government" fled from Budapest (July 31).

Rumanian occupation — national government

The Rumanians entered the undefended capital and began to loot and impose their own type of terror upon the much-suffering population.[4] Various moderates tried to form governments but they were unacceptable to the Allied Commission. The only hope of the nation was now the "Counter-Revolutionary Government" set up in the south of the country, but not yet officially acknowledged by the Allies. This government-in-exile had recruited a small "National Army", commanded by Admiral Miklós Horthy, which was however not allowed to proceed to Budapest where the Rumanians were "absorbing" western civilisation at an alarming rate. After months of negotiations, the Rumanians were induced to leave Budapest and Horthy's "National Army" entered the capital in November 1919. A caretaker government was formed and in January 1920 elections were held under Allied supervision. As a result, a moderate rightist government was elected. As the Entente forbade the restoration of the Habsburg dynasty, the Hungarian throne was declared vacant and Admiral Horthy was elected Regent (March 1920).

Following the collapse of the Kun regime (July 1919) Hungary had practically no law-enforcing agencies — these (gendarmerie, police, courts) had all been abolished by the Communists. Between July and November 1919 there were isolated, individual acts of revenge against those held responsible for the sufferings of the preceding months. There were also outbursts of anti-Semitic (or rather anti-Galician) feelings, as the most hated of the Bolshevik leaders (Kun, Szamuelly, Korvin) were Jews. This was the much publicised *"White Terror":* a series of regrettable, lawless acts, evoked by the "Red Terror" and made possible by the legal vacuum created by Kun and his regime.

The well-disciplined units of the National Army restored law and order and put an end to these excesses. Thus Admiral Horthy, whose name had been maliciously connected with the "White Terror", was, as commander of the National Army and then Head of State, the very person to stop these regrettable acts of revenge.[5]

The Trianon Treaty

The verdict of the Peace Treaty was given solely on the submissions of the Czech, Rumanian and Serb delegations. Neither the Hungarian submissions nor President Wilson's much vaunted 14 Points[6] were taken into consideration. Hungary was punished more severely than any other country: she lost 71.4% of her territory and 63.5% of her population; she was also ordered to pay reparations (in addition to the loot taken by the Rumanians) and to reduce her armed forces to 35,000, without heavy armement or national service. The country lost all her salt, iron, silver and gold mines and most of her timber

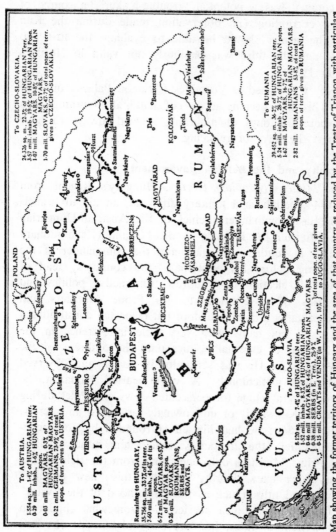

To CZECHO-SLOVAKIA.
24,326 sq. m., 22.3% of HUNGARIAN Terr.
3.57 mill. inhab., 19% of HUNGARIAN popn.
1.07 mill. MAGYARS, 30% of HUNGARIAN MAGYARS.
1.70 mill. SLOVAKS, 47.7% of total popn of terr. given to CZECHO-SLOVAKIA.

To RUMANIA.
39,452 sq. m., 36.2% of HUNGARIAN terr.
5.24 mill. inhab., 26.7% of HUNGARIAN popn.
1.67 mill. MAGYARS, 16% of HUNGARIAN MAGYARS.
2.82 mill. RUMANIANS, 53% of total popn. of terr. given to RUMANIA.

To AUSTRIA.
1554 sq. m., 1.4% of HUNGARIAN terr.
0.29 mill. inhab., 1.6% HUNGARIAN popn.
0.03 mill. MAGYARS, 0.3% of HUNGARIAN MAGYARS.
0.22 mill. GERMANS, 75% of total popn. of terr. given to AUSTRIA.

Remaining to HUNGARY,
35,756 sq. m., 32.7% of its terr.
7.60 mill. inhab., 41.6% of its popn.
6.72 mill. MAGYARS, 62.5% of MAGYAR popn.
0.26 mill. SLOVAKS, RUMANIANS, SERBS and CROATS.

To JUGO-SLAVIA.
8,129 sq. m., 7.4% of HUNGARIAN terr.
1.52 mill. inhab., 8.3% of HUNGARIAN popn.
0.46 mill. MAGYARS, 65% of HUNGARIAN MAGYARS.
0.38 mill. SERBS (in E. Terr.), 25.9% }of total popn of terr. given
0.15 mill. CROATS and VENDS (in W. Terr.), 10% } to JUGO-SLAVIA.

Map showing the former territory of Hungary and the area of that country as reduced by the Treaty of Trianon, with particulars of the partitions and allocation of the alienated territory to Czecho-Slovakia, Jugo-Slavia, Rumania and Austria.

– – – – – pre-war boundary of Hungary.
————— present boundary of Hungary.

Hungary's partition by the Trianon Treaty (1920)

and coal production. One-third of all Magyars were transferred to a foreign country.[7]

The arguments against Hungary were basically the following: Hungary had started the War, she had oppressed her minorities and the country was a potential "trouble-maker", a source of Communist corruption (an observation made during the Kun regime). The reader should be able to evaluate the first two arguments, and the third was obviously not valid in Horthy's Hungary in 1920.

The treaty was signed at Versailles (Trianon Palace) on June 4, 1920. This day became a day of national mourning in a country where the days of mourning seemed always to have outnumbered the days of rejoicing.

Miklos Horthy and the Bethlen government

Admiral Miklós (Nicholas) Horthy, Hungary's Regent from 1920 to 1944, had been a military diplomat, an aid to Francis Joseph, the last commander-in-chief of the Austrian-Hungarian Navy, the Minister for Defence in the "Counter-Revolutionary Government" in southern Hungary and the commander of the National Army before his election as the country's Head of State. After his election he withdrew from active politics and left the tasks of government to his Prime Ministers and Ministers, becoming a dignified, aloof but respected constitutional monarch in all but name with very little interference in the country's internal or external politics until the outbreak of the Second World War. He was scrupulously honest and observed the Constitution meticulously. A warm-hearted humanist, he made his country a refuge for persecuted Jews and Poles during World War II. Knowingly or unknowingly he started an interesting social evolution: he had himself surrounded by non-aristocratic personalities (the aristocrats treated him rather coolly). Of his 14 Prime Ministers only one came from the rich, aristocratic land-owner class. Horthy provided this "new nobility" with honours and titles (such as the knighthood of the "Vitéz" awarded for outstanding war service) — somewhat similar to the British system of titles, honours and knighthoods (he was a great admirer of the British). Thus he gradually created a new, non-aristocratic, leading class of Hungary.

After the 1920 elections the Christian and Smallholder parties formed a coalition government. After the signing of the Trianon

Treaty, Horthy appointed count *Pál Teleki* Prime Minister (1920-1921). Teleki, scion of an historic Transylvanian family, was a world-renowned professor of Geography, an honest and wise statesman and a devout Catholic. He was an unusual politician in that his bluff sincerity, monosyllabic oratory and bespectacled, schoolmasterly figure clashed with the Renaissance decor and Baroque atmosphere of the Hungarian Parliament.

In 1921 *King Charles* attempted twice to reclaim his Hungarian throne. On the first occasion Horthy convinced him that his restoration — though welcome in Hungary — was against the stipulations of the Peace Treaty. On the second occasion, armed confrontation occurred between Hungarian troops loyal to Charles and those loyal to Horthy, while the Czechs and Rumanians mobilised threatening armed intervention if Hungary restored the Habsburg dynasty. In order to avoid further bloodshed and foreign intervention, Charles surrendered.

The Entente Powers exiled Charles to Madeira in the Atlantic where he died in 1922. It was one of the many ironies of Hungarian history that this pious, honest and humane man, with outstanding intellectual and moral qualities, loved and respected by all Hungarians, was not allowed to remain on the Hungarian throne — he was the first Habsburg who would have been welcome to it.

Teleki resigned and Horthy appointed *count István Bethlen* Prime Minister (1921-1931). This able politician, scion of another historic Transylvanian family, was an excellent choice. His first task was to re-establish some measure of *financial stability*. In 1922 Hungary was admitted to the League of Nations. After three years of strenuous negotiations Bethlen managed to secure a substantial loan through the League for Hungary. (Foreign aid freely given to "developing" countries did not exist in those days). Interestingly enough, the greatest obstacle was created by the Hungarian emigrés, led by Károlyi in Britain, who did everything to discredit Hungary and have the loan withheld from a country ruled by "Horthy's reactionaries". Finally the loan was granted and Bethlen could stop the crippling inflation by introducing a new stable currency based on gold (1927).

An *industrial prosperity* of some sort began: a fourfold increase in manufacturing output brought relative affluence to

225

the urban workers who also enjoyed progressive social and free health benefits.

The government was, however, unable to solve the *agrarian question:* 3 million peasants (more than one-third of the country's population) lived more or less on subsistence farms of their own or as landless agricultural workers. The succession states carried out their much-vaunted agrarian reforms through the inexpensive device of confiscating former Hungarian landholdings. Hungary had no ex-enemy loot to divide — the land to be given to the peasants had to be bought from the owners. The Hungarians' scrupulous respect for proprietary rights prevented them from confiscating even the huge estates of the Habsburg family (confiscated everywhere else).

In 1921 the government commenced an agrarian programme involving about one million acres (6% of the country's arable land) distributed among 400,000 landless peasants. There is no doubt that much more should have been done to hand back to the Magyar peasants the soil for which a million of them died in two world wars.

Education progressed rapidly: eight thousand new primary schools, many high schools and universities were built during the ten years of the Bethlen government — not a bad record for an impoverished nation of 8 million. The *electoral* policy of the government was rather conservative: limitations of age, sex, residence, education and family status reduced the number of electors to about two-thirds of the adult population. The Parliament consisted of a Lower House (elected by secret ballot in towns and open voting in the rural areas) and an Upper House with its hereditary or appointed members and representatives of professions (similar to the House of Lords). The Regent appointed or dismissed the Prime Minister who did not have to be a member of the Parliament, but had to be supported by the majority party. The Prime Minister chose his ministers (not necessarily from members of the Parliament).

Law and order were maintained by a well disciplined and educated police and gendarmerie force (all commissioned officers were law graduates) and by well-qualified judges who meted out justice based on solid Roman Law as revised by the Code Napoleon and the Hungarian Articles of Law ("Corpus Juris"). In the public service bribery, embezzling and fraud were practically unknown but nepotism was rampant. The working classes —

urban and agrarian — showed remarkable self-discipline and patriotism during the trying years of reconstruction, depression and second World War. Strikes and demonstrations were rare in the industrial centres and non-existent in the country where the Magyar peasant continued to carry his thousand-year-old burden with enduring loyalty.

"Revisionism" and foreign policy

The idea that the Trianon frontiers needed a radical revision became the basic ideology in Hungarian politics as well as in education, art, literature and social life. The succession states and their protector, France, remained deaf to the Hungarian arguments for a peaceful revision of the frontiers (most Magyar-populated districts were contiguous to the Trianon frontier and their adjustment would have caused few demographic problems). The Hungarians reacted emotionally and the words "Nem, nem, soha!" ("No, no, never!"), rejecting the mutilation of the country became a national motto. Abroad, this propaganda, appealing to the heart rather than the mind, found a warm response in Italy, a somewhat amused acknowledgement in Britain and little success elsewhere.

The generations of young Hungarians brought up during these decades lived in the wishful dreamworld of the "restoration of Hungary's thousand-year-old frontiers". Though unattainable, this was a goal to strive for, to hope for, to struggle for and to demonstrate for. It was definitely a worthier cause to get excited about than some of today's causes. To the nation, the lofty ideal of revisionism gave a sense of dignity and self-respect, lifting the people's minds out of despair. On the other hand, this attitude certainly damaged the Hungarians' chances of establishing useful economic ties with their neighbours and it also proved harmful to the Magyar minorities in the succession states. Hungary's emotional (and ineffective) revisionism served as a pretext for the oppression of the Magyar minorities in Rumania, Czechoslovakia and Yugoslavia. Moreover, in order to guard the results of their victory, these three states formed a strong military alliance (called the "Little Entente") with the sole aim of preventing Hungary from recovering her lost territories.

It had not occurred to a single Hungarian politician to *pretend* to accept the terms of the Treaty and thus ease the tension and the Magyar minorities' plight.

The relations between Hungary and *Austria* were rather strained at the beginning of the period, as the Hungarians resented the fact that Austria had also accepted a slice of Hungarian territory under the Peace Treaty. *France,* the protector of the "Little Entente", maintained a hostile attitude toward Hungary during the entire period. The *British* did cast occasional, supercilious glances toward Central Europe, but the business of the Empire kept the British politicians from trying to counterbalance France's influence there, though the Hungarians were eager to approach Britain.

The first state to turn a friendly hand toward Hungary was *Italy.* A friendship pact with this country was Bethlen's greatest diplomatic success (1927).

By 1930 Horthy and Bethlen had achieved the seemingly impossible: the nation was back on its feet, the social and economic conditions were improving, the currency was stable and unemployment was minimal. Then, in 1931, the full force of the world financial crisis and depression hit the country's economy (still very much dependent on foreign trade, especially wheat exports).

Unwilling to lead the country through another crisis, Bethlen resigned in August 1931.

27. THE HEART AND THE HEIGHTS

(The settlement, land, art, customs and way of life of the people of Budapest and Northern Hungary)

Budapest: the Heart of the Nation

Budapest (population 2 million) arose from the union of two towns, Buda and Pest, in 1873. *Buda,* the older town, situated on the western hills, has been Hungary's capital since the XIVth century. It was under Turkish occupation for 145 years. Often besieged, damaged, destroyed and rebuilt the royal castle of Buda preserves the memories of many periods since the XIIth century. Near the royal palace, the seven-centuries-old "Our Lady" cathedral ("Coronation" or "Matthias" Church) was the scene of the crowning of several Hungarian kings. To the south lies the "Gellért" hill — named after Bishop Saint Gerard (Gellért), who helped Saint Stephen to convert the Magyars to Christianity in the XIth century. Seven bridges span the Danube between the two cities: all were destroyed at the end of World War II and rebuilt afterwards. On the east bank *Pest,* the administrative, business and cultural centre of the country, possesses innumerable buildings and monuments of historical or cultural significance, among which we have already mentioned a few in other chapters. The Academy of Sciences, built in 1862 in Italian neo-Renaissance style, and the monumental Szent István (Saint Stephen) basilica (1851, neo- Renaissance) deserve particular mention. A remarkable monument, the "Millenium Monument", stands near the City Park: a tall, slender column topped by the figure of a flying angel; the base is surrounded by many statues representing the important historical figures of Hungary. The work was created by the sculptor Gy. Zala on the occasion of Hungary's millenary

Fishermen's Bastion, Buda

S. Hollósy: Corn husking (Cf. pp. 209 and 238)

celebrations (1896). The replica of the historic castle of Vajda-hunyad in the City Park was built on the same occasion. The nearby Museum of Applied Arts is an interesting example of Ödön Lechner's "Magyar-Secessionist" style (1893).

Margaret Island, now a national recreation area, was named after Saint Margaret of the Árpáds (XIIIth century), who spent her life in prayer and work on this island.

Almost half of Hungary's industry is concentrated in and around Budapest, especially in some suburbs (Csepel, Ujpest, Kispest etc.). An interesting fact is that several suburbs and townships nearby (Szentendre) are inhabited by Slovak, Serb, German and other nationalities which have preserved their ethnic culture and way of life for centuries in the heart of the country.

The loyal North

Northern Hungary, or the "Uplands" ("Felvidék"), is the region of historic Hungary bounded by the northern Carpathians, the Danube and the Great Plain in the south. This area has suffered less from the vicissitudes of Hungarian history than the others. Since 1920, most of the area has belonged to the newly created state of Czechoslovakia. Since 1945 the eastern district (Ruthenia) has belonged to the Soviet Union.

The *population* of the Uplands consists of Slovaks, Magyars, Germans and Ruthenians (Carpatho-Ukrainians). The *Slovaks,* the largest group (2 million), are the only non-Magyar indigenous group in the Carpathian basin. During the thousand years as citizens of the Hungarian state, the Slovaks have kept their language, culture, way of life and national identity. Their numbers have increased considerably, partly because of the sheltered nature of the region, partly through immigration of neighbouring Slav elements. Though many Slovaks rose to the ranks of the Hungarian leading classes through services to the Church or State, the Slovaks of the mountain villages did not assimilate (no one told them to). There had been no antagonism between Magyars and Slovaks before the XXth century when external political agitation stirred up "independence" and "libera-tion" movements among them, with limited success. Before that time, the Slovaks had always been the Magyars' loyal comrades-in-arms in their common struggle against oppression, especially in Rákóczi's time. The Magyars have always found the mild-mannered, art-loving, industrious Slovaks close to their hearts. Thus it frequently happened that in villages with mixed Magyar and Slovak populations the Magyars integrated into the Slovak community. The opposite happened less frequently; in fact, large isolated Slovak settlements have maintained their ethnic identity in the south of the Great Hungarian Plain.

The *Ruthenians or Carpatho-Ukrainians* (about 500,000), who migrated to the eastern districts of the Uplands during the Middle Ages, have been peaceful, honest and loyal subjects of the Hungarian state. They, too, wholeheartedly supported the Hungarians in their freedom struggles and earned the epithet given to them by Rákóczi: "gens fidelissima" ("the most faithful people"). The *Germans,* called Saxons, settled during the XIIIth-XIVth centuries in the central northern towns and have similarly been loyal citizens of the country of their adoption. During the struggles against Austrian-German oppression these German-speaking Hungarians stood faithfully by their Magyar brothers.

The *Magyar* population is concentrated in the southern counties of the region, but there are pockets of rural settlements everywhere, while the urban population was largely Magyar before 1920. Certain Magyar groups show marked ethnic cultural characteristics, such as the Palóc, the Magyars called "Matyós" etc. Due mainly to the isolation caused by the mountains, the people of these districts have developed different customs and folk-art, in spite of their common Magyar origin.

Some towns of historic and cultural interest

Kassa (today Kosice, Czechoslovakia) is the largest city of the northern central area, with memories of various freedom struggles. Its cathedral, named after Saint Elizabeth of Hungary and built in 1360, is the finest remaining example of Hungarian Gothic architecture. The remains of Ferenc Rákóczi and his mother, Ilona Zrinyi, rest in the crypts of the cathedral. The interior of the church contains many outstanding examples of XIVth-XVth century Hungarian wood-carving, painting and decorative art.

Pozsony (today Bratislava, Czechoslovakia), near the western border, used to be the administrative capital of Hungary in

Turkish times. Several Habsburg kings were crowned here and it was the seat of what passed for a Hungarian "Parliament" during the XVIth-XVIIIth centuries (until 1848).

Nearby is Trencsén, the centre of *"Mátyusföld"*, a region named after Máté ("Mátyus") Csák, a rich feudal lord who was Palatin of Hungary in the XIVth century. Csák, a descendant of a Magyar tribal chieftain of the IXth century and Hungary's chief minister, would have been amused to learn that certain imaginative historians have identified his name with the word "Czech" and claimed Czech supremacy over "Mátyusföld" during Csák's feudal tenure. (This was one of the "proofs" submitted to the Trianon Peace Treaty Commission . . .)

The northern "Saxon" towns (Löcse, Késmárk, Eperjes) present an interesting synthesis of Hungarian history and local German tradition.

The southern hilly fringe of the region belongs to Hungary. The largest city here is *Miskolc,* second largest city in Hungary. Near the industrial complex of Diósgyör lies the historic castle built by the Anjou kings (XIVth century). Near the Tokaj vineyards lies Rákóczi's castle of Sárospatak, famous also for its old Protestant College. *Eger* is rich in historic relics, such as the fort which István Dobó defended successfully in 1552. This archiepiscopal see has many Baroque and Renaissance churches. *Visegrád* is situated at the bend of the Danube. Its gothic palace built in the XIIIth and XIVth centuries was the favourite residence of the Anjou kings and Matthias.

Magyar folk art and crafts in the Uplands

The Magyars of this forested area use wood to a great extent to make carved furniture, wooden vessels, musical instruments and buildings. Timber belltowers, carved wooden steeples and ornamental carvings abound in Catholic villages of the area.

The most characteristic aspect of the Magyar folk art in this area is the colourful *folkwear,* which shows many different styles. In the districts closer to the Plain, brighter colour schemes, shorter skirts and lighter footwear types are found. The Palóc of *Boldog* are particularly famous for their elaborate headdresses ("párta") worn by the young brides. *Buják* is known for the vivid colours of the skirts worn over many petticoats.

Matyó folkwear

The rich peasants of *Martos* (now Czechoslovakia) wear golden and silver lace-decorated coifs and many silver chains.

The *Matyó* folkwear is world famous. These descendants of King Matthias' Magyar bodyguard live in a few villages around Mezőkövesd in Borsod county. Their characteristic folk art was inspired by the Gothic-Renaissance styles of Matthias' court. The magnificent costumes of the women, with lines of almost gothic delicacy, are richly embroidered. Though they use vivid colours as well, the aristocratic combination of white on black is their favourite. The women present a tall, slender figure in their ankle-length skirts, which flare out slightly at the bottom. The narrow apron is made of black or dark blue material with white embroidery. Men's articles are also multicoloured: their long, wide sleeves and shirt collars are embroidered, as are their aprons.

Embroidery is used — in addition to costume decoration — in ornamenting bedcovers, scarves and pillow-slips. *Home-weaving* is used for decorative material and recently there has been a marked revival in home-weaving and embroidery in the **Palóc** districts, where it is becoming part of a thriving rural industry.

Some folk customs of the Uplands

The *marriage customs* illustrate well the Palóc' strict moral code and colourful traditions.

When a boy has found a girl acceptable to his parents, he asks the girl's mother for the hand of the girl. If he is accepted, the girl gives him a token present (in Matyó villages: an apron). The boy announces his engagement by wearing a rosemary to church and the girl's gift, but does not disclose her name. They rarely meet in public. After a courtship of two to three months (carefully chaperoned) the wedding takes place usually in a day-long celebration. The groom sends his best man to fetch the bride. At the bride's home, the envoy performs the ceremony of "buying" the girl. This pantomime revives the memory of the pagan custom of kidnapping or buying the bride. (In Hungarian the groom is called: "völegény": the buyer). When they have concluded the "sale", the bride's trousseau is loaded on a cart and she is farewelled by her parents (cf. Chapter 18). After the church ceremony the banquet starts at the groom's house.

Palóc folkwear (Rimóc)

The bride and bridegroom often eat in a different room, accompanied by the bridesmaids. During the dance, following the banquet, the guests dance with the bride in turn and pay a token price for each dance (there are no other wedding presents given).

When the guests disperse, the young couple sleep in different rooms. Not until the bride opens the door of her own free will is the young husband allowed to join her.

The tedious task of *corn-husking,* the stripping of the leaves and shelling of the ears of corn (maize), provides a pleasant opportunity for social gatherings in Upland villages on winter evenings. Relatives and friends gather (with their children) at the farmer's house to help him. The entertainment includes tales told by old people, songs from the girls and boys and games. When someone finds an ear with red corn on it, the finder is entitled to kiss the person next to him (strangely enough, it is always a boy who finds the red corn and there is always a girl sitting next to him).

* * *

As a child I spent many magic winter evenings in these corn-husking gatherings, listening to ballads, songs, fairy tales and legends, sharing the warmth of belonging and love with those gay, simple artists of life. As the village of my birth had a mixed Magyar-Slovak population, the gatherings and games were often mixed, too. In fact at a very early period of my life I thought that the (rather delightfully) "different" children (i.e. girls) were Slovaks. Somehow I have liked "Slovaks" ever since . . .

I sincerely wish that no greater misunderstanding should ever come between Magyars and Slovaks. . .

28. "NEW MELODIES OF NEWER YEARS. . ."

(Hungarian literature during the first decades of the XXth century)

Endre (Andrew) Ady

Born of a Protestant family of ancient nobility in northern Transylvania (1877), he received a good education and chose the career of a journalist in the eastern Hungarian town of Nagyvárad. Here he met and fell in love with a married woman who became his great love, inspiring muse and tragic destiny, the "Leda" of his sensuous love poems. On Leda's invitation Ady went to Paris, where the modern trends of French art and poetry changed his outlook on life. On his return he settled in Budapest and published "New Verses" (1906). The collection had a shattering effect on the stagnating Hungarian literary life of this complacent era.

The violent attacks of the critics of the "establishment" only enhanced Ady's popularity with the young. He published several collections in the following years, each causing a storm of praise and attack for its prophetic, scolding patriotism, sensuous, sinful longing for love and for the poet's imaginative but obscure symbolism. The excesses of his stormy youth gradually destroyed Ady's health. He broke with Leda and found pure, youthful, true love in a girl much younger than himself whom he married. He was deeply shocked by the Great War, its senseless horrors and its destruction of human values. He died during the tragic month of January, 1919.

Ady created a *symbolic language* of his own to interpret his dynamic message. His exceptionally rich language uses picturesque, half-forgotten archaic words, racy folk-dialect, city slang and colourful composite words of his own creation. Frequently a sequence of allegoric images becomes the vehicle for his thoughts. This symbolism may take the form of a gothic image of his own captive soul in "an old, fearful castle" where "the lone, forsaken rooms ring hollow" — the prison of his frustrations — from where "rarely at the hour of midnight. . . my large eyes begin to flare. . ." ("The White Lady").[1] He often creates symmetrical structures of opposites or choices, as in the prophetic appeal to his nation presented in the form of a paraphrase of an old Magyar folk song: "Peacock"[2] where he challenges his somnolent nation to accept the "new Magyar miracles. . . new flames, new faith. . ." The nation must accept the demands of the new times because "either the Magyar words — shall have new senses, or Magyar life will stay sad. . ." The very titles of his collections carry symbolic messages: "Blood and Gold", "In Eliah's Chariot", "Craving for Affection", "This fleeing Life", "In Death's Foreranks".

The choice of *themes* often displays challenging contrasts. Life and death, the struggle between vitality and melancholy, often find a fatalistic harmony in the same poem with the thought of death almost welcome — in the midst of life's joys. The hauntingly beautiful "Autumn in Paris"[3] presents his death-wish in the association of autumn and death". . . songs within my spirit burned — I knew for death they yearned . . . then Autumn whispered something from behind. . ." It would be interesting to compare Ady's mystic death-wish with Petőfi's classic vision in his "End of September" (cf. Chapter 7). Another moving picture of fatalistic resignation uses the tone of the folk-tale in its sombre imagery: "The Horses of Death".[4]

Love is a lethal passion: Ady's thirst for love is akin to his resigned acceptance of death, which invades his most sensuous desires; "this kiss consumed we should peacefully — die without sorrow. . . " he says in "Half-kissed Kiss"[5] The poet is "Death's Kinsman", his kiss is the kiss of parting: "Her lips — to kiss I love who goes — not returning. . ."[6] The break with his "femme fatale", Leda, is motivated by his deep longing for pure, chaste, spiritual love: he "wants to be loved by somebody. . . and to be somebody's ("Craving for affection")[7]. In the calm, sad moments of regret the memories of his childhood return: "A Familiar Lad" — his childhood innocence — mourns his approaching death[8].

Ady was deeply concerned with the tragic fate of his *Magyar nation*. He saw the faults of the present and he despaired of the nation's future. He raised his scolding, prophetic words against his people, like an angry parent, called them his "detestable, lovable nation"[9]. His is the tragic mission of the tormented Messiah[10], the task of awakening his nation with "new melodies of newer years[21]. The mystic attraction of the Hungarian soil is expressed in the moving picture of the "Outcast Stone" (cf. Chapter 7). As the apocalyptic destruction of the War progresses, he despairs for his nation in the face of that monster devouring the youth of the Magyar people. His visionary poem, "Remembrance," written on the day the War broke out, conjures his fearful vision of War with the imagery of a folk-ballad[12].

Ady's tormented heart repeatedly found peace in his never-failing refuge, *God's love*. He remained indeed throughout his sinful, cursing, prophetic career a God-seeking, repenting Christian psalmist echoing David's eternal human cry from the depths of his misery and passion. He is his nation's prophet, and the prophet's destiny is loneliness as his mission is "sad, between Heaven and earth to wander. . ."[13]. He knows that when he is deserted by humans he can find refuge and peace in the Lord, because He "took me in His embrace."[14] Like the ancient poet of his Bible, he found God the greatest consolation and satisfaction. He faces death calmly because: "I've found Him and have clasped Him in my arms, — in death we'll be united, never to part. . ." [15]

Ady's poetry can only be understood if approached with respect and compassion.

The poets of the "Nyugat" circle

Ady's appearance on the literary scene heralded the beginning of a new era in Hungarian literature. His courage inspired a number of poets, essayists and critics rallied around the literary review "Nyugat" ("The West"). Though the writers of this group showed some degree of social concern, their basic philosophy was that of universal humanism. This explains also their interest in foreign literature, especially French contemporary poetry and philosophy.

241

Mihály Babits (1883-1941), classic poet, aesthete, novelist and critic was a virtuoso of the language and a brilliant interpreter of foreign literature: Latin and western. He was a defender of pure poetry: his goal was aesthetic self-expression without any utilitarian or ideological aspects. The best known of his *novels and novelettes* are: "Stork Calif", a masterly portrait of a split personality, "Pilot Elsa", an Orwellian satire of a future society engaged in eternal wars, and the "Son of Virgil Timar", an emotional parallel between spiritual love and cynicism.

Babits' many collections of *poetry* reflect his warm humanity and classic taste. Even self-pity takes the form of compassion in "Gypsy Song", where he bemoans his own "exile" from the capital in the symbolic image of the homeless gypsy.[16] His pacifism lacks Ady's bitterness and mirrors the classicist's sorrow for the loss of human values ("They sang. . .")[17]. His lofty philosophy resulted in a certain degree of spiritual isolation.[18]

Gyula Juhász, the poet of deep, tender melancholy, searched in vain for sympathy; even his memories failed to console him.[19]

Árpád Tóth, a sensitive impressionist, was a subtle artist of the language and a true interpreter of French poetry. He described the melancholy feelings of the city-poet in exquisite sonnets[20].

Dezsö Kosztolányi, poet, translator, novelist, critic and essayist was a charming, witty, optimistic person, an independent and true aesthete. His prose shows an interest in modern psychology. His short stories (many translated into English) describe middle-class city society in colourful, humorous and vigorous style. His poems show his volatile temperament, all shades of light and gloom, vitality and refined decadence. His early farewell to the scene of his youth, "The Trees of Üllöi Ut", is a moving tribute to Budapest.[21] He understands the timeless beauty of married love threatened by the dull routine of the home. The witty "To My Wife"[22] is that rare phenomen, a love poem to the poet's own wife.

His translations opened new horizons: he interpreted subtle Chinese and Japanese poetry, but also modern American poetry.

Attila József (1905-1937), the son of a deserted mother in a Budapest slum, was the representative of the urban proletariat in modern Hungarian poetry. After his expulsion from the University he joined the illegal Communist Party but was soon expelled from it for his individualistic views. The hardships of his life during the depression affected his mental health and he eventually committed suicide.

His poetry shows flashes of vitality, even humour, but it remains basically pessimistic. His witty, cynic, sad humour is best illustrated in his poem "On My Birthday" mentioned in Chapter 7. Some of his most moving poetry is dedicated to his mother's memory ("Mama")[23]. His basic philosophy is characterised by his sincerity and classic realism. His imagery, naturalistic as it may be, impresses with its truth and lucidity, such as the lines where he describes how he feels mental illness approaching: "I feel my eyes jump in and out. . . when I squint with my whole reality. . . "

The "Ars Poetica"[24], the basic creed of his art, stresses the role of the intellect in poetry. It is surprising to see this highly emotional, often unruly spirit stress the need of conscientious effort involved in writing poetry. We cannot help remembering Petöfi, a kindred spirit who used a similarly classic, realistic, pure language to convey his revolutionary message.

József's own suffering arouses his compassionate approach to his surroundings. The memories of his difficult slum childhood evoke nostalgic tableaus of happier children ("Lullaby")[25]. His deep, humanistic Christianity is expressed in "The Three Kings"[26], a Magyar Christmas scene, reminiscent of the "Bethlehem plays" of the people.

Though bitter and "an exile" in his own country, József still felt one with his Magyar nation: "My dear country — take me to your heart — I want to be your faithful soul. . ." he said in his credo which could be his epitaph.

Some novelists of the period

Géza Gárdonyi (1863-1922) was born of Catholic peasant parents in Transdanubia. He spent his life teaching as a village teacher. His marriage was tragic and he died a melancholic, lonely man in the northern Hungarian town of Eger.

Gárdonyi was successful in many literary genres, but most of all as a novelist. He was a realist, like Mikszáth, but his gentle, shy person lacked malice and cynicism. He was also a good psychologist and could search the soul of the child and the peasant with perfection. However, his portraits of women were tinged with bitterness and mysogony — obviously the result of his unfortunate marriage.

His best novel is the *"Invisible Man"* (also translated: "The Slave of the Huns") which displays imagination, genuine historical sense and the ability to characterise young people in love. Set in the age of Attila and told by Zeta, a Greek slave, the novel is a good synthesis of history and romance. The background of historical events up to Attila's death highlights the love story of Zeta and the Hun girl, Emőke. The characters are real and credible, and the aim of the narrative is to search for the real ego of the principal characters — hence the title.

Gárdonyi's other historical novels "The Stars of Eger" (the epic saga of Eger's defence in 1552) and "God's Captives" (the story of Saint Margaret of the Árpáds), describe historical events and characters behind romantic plots of gentle youthful love — in the first novel ending in happy marriage, in the second remaining pure and platonic.

Gárdonyi's social novels are spoilt by his distrust of women and his aversion to the institution of marriage. His *short stories,* especially those resulting from his long observation of village life, are idyllic, charming and colourful tableaus of peasant life.[27]

He also wrote many plays, revolving around the problems of village life. The best-known is "Wine", the story of the peasant who promises to give up drinking but breaks his promise. The near-tragedy is prevented by a timely application of peasant common-sense and all ends well.

The work of his sensitive, lonely man has provided immense enjoyment to countless readers. His choice of historical and rural topics limits his appeal to foreigners, though some of his works are available in excellent translations.

Zsigmond Móricz (1879-1942) was born in eastern Hungary of a poor, Protestant family. His novels, short stories and plays present a compassionate and realistic picture of the misfits of Hungarian society during the first decades of the century: the selfish peasant, the irresponsible gentry, the foolish, frustrated middle-class woman, the violent outlaw ("betyár") and the greedy village-merchant. He paints a gloomy picture of a decaying society with coarse naturalism, in racy idiomatic Hungarian. His view is limited: he only sees the misery, servility, conceit, greed and lewdness of his world without bothering to reveal the good and promising side of Hungarian society.

"Be Faithful unto Death" shows a different Móricz: this gentle, warm story of a sensitive boy's schooldays has been his most popular work (filmed and adapted to the stage as well as in its original novel form). The historical trilogy, "Transylvania" is a fine analytical study of the XVIIth century with a lively plot and true, realistic portrayal of the leading personalities of the Principality.

Gyula Krudy (1878-1933) was a unique novelist who described hazy, undefined personalities in an impressive, dreamy atmosphere where realities and character delineations disappear, plots become blurred and the present and past are intertwined. His portraits of Budapest middle-class people or country gentry are reminiscent of a surrealistic painting. ("The Sindbad cycle", "The Red Mailcoach").

Christian renaissance

Bishop *Ottokár Prohászka* (1858-1927) who watched the spread of materialism with anxiety, became the inspired voice of the Christian conscience of millenary Hungary. He expounded the principles of modern Catholic social justice in his writings, sermons and lectures; sought out the roots of the spiritual, social and economic problems of his period and pointed to the resources of true Christianity. The mystic depth of his religious writings and the progressive humanism of his social ideas met with mixed response from his contemporaries.

Only after his death did his teachings find their echo among the writers of the short-lived Christian renaissance of the twenties and thirties.

The most popular of the post-war Catholic poets was the gentle humanist, *László Mécs* (1895-), a priest-poet of Northern Hungary. Unfortunately, the imaginative symbolism and colourful language of his poetry defy translation.

The other Catholic poets and writers (Sándor Sik, Lajos Áprily, Lajos Harsányi, Bishop Tihamér Tóth) and the great protestant Bishop, László Ravasz were the leaders of a promising Christian literary revival which ended abruptly with the collapse of the old social structure of Hungary in 1945.

245

Bishop O. Prohászka, (1858-1927)
the voice of Hungary's new Christian conscience.

29. NO WAY OUT

(Hungary's history from the Depression to the end of World War II)

This chapter records some of the events that have shaped the present world. As the documentation of the events and developments described is still incomplete and the historical perspective is insufficient, we shall only present a chronological record of the main events and introduce the makers of Hungary's recent history, leaving it to the reader to analyse their motives and assess the results of their actions.

*   *   *

The crisis years

In consequence of the world financial crisis of the 30s, no foreign loans could be raised for the Hungarian economy and some of the existing loans were foreclosed. Banks, businesses and industries collapsed and many farms were ruined because of the 75% fall in the export price of wheat. Unemployment rose causing unrest and demonstrations in the cities.

This was the situation which Bethlen's successor, *count Gyula Károlyi,* faced as Prime Minister (1931-1932). He instituted harsh austerity measures, including a 50% cut in public expenditure (he travelled by bus to his office every day. . .), increased taxation and ordered reductions in salaries and wages. When these restrictions failed to remedy the situation, he resigned.

Horthy appointed the leader of the young radicals in the government party, general *Gyula (Julius) Gömbös,* as Prime Minister (1932-1936). Gömbös was an ardent nationalist with progressive social ideas. The conservatives in the government advised against radical social reforms and so Gömbös and his brilliant Finance Minister, Béla Imrédy, concentrated on the economic problems. Some foreign loans, expertly negotiated by Imrédy, further cuts in government expenditure and an improved taxation policy set the nation on the road to recovery.

The basis of Gömbös' *foreign policy* was revisionism (cf. Chapter 26), which he sought by peaceful means. He turned first to Italy, the country which seemed to show some understanding of Hungary's problems. When he saw that Hitler was endeavouring to effect a revision of the Versailles Treaty, he suggested closer Italian-German co-operation by forming a "Berlin-Rome Axis" (a term invented by Gömbös). Later, on seeing the increasing German aggressiveness toward Austria, he initiated the Italian-Austrian-Hungarian alliance (Rome Protocols, 1934) in order to resist German pressure. After the assassination of the Austrian Chancellor, Dolfuss, Gömbös realised that nothing could stop the German annexation of Austria and adopted a more Germanophile attitude.

The 1935 election brought victory to his young followers and Gömbös was ready to proceed to his ambitious social programmes. He was then struck by a disease and died at the age of 50.

Horthy, who had not been very happy with Gömbös' pro-German policies, appointed *Kálmán Darányi* in his place (1936-1938). Darányi began by steering a middle-of-the-road policy in both internal and external politics and kept a firm control on all extremists of the left and right. It was at this time that the first National Socialists appeared on the Hungarian political scene. They formed various small parties but could not form a united front. The philosopher of "Hungarism", (the Hungarian National Socialist ideology), Ferenc Szálasi, made his debut in politics and was imprisoned several times — a fact which increased his political charisma and the number of his followers.

Darányi introduced a much-needed electoral reform bill (with secret and compulsory vote for men and women). After Austria's annexation by Germany, Darányi launched a massive rearmement programme. In his foreign policy he favoured, by necessity, Germany, Hungary's new, powerful neighbour. Trying to cede to German pressure, Darányi introduced the First Jewish Law.[1]

Alarmed at his policies, Horthy asked Darányi to resign.

Admiral M. Horthy, Regent of Hungary (1920-1944)

In the shadow of Germany

Béla Imrédy, a devout Catholic, and known to be an Anglophile at that time, seemed the right choice for the post of Prime Minister (1938-1939) in the year of the Eucharistic Congress held in Hungary in connection with the 900th anniversary of Saint Stephen's death.

In August of that year, Hitler invited Horthy and Imrédy to Germany. The German leader suggested that Hungary should attack Czechoslovakia, seeing this as an excuse for Germany to step in and crush the country. Horthy and Imrédy rejected his proposals. Then Horthy and his Foreign Minister, Kánya, gave Hitler and Ribbentrop some unsolicited advice on their warmongering policies and the talks broke up in a hostile atmosphere.[2]

At the famous Munich meeting of the four Prime Ministers (29 September, 1938) only Germany's claims against Czechoslovakia were settled. The Hungarian government began negotiations with the Czech government without success. Hungary then appealed to France and Britain, but the two powers suggested that Germany and Italy should mediate. Thus Hungary asked for and accepted the decision of Germany and Italy, given in the so-called *First Vienna Award* (30 October, 1938) which returned to Hungary the Magyar-inhabited southern strip of Slovakia and Ruthenia.[3] The British and French governments acknowledged the territorial changes.

The western powers' reluctance to participate in Central European politics convinced Imrédy that the region had been left to the mercy of Hitler's Third Reich. Thus he changed his anti-German attitude. Hungary joined the Anti-Comintern Pact of Germany, Italy and Japan, left the League of Nations and introduced the Second Jewish Law.[4]

Then someone found proof that one of Imrédy's ancestors was (probably) Jewish. Faced with this evidence, Imrédy resigned.

Horthy turned to his old friend, the former Prime Minister, count *Pál Teleki,* who reluctantly agreed to head the government (1939-1941). In March, 1939, Hungary, simultaneously with the German action against Czechoslovakia, occupied Ruthenia (the easternmost province of the dismembered Czechoslovakia, formerly a Hungarian district). The Hungarophile Ruthenes were pleased, and so were the Poles, who now had a common border with their friends, the Hungarians.

Before their attack on Poland, the Germans asked for permission to move troops across Hungary. Horthy categorically refused.[5]

The coming of World War II

When the war broke out, Hungary remained non-belligerent but helped the Poles unofficially with volunteers and by admitting about 200,000 refugees (including many Jews).

In the summer of 1940, Hungary suggested negotiations with Rumania with a view to a revision of the frontiers in Transylvania. When Rumania refused to negotiate, Hungary mobilised. Rumania then asked Germany to mediate. Thus Germany and Italy handed down the *Second Vienna Award* (30 August, 1940) which returned to Hungary about 40% of the territory given to Rumania at the Trianon Peace Treaty.

In September 1940 Hungary joined the Tri-Partite Pact (Germany-Italy-Japan). Teleki then negotiated a Friendship Treaty with Yugoslavia with a hardly disguised anti-German edge. Yugoslavia was then persuaded to join the Tri-Partite Pact. On the day of the signature there was a coup d'etat in Belgrade and the new Yugoslav government repudiated the pact with Germany and accepted a British guarantee instead. Hitler decided at once to punish Yugoslavia and again he suggested that Hungary should attack first. Horthy and Teleki refused the suggestion.

The Hungarian government decided not to interfere in the German-Yugoslav conflict unless Yugoslavia disintegrated or the Magyar minorities were in danger. Teleki sent this information to London, asking for Britain's understanding of Hungary's position. Britain answered by threatening a break of diplomatic relations if Hungary allowed the Germans to cross her territory and said she would declare war if Hungary attacked. In the meantime, German troops began to move against Yugoslavia across Hungary. Teleki, on receiving the British note and the news of the German troop movements, shot himself in protest against Hungary's involvement (3 April, 1941). The circumstances of the German troop movements and of Teleki's death are still unclear.

Involvement

After Teleki's death the Foreign Minister, *László Bárdossy,* was appointed Prime Minister (1941-1942). Germany attacked and overran the Yugoslav defences, and on the 10th of April Croatia declared her independence. Yugoslavia now ceased to exist and the Hungarian government sent some troops to the Magyar-populated Bácska district.

When Germany attacked the Soviet Union (22 June, 1941), Hungary declared her intention to remain non-belligerent. A few days later the Hungarian town Kassa was bombed, allegedly by Soviet planes. After some talks with Horthy and the government, Bárdossy declared to the Parliament that a *state of war* existed between Hungary and the *Soviet Union*.[6] The circumstances of this declaration are similarly unclear.

A small force — the Mobile Corps — was sent to the Russian front. Britain declared war on Hungary in December 1941. Hungary declared war on the U.S. simultaneously with the other Tri-Partite states. In the spring of 1942 the Germans demanded more substantial help in Russia, hinting that as the Rumanians had sent two armies, Germany might return Northern Transylvania to them. So the Hungarian 2nd Army was sent with 10 divisions for front line service, and a few added divisions for occupation duty.

There had been some partisan activity in the Hungarian-occupied Bácska (the Magyar inhabited district of former Yugoslavia). The impetuous Hungarian commander — a pro-German general — took unwarranted, brutal steps to suppress the partisan activity and had many partisans and suspects executed, without the knowledge of the Budapest government. An investigation followed but the general eventually fled to Germany with some of the other officers involved in this so-called *"Ujvidék massacre"*.

As the Regent was in his 75th year, the question of succession had to be considered. The Parliament elected the Regent's son, *István Horthy, as Deputy-Regent*. Upon his election, the Deputy-Regent, a reserve officer in the Hungarian air force, joined his unit fighting in Russia. A year later, during one of his missions, his plane crashed and István Horthy died.

Hungary's unwilling participation in the war created among many of the nation's leaders, Churchmen, moderate politicians and intellectuals strong anti-German and anti-war feelings which developed into a powerful *silent resistance*. They sought peaceful and legal ways to extricate Hungary from her ever-increasing commitments on the side of Germany. Tibor Eckhardt, the leader of the largest opposition party (the Smallholders), went to the

U.S. in 1941 to prepare a possible government-in-exile should the German pressure become unbearable. Horthy knew about the aims of the group and discreetly supported them.[7]

In the spring of 1942 Horthy appointed *Miklós Kállay* (1942-1944) Prime Minister and entrusted him with the task of extricating Hungary from the war and restoring the country's independence.[8] Kállay began an astute course of diplomatic balancing acts, pretending to be a pro-German and in the meantime preparing the way to regain Hungary's freedom of action. Hungarian humour has dubbed this policy the "Kállay Double Dance" from the famous folk dance of the Premier's native district. To begin with, he brought in the Fourth Jewish Law[9] (after having discussed it with the Jewish leaders). At that time more than 100,000 Jewish refugees from other countries lived in Hungary in addition to the 700,000 Hungarian Jews. Thanks to Horthy and Kállay, they remained in security (though under some restrictions) until the German occupation in March 1944.[10]

Kállay also instituted *secret peace initiatives* abroad but the western responses were evasive. The Casablanca Conference had already stated (1943) the demand for "unconditional surrender", while the Teheran Conference assigned Hungary to the Soviet sphere. These two decisions strengthened the arguments of the pro-German elements and frustrated the efforts of the peace-seekers. The vague verbal promises and agreements reached with Britain and the U.S. were later conveniently forgotten.

In January 1943 the *Hungarian 2nd Army* was holding 200 kilometres of the Don line in Russia with 9 "light divisions" (brigades). The army's armoured division and air-brigade had been placed under German command and used elsewhere. The army had few heavy weapons, hardly any winter equipment (it was −45 degrees) and insufficient ammunition, though the Germans had promised to supply everything.

On January 13, a Russian army group and a tank army attacked the Hungarians. The Hungarian army of about 200,000 suffered 150,000 casualties, among them 100,000 dead. The bitter fighting lasted for three weeks. One Hungarian corps was surrounded and its commander captured fighting; the other divisions were annihilated or thrown back. The men fled in 40-50 degree cold, without transport, as the Germans monopolised the few roads and shelters.[11]

The German occupation of Hungary

Hitler at last learned about Kállay's tentative attempts to "jump out" (in the Budapest cafés everybody knew the exact details). He invited Horthy to Germany in March, 1944, then faced the Regent with an ultimatum: unless Horthy replaced Kállay with a pro-German premier and placed Hungary's full potential at Germany's disposal, Hitler would order Rumanian, Slovak and Croat troops to occupy Hungary. During these "talks" German troops occupied the key positions in Hungary.

Horthy had no choice — Hungary had no fighting troops left to resist. So he appointed *Döme Sztójay* as Prime Minister and accepted pro-German ministers in the Government. German police and SS arrested many moderate and left-wing politicians and anti-German intellectuals. Leading personalities in the administration and army were replaced with pro-German appointees. The SS ordered the concentration of Hungarian Jews in ghettoes, then, without Horthy's or the government's knowledge, and with the connivance of some pro-German officials of the Interior, began to move the Jews to German concentration camps ostensibly for "work".

On learning of the deportations, Horthy defied the Germans and dismissed Sztójay and the officials who had collaborated with the SS in the deportations. He then appointed general *Géza Lakatos* to head the government of generals and non-political experts and ordered him to end Hungary's participation in the war.

After Rumania's volte-face in August 1944, the Soviet troops began to move into Transylvania. There were no Hungarian troops strong enough to stop them and the Germans refused to use against the Russians the panzer divisions occupying Hungary. By October the Russians stood near Debrecen.[12]

The armistice. Hungary's second German occupation

Horthy sent a delegation to Moscow to ask for an armistice. A preliminary agreement was signed there on the 11th of October. After the final Crown Council on the 15th of October, 1944, Horthy announced to the nation that he was asking for an armistice and ordered the troops to stop fighting.

What followed is not clear. There are so many different accounts of the events that one can only state the results:

Horthy was arrested by the Germans and the capital was taken over by the SS and the Hungarian National Socialists. Horthy learned that his (only) son had been kidnapped by the SS. In addition, all the strategic points of Budapest were in German hands (there were hardly any Hungarian troops in the capital). The Regent was forced to rescind his proclamation and to appoint Ferenc Szálasi as Prime Minister, replacing Lakatos arrested by the Germans. Horthy then abdicated and was taken to Germany as a prisoner, where he and his family were kept in custody until the end of the war.

Ferenc Szálasi formed a right-wing coalition government and, in November 1944, was elected "Leader of the Nation" by what was left of the Parliament. The Hungarian army was reorganised and many civilian and military leaders were arrested, taken to German concentration camps or executed (such as the members of the anti-German "Committee of Liberation", led by Endre Bajcsy-Zsilinszky). In Budapest, certain criminal elements, claiming adherence to the "Arrow-Cross" (the Hungarian National Socialists), took the opportunity to commit atrocities against the Jews and opponents of the regime. The retreating Germans took to Germany all the livestock, equipment and machinery they could dismantle.

The entire Hungarian army continued fighting the Russians, their resistance strengthened by the horrifying news of the lootings, rapings and other atrocities in the Soviet-occupied Hungarian territories. For the same reason, hundreds of thousands of refugees moved west with the retreating troops.

In December, the Russians encircled Budapest, which was defended by Hungarian and German troops under the command of general Ivan Hindy. After the fall of Pest, the Germans blew up all the Danube bridges and the defenders continued the fight in Buda. During the seven weeks' siege most of Pest and Buda, including the royal castle, was destroyed. Buda fell on the 13th of February, 1945 (it had been held longer than Stalingrad).[13]

In the west the exhausted Hungarian-German troops fought on bravely, (one town, Székesfehérvár, changed hands seven times), defending Hungarian territory against superior Russian forces until the 4th of April, 1945.

Under Russian occupation

On receiving Horthy's armistice orders, general Béla Miklós, commander of the First Hungarian Army, surrendered to the Russians. He and the members of Horthy's Moscow armistice delegation were taken to Debrecen, occupied by the Russians. Here a "National Assembly" was hastily collected and it appointed *Béla Miklós* Prime Minister. His first government consisted of the members of the armistice delegation, politicians of the moderate or left-wing parties and three Communists (who held the key positions). This *"Provisional Government"* signed an armistice with the Soviet Union and duly declared war on Germany — though no Hungarian unit ever fought against the Germans. The government was later moved to Budapest and received its orders from Marshal Voroshilov, Soviet Commander-in-Chief.

It is impossible to give an accurate account of Hungary's *military and civilian losses*. Of the more than 1 million Hungarians in the services, conservative estimates put the number of dead and missing at 200,000. At least a similar number of civilians perished as a result of bombings, atrocities and deportations, in addition to the 120,000 to 200,000 Jews who died in German concentration camps (it is impossible to determine the exact numbers as many of them were refugees from other countries). Altogether some 550,000 to 650,000 Hungarians perished during the war (total losses of the U.S.: 290,000).

The material losses were incalculable: some cities, most industries, transport installations and rolling stock were totally destroyed; the loss of agricultural produce and private property was immense. About one million soldiers and civilian refugees left the country at the end of the war, though many have returned since ("here you must live and die. . .").

30. "EVERYBODY IS HUNGARIAN..."

(Hungarian travellers and settlers in the world)

About one third of the 15 million Hungarians live outside the present frontiers of Hungary. Three million live "abroad" without ever having left their country in the Carpathian basin: their home territory was transferred from Hungary to various succession states by the Trianon Treaty in 1920. We have studied their way of life, art and customs in the various chapters describing the regions of the Carpathian basin.

In this chapter we are looking only at some Hungarians who left the Carpathian basin for various reasons and settled or lived in foreign countries for a considerable period.

The Middle Ages

Several princesses of the Árpád dynasty married into foreign ruling families. We have already mentioned Saint Stephen's daughter, Agatha, and her daughter, queen Saint Margaret of Scotland (Chapter 5). The daughter of king Saint László, *Piroska* ("Irene" in Greek), married to the Greek emperor, was the mother of Manuel the Great (1143-1180), the last great ruler of Byzantium. After her husband's death Irene retired to a convent in Contantinople where she died and is known today as Saint Irene.

Saint Elizabeth of Hungary, daughter of king Endre II, was married to the Prince of Thuringia. After the death of her husband, Elizabeth dedicated herself to the care of the poor and the sick. Her niece, also called Elizabeth, Princess of Aragon, is known today as Saint Elizabeth (Isobel) of Portugal. We

257

know little of Clemence of Hungary, wife of France's Louis X in the XIVth century. She was an Árpád on her mother's side and sister of Hungary's king, Charles Robert. Her son, John I, was assassinated when he was five days old.

Queen Saint Hedwig (Jadwiga) of Poland was the daughter of Louis the Great. She inherited the Polish throne after her father's death (1382). Then she married the pagan Jagiello, Prince of the Lithuanians, converted him and his people to Christianity and united the two countries.

We have already mentioned the four Dominican monks who travelled to the borders of Europe and Asia in the XIIIth century in search of the "Greater Hungarian Nation" (Chapter 5).

The XVIth - XVIIIth centuries

One of the tragic results of the Turkish wars was the deportation of hundreds of thousands of Magyars of all ages by the Turks as slaves. Estimates indicate that about 2 million Hungarians were subjected to the horrors of slavery. The families were, of course, separated and the children lost their national identity. Many boys were trained in special institutions to become Janissaries, the Turks' elite soldiers. They lost all recollection of their birth, name, religion or family.

Brother György (George) Hollósi who accompanied a troop of Spanish "Conquistadors" in 1541 in Mexico, lived for 40 years among the Zuni Indians of that country. He converted them and protected them from the greedy Spanish conquerors. He died among his Indians who wrote on his tombstone: "Here lies Brother Gregorio Hollósi, brother of all men, who brought light to those who were living in the dark."

Poland's great king, Stephen Báthori was mentioned in Chapter 13.

Among the emigrés accompanying Prince Rákóczi to France in 1711 was count Ladislas Bercsényi, son of the Kuruc commander, Miklós Bercsényi. Young Ladislas settled in France, founded a hussar regiment which still bears his name and eventually became Marshal of France.

The adventurous count *Móric Benyovszky* (1741-1784) began his career as an officer in the Seven Years' War. Seeking further adventures, he went to Poland and joined the Polish freedom fighters against Russia. He fought so well that the Poles appointed him general and made him a count. He was eventually taken prisoner and deported to East Siberia (Kamchatka). Here he rallied his fellow prisoners and managed to capture the fort of the governor and the heart of his daughter. He then commandeered a Russian battleship and set out to explore the Pacific. Having visited Japan, Hongkong and various islands, he spent some time on Formosa (today Taiwan) straightening out the local political situation. He then sailed on and inspected the huge island of Madagascar off the African coast, then still independent and ruled by countless native chieftains. He eventually arrived in France, where he suggested to the king (Louis XV) that he should establish a French colony on Formosa or Madagascar. The king appointed him a general, gave him the title of count and a few promises, and sent him off to Madagascar. Equipped with his titles (and not much else) he landed in Madagascar, befriended some tribes, defeated the others and in 1776 was proclaimed by the assembled chieftains king of Madagascar. He ruled the island wisely for three years. Among other things he introduced Latin script — with Hungarian spelling — for the Madagascar language. The islanders still use his script and spelling. Then — probably at the urging of his family (he had several, in fact) — he returned to France seeking closer trade and political ties.

This time the French ignored him, so he returned to his native Hungary, where queen Maria Theresa made him a count and appointed him general. But she was not interested in African colonies(she had Hungary, after all . . .) So Benyovszky went to Britain and then to the new Republic of the United States. There he loaded his ship with goods for Madagascar (before they could make him a count and appoint him general) and sailed back to his kingdom. To his surprise, he found a French military establishment there (led probably by a general who was also a count). He fought to regain his kingdom but died during the fighting. Some native legends and street names (and a few generals and counts) keep his memory in Madagascar.

The first Hungarian known to have landed in *North America* was Parmenius of Buda, a naval officer in the British service (1585). Several Hungarian missionaries worked among the natives of South and North America during the XVIIth and XVIIIth centuries. Colonel M. Kovats was a distinguished officer in Washington's army during the War of Independence.

András (Andrew) Jelki, the enterprising boy from Hungary, set out to see the world in 1750 and became a sailor. After having been shipwrecked, captured by pirates and sold in slavery, he reached the Dutch East Indies (alive) where he again landed among some primitive natives who wanted him for (their) dinner, but he "got out of the frying pan" by marrying the daughter of the local chief and eventually became the chief of the tribe himself. Then we find him in Batavia, the capital of the Dutch East Indies, as a prosperous businessman (without his native wife). At a later date we find Jelki in Japan as the Dutch Ambassador there. He died in 1783.

László Magyar reached Portuguese West Africa (Angola) at the end of the XVIIIth century. He began mapping the interior of the colony in Portuguese service and discovered the source of the Congo river. Then the fate of seemingly all Hungarian adventurers caught up with him: he married the daughter of the Sultan of Bihé (Bié) and in due course became the king of the country himself. He died in Bihé under obscure circumstances (possibly during a state dinner. . .)

The XIXth century

Sándor Körösi-Csoma (1784-1842), the brilliant Székely scholar, wished to study the origins of the Hungarians. He decided to explore Central Asia first. Being very poor, he travelled to India mostly on foot, equipped only with the knowledge of a dozen languages. After an adventurous journey he reached India in 1822. Commissioned by the Indian (British) government to prepare a Tibetan-English dictionary, he spent 16 months in a Tibetan monastery, studying the Tibetan language and literature, completing his dictionary and translating some Tibetan literature into English. He then travelled to various Tibetan towns (the first European to move about in Tibet freely) and studied data concerning possible ties between Hungarians and the Central Asian races.

On returning to India he published his dictionary and Tibetan grammar which are still the most important source of Tibetan linguistic studies. Having completed his research, he set out to re-enter Tibet and move from there to the area inhabited by the "Ujgur" or "Djungari" people, north of Tibet, whom he suspected of being related to the Hungarians. On his way he

S. Körösi-Csoma (1784-1842)

contracted malaria and died in Darjeeling on the Tibetan border. His memory still lives in Tibet. In 1935 he was proclaimed a "Saint" of Tibetan Buddhism. Various Indian scientific institutions preserve his memory.

Sir Aurel Stein, the Asian explorer, was born in Budapest. He carried out archeological explorations for the Indian (British) government in Central Asia and discovered the so-called "buried cities" in Mongolia.

During the *American Civil War* many Hungarians, mostly refugees from the Freedom War of 1848-49, settled in the United States. Many fought in the Union armies (none with the Confederates), such as generals Stahel and Asbóth, Colonels Mihalótzy and Zágonyi and several units of Hungarian soldiers. Ágoston Haraszty was a pioneer of California, a wine-grower, a businessman and a diplomat.

General *István Türr* (1824-1908) took part in the Italian freedom war in 1860 as Garibaldi's Chief of Staff. He then assisted Klapka in organising the "Hungarian Legion" (cf. Chapter 22). After the Compromise he returned to Hungary and his original profession, engineering. He later worked at the construction of the Suez and Panama canals.

Hungarian-born *Joseph Pulitzer* of newspaper fame served first as a cavalry officer during the Civil War. After the war he became interested in newspaper editing and eventually owned a chain of newspapers. He left his huge estate (about $20 million) to a foundation bearing his name and a school of Journalism.

János Xántus, a self-educated scientist and explorer, discovered several hundred animal and plant species in North America and South-East Asia between 1855 and 1871.

The XXth century: science, art and literature

Eight scientists of Hungarian birth received the Nobel Prize between 1914 and 1976. Only one worked in Hungary when he received the Prize (Albert Szentgyörgyi). Of the others Fülöp Lénárd, Richard Zsigmondy and György Hevesy lived in Germany, Robert Bárány in Austria, György Békésy and Jenö Wigner in the U.S. and Dénes Gábor in Britain when they received the award. It was said that if two members of the U.S. Atomic Commission had been absent, the others could have held their meeting in Hungarian. The most eminent of these Hungarian-American scientists was Professor *Leo Szilárd,* who demonstrated the possibility of atomic fission in 1939. With his friend, Einstein, he suggested to President Roosevelt that he should set up an atomic research programme in the United States. The team of Szilárd, Teller, Wigner and Neumann — all Hungarians — with the half-Hungarian Oppenheimer and the Italian Fermi constituted the successful Atomic Commission which eventually assured the United States the possession of the atomic bomb.

Todor Kármán, engineer and scientist made himself famous in the U.S. through his many inventions and innovations in the field of aerodynamics and rocket research.

In the field of *economics,* Hungarian emigrés have enriched both "worlds": Jenö Varga was the leading economist of Soviet Russia and György Lukács the leading philosopher of Marxism, while Lord Thomas Balogh and Lord Miklós Káldor were the British government's chief economic advisors until recently.

Before World War II the American *film industry* seemed to be Hungary's only colonial empire. The malicious saying "It is not enough to be Hungarian, you gotta have talent too. . ." was wrong, of course, as quite a few had little talent, only "Hungarian connections". But the names of Adolf Zukor, Michael Kertész, Sir Alexander Korda, Zoltan Korda and many others assured Hungarian hegemony in the fledgling art of the film. Some film-stars are also of Hungarian birth, such as Peter Lorre, Tony Curtis, Cornel Wilde and Ilona Massey — they were obviously not born with these well-known names. Others seem to be quite proud of whatever they were born with: the Gábor sisters, Marika Rökk, Éva Bartók and many others.

As Hungarian *writing* is not easily translated, Hungarian writers best known abroad are those who learnt to write in English or German, such as Arthur Koestler ("Darkness at Noon") and Hans Habe. *George Mikes* has achieved the difficult synthesis of Hungarian humour and British satire. His delightful racial tableaus ("How to be an Alien", "Milk and Honey" etc.) delight everybody (including the people he is satirising).

Lajos Zilahy, a well-known novelist before his migration to the U.S., wrote his controversial historic novels, "The Dukays", in America.

József Reményi (1892-1956) was the first great Hungarian-American author, essayist and literary historian.

Albert Wass (1908-) was also a noted Hungarian author in Transylvania before 1945. In 1952 he migrated to the U.S., and became a professor of Florida University. His Hungarian and English writings include novels, short stories, poetry, essays and research work of historical, sociological and folkloric nature.

Ferenc Molnár (1878-1952), the most successful playwright of recent Hungarian literature was also a remarkable novelist and author of short stories. His novel "The Boys of Paul Street", an exquisite tableau of adolescent life has become a world best-seller in many translations. His mystery-drama "Liliom" has achieved world fame through its American stage and film-version "Carousel". Molnár settled in the United States before World War II and continued his career as a successful writer for stage and film.

The playwright *Menyhért Lengyel,* noted for his interest in social problems in his dramas written in Hungary before 1914 ("Typhoon"), migrated to the United States after World War I and became a popular film-script writer.

The authoresses Yolanda Földes and Christa Arnóthy in France and Claire Kenneth-Bardossy in the U.S., are well known for their pleasant novels of lighter nature.

Áron Gábor, a journalist living in Germany, presents a staggering indictment of man's inhumanity to man in his auto-biographical work "East of Man".

The number of talented authors: poets, novelists, philosophers and historians living abroad and using the *Hungarian language* in their writings is immense. Their opus represents an important segment of contemporary Hungarian literature, the study of which is, however, beyond the scope of this book.

Music is another field where Hungarian participation has assumed proverbial proportions. The number of well known Hungarian conductors living abroad is truly impressive (Sir George Solti, Eugene Ormandy, George Széll and many others). Since Liszt and Reményi, many Hungarian performing artists, especially of the violin and piano have lived abroad, such as Emil Telmányi, Joseph Joachim, Joseph Szigeti, Johanna Darányi violin virtuosos and Géza Anda, the pianist. Miklós Rózsa and Sigmund Romberg have become well-known for their film and operetta music.

In *Fine Arts* the adage that a Hungarian painter can only succeed abroad has proved true in many cases. Some talented Hungarian artists lived abroad all their creating life, such as Fülöp László, portrait painter in Britain, Ferenc Martyn, avant-garde painter in France, Marcel Vértes, graphic artist, Victor Vásárely, creator of three-dimensional "op-art" in France, György

"Ballet" by V. Vásárely

Buday, graphic artist in Britain, Sándor Finta, the shepherd-boy who became a famous sculptor, author and teacher, László Moholyi-Nagy founder of the "New Bauhaus" movement, György Kepes, professor of Art, M.I.T., and colour woodcut artist József Domján in the U.S.A., Amerigo Tóth in Italy, Zoltán Borbereki-Kovács in South Africa and many others.

Hungarians in Australia

The first Hungarian migrants arrived in Australia in the middle of the XIXth century: many of them were ex-officers of the 1848-49 freedom war.

Most of the immigrants before 1930 were single men who married Australian girls and integrated into Australian society. The 1930s and 40s saw the arrival of the Hungarian migrants who left Hungary because of the oppressive atmosphere in Hitler's Central Europe. They were mostly Jewish intellectuals and businessmen. Hard-working and ambitious, they became respected members of Australian society, but they cherished their Hungarian culture and helped to dispel some misapprehensions about Hungary's role during World War II. The Australians learned through them that Hungary was, during the Nazi oppression, the refuge of the Jews in Europe.

About 15,000 Hungarians arrived in Australia as "displaced persons" between 1949 and 1953. The bulk of them were professional and middle-class people, most of them with families. Having met the earlier Hungarian migrants, the two groups could find a common reason why they came to Australia: to flee the tyrannies of one kind or the other.

After 1956 another 15,000 Hungarians came. As these were mostly single men, many of them assimilated rapidly. On the other hand, those who came with families — at any period — usually kept the Magyar ethnic consciousness in the family and their children learned to appreciate the values of their ethnic heritage (through Hungarian schools, Scout and other youth activities), without interfering with their harmonious integration into Australian society and culture.

In the 1960s many migrants came from Yugoslavia: most of these were Hungarians, members of the Magyar minority in that country. They usually came with their families and often settled close to each other, assisting each other in a form of co-operative. They have mostly kept their Hungarian identity.

It is estimated that in 1970 about 50,000 Australians had Hungarian ethnic origin. This number does not include the children born in Australia.

Only 0.4% of Australians are of Hungarian origin (or, as the Magyars put it, 99.6% of Australians are of non-Magyar origin), but their involvement in certain professions and occupations is well above that rate. They favour occupations in which independence, initiative and imagination prevail and industry assures success.

There were some 50 professors and lecturers at various Australian universities in 1970. Some academics are well-known such as professor George Molnár who is also a political cartoonist. In their specific fields there are many outstanding scientists, such as the entomologist József Szent-Ivány, the international jurist Gyula (Julius) Varsányi, the anthropologist Sándor Gallus, the demographer Egon Kunz, the historian Antal Endrey and Ákos Györy who, at the time of his appointment, was the youngest professor of Medicine in Australia. Dr. A. Mensáros, a member of the West-Australian government, was the first non-British Cabinet Minister in the State.

In *art and music* Australia lacked the attraction of some other countries, thus only a few well-known artists settled here. The conductors Tibor Paul and Robert Pikler are the best known names in music. The Fine Arts are represented by the late Andor Mészáros, the sculptor and engraver, Desiderius Orban, one of the "Group of Eight" (cf. Chapter 25), Judith Cassab painter, Stephen Moor and György Hámori decorative artists.

There are many eminent *businessmen* and architects of Hungarian origin in Australia and the number of small businessmen is immense. It seems that some businesses, such as espressos, small-goods manufacturing and clothing manufacturing are Hungarian monopolies.

In *sport,* table tennis was made popular by Hungarians. Australian soccer owes its origins and success to Hungarian coaches, organisers, players and patrons. A Hungarian-founded and sponsored team, the "Budapest" (later: "Saint George- Budapest") has been the most successful team in the country. In chess, Lajos Steiner and other Hungarian players dominated the national championships for two decades. Fencing, a typical Magyar sport, owes its increasing popularity in Australia to Hungarian sportsmen and trainers (G. Benkö, A. Szakáll).

*   *   *

There are today almost 2 million Hungarian expatriates who have invaded the farthest corners of the world. Hungarians can

Canterbury Altar by A. Mészáros

be found anywhere — and they usually are. As false modesty is not one of their national vices, they do not conceal their presence nor the fact that they are Hungarians. In fact, their vitality, industry and extrovert friendliness make them more conspicuous than population statistics would suggest. One is tempted to accept the thesis of the Hungarian writer, Mikes: "Everybody is Hungarian. . ."

There are about 15 million Hungarians in the world today: not quite 0.5% of mankind.

Without them the sun would still rise and life would still go on — but the rainbow would be a little paler, music a little duller, women a little sadder and mankind a little poorer.

APPENDIX

(NOTES, DOCUMENTATION, SELECTED TEXTS IN ENGLISH TRANSLATION)

THE UNSUNG SAGA

1. From: "Selected Hungarian Legends" F. B. Kovács ed., transl. by E. Wass de Czege, Danubian Press, Astor Park, 1971.

CHAPTER 1

1. Prof. Gy. László: "A Kettös Honfoglalásról" ("The two Conquests"), "Archeologiai Értesitö", 97, pp. 161-190; Prof. P. Lipták: "Origin and development of the Hungarian People", "Homo" XXI (4), pp. 197-210.

CHAPTER 4

1. Recent historical research throws a different light upon this covenant. It seems that the Hungarian tribal federation was led, in the IXth century, by a (nominal) head of state, the "kende", who shared his rule with the military commander, the "gyula" (or "horka"). At the time of the Settlement the "kende" was Kurszán (Kusid or Kursan), and the "gyula" was Álmos, then his son, Árpád, who planned and conducted the military operations of the conquest. "Kende" Kurszán was killed during a raid in 904 and "gyula" Árpád became the sole ruler of the new nation. After having secured the succession for his son (Solt or Zoltán), he conferred the office of the "gyula" on another tribal chief. (Cf. the "Gyula" mentioned in chapters 4, 5 and 14). The "Blood Treaty" may have been fully or partly invented by the medieval chroniclers in order to justify the succession of the Árpád dynasty.

CHAPTER 6

1. *Yonder lies a round, black (!) sward. An enchanted stag
   grazes on it. His marvellous head carries a thousand antlers.
   On the thousand antlers a thousand mass-candles burn
   without being lit — and they go out by themselves.
   My hiding place is the old law, hola, I hide in songs . . .*
   (Recorded in Zala county, Transdanubia).
2. *Get up father, get up mother, the Ancient Ones have come.
   My hiding place is the old law, I hide in songs!*
   (Recorded in Udvarhely county, Transylvania).
3. *Stork, stork, turtle-dove,
   Why are your feet bleeding?
   Turkish children cut them,
   Magyar children heal them,
   With pipes, drums, and reed violins . . .*
4. *Tall is the "ruta" tree — leaning over the great sea.
   Fair Ilona Magyar wears — a crown of pearls
   In her golden-silky hair . . .*
   (Recorded in Nyitra county, Northern Hungary).

CHAPTER 7

1. **Sándor Petöfi:**

(In Hungarian:) **Szeptember végén**

*Még nyilnak a völgyben a kerti virágok,
Még zöldel a nyárfa az ablak elött,
De látod amottan a téli világot?
Már hó takará el a bérci tetöt.
Még ifjú szivemben a lángsugarú nyár
S még benne virit az egész kikelet,
De ime, sötét hajam öszbe vegyül már,
A tél dere már megüté fejemet.*

*Elhull a virág, eliramlik az élet . . .
Ülj, hitvesem, ülj az ölembe ide!
Ki most fejedet keblemre tevéd le,
Holnap nem omolsz-e sirom fölibe?
Oh mondd: ha elöbb halok el, tetemimre
Könnyezve boritasz-e szemfödelet?
S rábirhat-e majdan egy ifjú szerelme,
Hogy elhagyod érte az én nevemet?*

Ha eldobod egykor az özvegyi fátyolt,
Fejfámra sötét lobogóul akaszd,
Én feljövök érte a siri világból
Az éj közepén, s oda leviszem azt,
Letörleni véle könnyüimet érted,
Ki könnyedén elfeledéd hivedet,
S e sziv sebeit bekötözni, ki téged
Még akkor is, ott is, örökre szeret!

(In English:) **At the End of September**

Garden flowers still bloom in the valley;
The poplar is still verdant at the window;
But can you see the winter world over there?
Already the peaks are covered with snow.
My young heart is still filled with summer rays
And within it the whole springtime in blossom.
But lo, my dark hair is flecked with grey
And my head has been struck with winter's frost.

The flower drops and past life races . . .
Sit, my wife, sit here on my lap now!
Will you, who on my breast her head places,
Not bend over my grave tomorrow?
O, tell me, if I die before you,
Will you cover my body with a shroud — weeping?
And will love of a youth sometime cause you
To abandon my name for his keeping?

If one time you cast off your widow's veil,
Let it hang from my headstone, a banner!
I will come up from the world of the grave
In the dead of the night and take it with me
To wipe from my face the tears shed for you,
Who has lightly forgotten her devotee,
And to bind the wound in the heart of one,
Who still then in that place, loves you forever.

(Transl. by Paul Desney).

2. Endre Ady:

(In Hungarian): **A föl-földobott kö**

Föl-földobott kö, földedre hullva,
Kicsi országom, ujra meg ujra
Hazajön fiad.
Messze tornyokat látogat sorba,
Szédül, elbúsong s lehull a porba,
Amelyböl vétetett.
Mindig elvágyik s nem menekülhet,
Magyar vágyakkal, melyek elülnek
S fölhorgadnak megint.
Tied vagyok én nagy haragomban,
Nagy hütlenségben, szerelmes gondban
Szomorúan magyar.
Föl-földhajtott kö, bus akaratlan,
Kicsi országom, példás alakban
Te orcádra ütök.
És, jaj, hiába mindenha szándék,
Százszor földobnál, én visszaszállnék
Százszor is, végül is.

(In English): **The Outcast Stone**

The stone cast up into the air comes down to earth;
Again and again your son will return,
To you, my little land.
He visits distant towers one by one and then
Reels crestfallen and drops into the dust again,
From which you toss him up.
Always breaking loose, he cannot get away,
With his Magyar cravings which die down
Only to take hold of him again.
I am yours in great anger and defection,
In unfaithfulness, unfortunately Magyar
Weighed down by thoughts of love.
A stone driven upwards unwittingly,
By way of example, my small country,
I fall back onto you.
And whatever the intention, it's all in vain
For though I am tossed away a hundred times,
I will alight until the last.

(Transl. by Paul Desney).

3. Attila József:

(In Hungarian): **Születésnapomra**

Harminckét éves lettem én —
meglepetés e költemény
csecse
becse:
ajándék, mellyel meglepem
e kávéházi szegleten
magam
magam.
Harminckét évem elszelelt
s még havi kétszáz sose telt.
Az ám,
Hazám!
Lehettem volna oktató,
nem ily töltötoll-koptató
szegény
legény.
De nem lettem, mert Szegeden
eltanácsolt az egyetem
fura
ura.
Intelme gyorsan, nyersen ért
a "Nincsen apám" versemért,
a hont
kivont
szablyával óvta ellenem.
Ideidézi szellemem
hevét
s nevét:
"Ön, amíg szóból értek én,
nem lesz tanár e földtekén" —
gagyog
s ragyog.
Ha örül Horger Antal úr,
hogy költönk nem nyelvtant tanúl,
sekély
e kéj —
Én egész népemet fogom
nem középiskolás fokon
tani —
tani!

273

(In English): **For my Birthday**

I am thirty-two, how nice:
this poem is a fine surprise,
a bric —
a brac.
A gift to surprise now in jingle
in this lonely café ingle
my self
myself.
My thirty-two years went away
without earning a decent pay.
How grand,
Homeland!
I could have been a teacher then
not one who lives by fountain-pen
as I,
poor guy.
But so happened at Szeged town
the Varsity boss sent me down,
funny
man he!
His warning roughly, rudely came,
for my "I have no God" poem
his hand
the land
defended boldly and with rage.
I quote herewith for future age
his theme
and name:
"As long as I have here a say
you won't be a teacher" — turned away
muttered,
stuttered.
Should Mr. Horger gloat with glee
that grammatics is not for me,
his bliss
dismiss.
For my words the entire nation
beyond high school education —
will reach
to teach.
    (Transl. by Egon Kunz).

274

CHAPTER 12

1. *Though they stoke the fire,*
   Still it dies away;
   There is not that love
   Which does not pass away.
   Love, oh love, oh love,
   Accursed misery,
   Why do you not flower
   On the leaves of every tree?

(Northern Hungary. Transl. by Paul Desney)

2. *Soft spring winds are waters wooing,*
   My flower, my darling.
   Birds are choosing, mates are wooing,
   My flower, my darling.
   Whom shall I choose then and woo, Dear,
   My flower, my darling.
   You choose me and I choose you, Dear,
   My flower, my darling.

(Moldavia, a Csángó-Székely song. Transl. by J. C. Tóth).

3. *Gazing round the battlefield of Doberdo,*
   I admire the starry heaven's wonder bow;
   Starry heavens, lead me to my Magyar country,
   Show me where my darling mother weeps for me!
   Dearest mother, wonder where my end shall be?
   Where my crimson blood shall flow away from me?
   In the heart of Poland you will find me buried;
   Dearest mother, never, never weep for me!

(Békés county, Southern Hungary, transl. by J. C. Tóth).

4. *The bird is free to fly*
   From branch to branch,
   But I am not allowed
   To visit my beloved.
   God bless, oh bless my Lord
   The house of my beloved,
   But strike God, strike
   Those who live in it.
   Not even all of those,
   But only her mother;
   Why has she not given
   Me her only daughter?

If she is her daughter,
My lover is she too;
If she is dear to her,
Dearer is she to me.

(Transylvania. Transl. by Paul Desney).

5. *I have left my lovely homeland!*
Left a famous little old land;
Sadly I turned once more to see
Through my falling tears its beauty.
Bitter food and bitter my days!
On and on their bitter tang stays;
Tearfully I gaze at the sky,
Numbering the stars as they die.

(Békés county, Southern Hungary. Transl. by J. C. Tóth).

6. *Rain is falling, softly gently falling,*
Spring will soon be coming;
How I wish I were a rose bud,
In your garden blooming!
Rose, my Dear, I cannot be,
Franz Joseph is with'ring me
In his famous great Vienna barracks
Boasting of three stories!

(Békés county, Southern Hungary. Transl. by J. C. Tóth).

7. *I shall plow the king's court with my sighs;*
Sow it with my country's bitter cries;
Let him see and know, the great emp'ror!
What grows in the heart of his Magyar.
Sorrow grows in it from sorrow's seeds;
Wounded is the Magyar heart, it bleeds;
Take, o Lord, the king and emperor!
Let him not oppress his poor Magyar!

(Gömör county, Northern Hungary. Transl. by J. C. Tóth).

8. *Jolly hussar, jolly hussar, jolly when he's dancing;*
Jingling saber, jingling saber, jingling as he's prancing;
Jingling, jingling, go on jingling, click your, click your spurs too!
Louis Kossuth's listing crew is making music rouse you.

(Veszprém county, Western Hungary. An 1848 song. Transl. by
J. C. Tóth).

276

9. (a) *There where I am passing, even trees are weeping.*
From their tender branches golden leaves are falling.
   Weeps the road before me, grieves the path forlornly;
Even they are saying: Farewell, God be with thee.
(Csik county, Székely district. Transl. by J. C. Tóth).

   (b) *I'm a goin', goin', far away a goin',*
From the dust of roamin', I've a mantle formin'!
   All my grief and sorrow, sadly twine around it,
While my falling tears drop buttons shining on it.
(Csik county, Székely district. Transl. by J. C. Tóth).

   10. *Leaves and branches make a forest;*
   Grief and sorrow mould the heart best;
   Grief and sorrow, like a light breeze,
   Where I go they follow with ease.
    Gleaming sun is on the meadow
   Shines on ev'ry maiden's window;
   Tell me, o Lord: why not on mine?
   Why does mine not see the sunshine?
(Bukovina, a Csángó-Székely song. Transl. by J. C. Tóth).

   11. (a) *How I wish I were a morning star-beam!*
   I would shine on you, my dear, when you dream;
   I would shine on you early, right early;
   One last kiss, I'd ask you then to give me.
(Great Plain. Transl. by J. C. Tóth).

   (b) *Fragrant are the woods when they are green!*
   Lovely when the wild dove's nest is seen!
   Like a dove a maiden longs to be
   Close beside her lover constantly!
    I am not to blame for being sad!
   Only Mother is, for if she had
   Given me to my own chosen love,
   I would be as happy as a dove!
(Nyitra county, Northern Hungary. Transl. by J. C. Tóth).

   (c) *Leaving with the waning of the morning star,*
   My dear love is walking to her home afar.
   Shining boots are gleaming on her pretty feet;
   Glowing starlight beams up on my little sweet.

This I wish for you my dearest, ev'ry day:
Lush green meadow, turn to roses on your way.
Fresh green grass too, rosy apples for you grow;
And your heart will never forget I love you so!

(Békés county, Great Plain. Transl. by J. C. Tóth).

(d) *Lovely leaves and branches make a citron tree!*
Dearest heart, how can they part us, you and me?
Like the star when parted from its shining beams,
So shall I be parted from my sweetest dreams.

(Bukovina, a Székely-Csángó song. Transl. by J. C. Tóth).

(e) *Cricket lad is marrying Lord Mosquito's daughter,*
Slipping, slopping is the louse, best man should be smarter;
Jerking, jumping up the flea, best man, too, pretending;
Ev'ry kind of ugly bug wants to be attending.

(Tolna county, Transdanubia: humour. Transl. by J. C. Tóth).

(f) *Rugged rock a-looming, roses on it blooming:*
Love is such a splendid thing!
Love is but a dream though, if you've never known its glow;
O how sad if it is so!

(Nyitra county, Northern Hungary. Transl. by J. C. Tóth).

CHAPTER 14

1. Cf. Vopiscus: *"Vita Aureliani"* 39: (Aurelianus) *". . . provinciam Daciam a Traiano constitutam sublato exercitu et provincialibus reliquit. . ."* Also: Eutropias IX.15: *". . . abductosque Romanos ex urbibus et agris Daciae. . ."* These and other contemporary Roman and Greek historians state that emperor Aurelianus evacuated the entire Roman population both from the towns and rural areas of Dacia.

2. According to F. J. Sulzer (Geschichte Daciens, Vienna, 1781) and E. R. Rösler (Romänische Studien, Leipzig, 1871), the original home of the Vlach (Wallachian, Rumanian) people was in the south of the Balkan peninsula (between Albania, Greece and Bulgaria). After the IXth century these nomadic herdsmen moved to the north and north-east. One branch crossed the lower Danube and moved into the Wallachian Plain (between the Carpathians and the lower Danube). A Byzantian source (Anna Comnena)

mentions them here first in the XIth century. From here some of them crossed the Transylvanian mountains into Hungary. A Hungarian document from 1224 mentions first the presence of some Vlach shepherds in the Fogaras district (south-western Transylvania). (Cf. Zathureczky: Transylvania. Anderson Research Center, University of Florida, 1963).

According to the Rumanian linguist Cihac, the vocabulary of the Rumanian language contains 45.7% words of Slavonic origin and only 31.5% of Latin origin.

3. *That's how the Hungarians sow*
   Their oats very slowly!
   That's how the Hungarians reap
   Their oats very slowly!

   That's how the wife
   Steals the oats, steals the oats!
   That's how the wife
   Drinks its price, drinks its price!

4. *It is time to go*
   And to get married.
   The question is only
   Whom should I marry?
   If I marry a town girl,
   She can't spin, weave,
   I'll have to buy my
   Pantaloons myself.
   If I marry an old one
   She'll be always sullen,
   And whenever she'll speak,
   It'll be like thunder.
   Only one hope I have
   To keep me going,
   I'll remain a bachelor,
   Forever, perhaps . . .

   (Extracts)

CHAPTER 15

1. *I shall die indeed,*
Mother, my dear mother,
For Helen Görög,
For her slender waist,
For her full lips,
For her rosy cheeks . . .
For blue-eyed Helen Görög.

. . .

Do die, my son, do,
Ladislas Bertelaki,
They'll come here to see
The marvellous dead
Virgins and fair maidens.
Your love will come too,
Your fair Helen Görög.

. . .

— Arise, my son, arise,
Ladislas Bertelaki,
She for whom you have died
Is standing at your feet . . .

(Extracts. Transl. in Leader: Hungarian Ballads).

2. (The concluding verses:)

Her little son set out crying,
He set out crying to the tall castle of Déva.
Three times he shouted at the tall castle of Déva:
"Mother, sweet mother, speak but one word to me!"
"I cannot speak my son, for the stone wall presses me,
I am immured between high stones here."
Her heart broke, so did the ground under her.
Her little son fell in and died.

(Extract from N. Leader: Hungarian Ballads).

3. (The concluding lines: after the boy's suicide)

. . . His mother sent
River-divers,
They took them out dead;
The girl in his arms;
One of them was buried
In front of the altar,

The other was buried
Behind the altar.
Two chapel-flowers
Sprang up out of the two,
They intertwined
On top of the altar. . .

(Extract from N. Leader: Hungarian Ballads).

4. (The first and last lines:)

"Aye! Come home, mother,
Father is ill!"
"Wait, my daughter, a little,
Let me dance a little,
I'll go at once,
I just spin and dance a little,
I'll be at home soon" . . .

. . .

"Aye! Come home, mother,
We have buried father."
"Oh, aye, my bedlinen,
I may get a new husband,
But I can't make bedlinen,
Because I cannot spin or weave . . ."

(Extracts from N. Leader: Hungarian Ballads).

5. *Once upon a time out went fair maid Julia*
To pluck cornflowers in the cornfield,
To pluck cornflowers, to bind them into a wreath,
To bind them into a wreath, to enjoy herself.

Up, up she gazed into the high heaven,
Behold! a fine pathway came down from it,
And on it descended a curly white lamb.
It carried the sun and the moon between its horns,
It carried the sparkling star on its brow,
On its two horns were ay! two fine gold bracelets,
Ay! at its two sides were two fine burning candles,
As many as its hairs, so many the stars upon it.
*   Up and spoke to her the curly white lamb:*
"Do not take fright at me, fair maid, Julia,
For now the host of virgins has fallen short by one.
If you were to come with me, I would take you there,

To the heavenly choir, to the holy virgins,
So as to complete their pious host;
I would give the key of Heaven into your hands.
At the first cockcrow I would come and see you,
At the second cockcrow I would propose to you,
At the third cockcrow I would take you away."

Fair maid Julia turns to her mother,
And up and speaks to her: "Mother, my sweet mother,
(. . . she tells her mother what happened and continues:)
Lament for me, mother, lament. Let me hear while I still live,
How you will lament when I am dead."

"My daughter, my daughter, in my flower garden,
You the wee honeycomb of my first bee-swarm,
You the golden wax of this wee honeycomb,
The earth-spreading smoke of this golden wax,
The earth spreading smoke, its heaven-breaking flame!

The heavenly bell, untolled it tolled,
The heavenly gate, unopened it opened,
Alas! my daughter, she was led in there!"

(Complete text — except for repetition in verse 4 — from
N. Leader: Hungarian Ballads).

6. (Extracts):

Once a prince of old
Thought he could find a sweetheart.
He decided right there
Dressed up as a coachman.

(He went to the rich judge's daughter, asked her hand in
marriage but she said:)

I would never wed, no,
A poor coachman fellow!
Ask my poorest neighbour!
Basket-weaver's daughter.

(He did and the basket-weaver's daughter said):

Yes, I will, I like you!
I'll be waiting for you!

(Dressed as a prince he went back to the judge's daughter,
who said she would be delighted to marry him, but the prince
told her that he was marrying the poor girl. The prince then
went to the basket-weaver's daughter who could not recognise
him and refused:)

> *I refuse to do so!*
> *Handsome prince, I say no!*
> *I have promised my hand*
> *To a handsome coachman!*

(The prince removed his royal disguise and saiᴏ):

> *I am he, no other!*
> *Let us kiss each other!*

(They did).

(Transl. by J. C. Tóth).

7. (Passage from the Tale of a King, a Prince and a Horse):

". . . *We are passing through the glittering Glass Mountain of Fairyland*" — *said the "táltos" horse.* "*You see, those who want to carry off a "Tündér" (fairy) girl for a wife must cut their way through the Glass Mountain. But there is no other horse except me that could do it. You know now why I have asked for the diamond shoes. Without them we would not be able to cross the Glass Mountain . . . Bind up your eyes and let us go ahead.*"

(So they did. The Prince bound up his eyes and the horse set forth at a great speed). "*Now, dear master, you can untie your eyes,*" *the "táltos" horse said. The boy looked around and saw around him a beautiful meadow undulating with the ripple of pure silk and with every blade of grass in it as bright as a pin. Right in the middle of that meadow there lay a man. As the man lay there his sword went round and round him.* "*He is the old comrade your father is yearning to see*" *said the táltos horse . . . (When the old man woke up) the boy greeted him:* "*May God bless you with a happy day, uncle.*" "*God bless you too, my son. What brought you here, beyond the beyond, far even for the birds to come?*" . . . "*I am a Prince, the youngest son of the King who weeps with one eye and laughs with the other. It was his wish that I come here to lead you to him, because you are his dear old comrade, and just like him, you weep with one eye and laugh with the other. But he feels sure that if he could see you again, both his eyes would weep first and then laugh for joy.*"

(The Prince brought the old man back to his father then went back and) . . *married the princess of Fairyland ("Tündérország"),*

and they had a big wedding feast . . . and if they are not dead, they are still alive to this day.

(From "Folktales of Hungary", ed. L. Dégh, transl. by J. Juhász, Uni. of Chicago Press, 1965).

8. (The conclusion of the legend "Blood Treaty")

. . . Chieftain Álmos turned toward the people and spoke: "The time has come when we shall retake the land which is our rightful legacy, the land of Atilla. According to the customs, the people of the Magyars must select a ruler who shall lead them in war and in peace. . . The tribes must unite into a nation again, and have one leader and one mind, as it was in the days of Atilla. . . The chiefs have chosen my oldest son, Árpád, to be your ruler for life."

The seven chiefs held a shield in front of Árpád. As Árpád stepped on it, they raised him high above their heads. He stood straight on the uplifted shield and in his hand sparkled the Sword of God (Atilla's sword). . .

The people around him broke out in cheers and the Táltos stepped forward with Atilla's wooden cup in his hand.

"Come before me, ye seven Chiefs," said the Táltos in a loud voice, "and you Kabars, who are joining us, do the same. Pledge your oath to your leader, Árpád, and his descendants!"

One by one, the Chiefs slit the flesh of their fore-arm and let their blood flow into Atilla's cup. . . The Táltos mixed wine with the blood, poured a small amount on the ground, and sprayed a few drops into the wind, in four directions. Then he gave them the cup, and one by one, they drank from it.

(Extracts from "Selected Hungarian Legends" ed. A. Wass, Danubian Press, 1971. Transl. by E. Wass de Czege).

9. (The last episode from "Matthias and his Barons")

Once the king and his barons were walking past a reedy swamp. A hot day it was. "A bit of rain would be just in time for these reeds," said the king though the reeds stood in water. The barons caught each other's eye and began to laugh. 'What need was there of rain when the reeds stood in water?' The king made no reply. When they got home, he gave orders to serve them the finest dishes generously salted and without any drink to wash the meal down. And at his orders big bowls were placed under the table, at the feet of each baron. The bowls were filled with water, and the barons had to put their feet into the bowls. When they had finished supping, the barons desired some drink as the good dishes made them thirsty. They asked the king to let them have some water as they were nearly dying with thirst.

Said the king: "What for? Your feet are in water. You were laughing at me when I said the reeds wanted a good rain. You said, 'Why should they want rain as they stood in water?' Well, why should you want water when your feet are in it? You will get none."

(From "Folktales of Hungary", d. by L. Dégh, transl. by J. Juhász, Uni. of Chicago Press, 1965).

10. In the far-off days when Jesus and Peter were still going about in the world, they were making for the Hungarian "puszta" (Plain) when they came to a village inn. Peter, who was tired, said "Let us go in." The Lord said then, "All right, let us take a little rest in there."

Inside the inn, some "betyárs" (outlaws) were making merry, shaking their legs in a lively dance.

The two wanderers lay down by the wall to rest for a while. But Peter, who was lying nearest the dance floor, received so many kicks in his side as the dancers went dancing past him that before long he felt anything but pleased at their manners. So he thought that it would be quite a good idea to change places with the Lord.

"Let us change places, Lord," he said, "and let me lie next to the wall for a while."

"All right, Peter, let's change places."

But now the dancers thought that for a change they should give a few kicks to the man lying next to the wall, and it was Peter again who got all the kicks.

(From "Folktales of Hungary").

CHAPTER 17

1. (a) (The first verse of the "Siege of Eger":)

You, Hungarians worship God now,
And indeed give thanks to Him,
Of valiant soldiers in Eger speak highly,
I tell you a chronicle, give me hearing . . .

(b) (Extracts from "Of the many Drunkards":)
You many drunkards, hear about your morals,
About the sins committed in your drunkenness against God,
For many a time you forget your God . . .
. . . . .
In thirst this was composed by one called Sebestyén,
In Nyirbátor in 1548,
The stewards did not give me wine, be cursed . . .

2. (Extracts):

> *Soldiers, what men could be*
> *More blessed on earth than we,*
> *Here in the frontier command?*
> *For in the pleasant spring*
> *Merrily songbirds sing,*
> *Gaily on every branch!*
> *Sweet is the meadow rose,*
> *Sweet dew the sky bestows;*
> *What men know life like our band!*

(Transl. by Paul Desney).

3. (In a similar vein he grieves, in Christian humility for the sins of his youth):

> *Unhappy is my lot;*
> *My pangs are great, God wot;*
> *My youth is turned to sighing.*
> *For toil is hard to bear,*
> *My yoke is harsh to wear*
> *In spite of all my trying.*
> *The good old times have flown*
> *By winds of evil blown,*
> *And left me to my crying.*

("Farewell" — first verse. From Kunz: Hungarian Poetry. Transl. by W. Kirkconell)

> 4. *When autumn dews are done,*
> *Across the waning sun*
> *November winds come blowing.*
> *They snatch the falling leaves,*
> *Across the bitter eves*
> *Their yellow fragments strowing*
> *Soon where I walk today*

286

Along the greenwood way
Strides winter with its snowing.
("Farewell": as above)

5. (From: "Greeting on finding Julia"):
I do not even want the world without you, my sweet love,
who now stands whole beside me, my sweet soul.
The joy of my sad heart, sweet longing of my soul,
you are the happiness of all; the pledge of God be with you.
My precious palace, fine scented red rose,
beautiful queen-stock, long life, fair Julia!
(Extract. Transl. by Paul Desney).

6. (Extract from Peter Pázmány's "The Guide to the right Faith):
Men build slowly, but they are quick to destroy their beautiful
buildings. Not so Almighty God. For he builds quickly. In six
days He created Heaven and Earth in all their fairness and
splendor, but he took seven days to lay siege to a single city,
Jericho. He decided to bring Niniveh to dust and ashes and yet
He tarried forty days.
Nor will He hasten to bring this world to dust and ashes.
He waits with great patience, as He does now. When the time
will approach, He will give terrifying signs. Do you know, o
Christians, why God has willed that there be great and manifold
horrors before the Last Judgement? Because our God is infinitely
good and full of mercy. He threatens us, so that we may know
there is still time to come to Him.
(From: B. Menczer: A Commentary. . . Amerikai Magyar Kiadó,
1956).

7. The concluding strophes of Zrinyi's "Peril of Sziget" express
the poet's pride in his achievements both in poetry and in warfare.
Whilst his somewhat exaggerated claim to poetic immortality is
in keeping with the typical baroque style of his age, he realises
that his true destiny is to "fight the Ottoman moon":
My work is done, a monument whose grace
No spiteful stream of time can wash away,
No fire's rage can harm, nor steel deface,
Nor gnawing envy cause its slow decay.
I seek my fame not only with my pen,
But also with my sword so feared by men;

And all my life I'll fight the Ottoman moon,
And gladly for my country die, be it late or soon.

(Transl. by W. Kirkconnell. From: "Hungarian **Poetry**").

8. (The folk-song variation of "Rákóczi's Farewell" — as recorded in an eastern-Hungarian village in Szatmár county):

> *Listen to my speech,*
> *My dear Hungarian people,*
> *Advise me, my brave soldiers,*
> *What should I do?*
> *The Germans are coming,*
> *Destroying everything,*
> *By sword and fire.*

(The "Rákóczi-song" — the work of a skilled poet):

> *Alas, Rákóczi, Bercsényi,*
> *Leaders of brave Magyars,*
> *Bezerédi!*
> *Where are you now,*
> *Living idols of*
> *Our Magyar people!*

> *Alas, you great, old*
> *Magyar people,*
> *How the enemy is*
> *Ravaging you!*
> *Once a beautiful,*
> *Ornate picture!*

CHAPTER 18

1. (As the bride leaves her parents' house for the church she says):

The hour has come to start out on my road,
To reach the goal with my beloved mate,
That we may be linked with the chain of love
In the house of God, that we may have another.
My dear parents, your tears spring from
The painful feeling in the parental heart.
Although I was a flower blooming in your garden,
I desired an even greater happiness than that.
Let me go on my road now,

I leave you in the protection of the Lord,
I greet you with all my heart.
   (As she enters the house of her mother-in-law:)
My dear mother, I wish you good evening,
I stand at the door of your house with fear.
As the migrating bird leaves her nest,
So I left that of my dear parents.
So does a single bird fly about alone
Until it finds its mate at last.
But your dear son is no longer alone,
Having found his loving mate already.
I have become a companion to your dear son today,
Receive me as your daughter now. . .

(From: Fél - Hofer: Proper Peasants, Corvina, Budapest, 1969).

2. (Good-wish song — usually sung by the children of the family):

> *Arise, brave people,*
> *Dawn is smiling,*
> *Approaching, like an angel*
> *On wings of golden feathers.*
>   *Green blades of grass,*
> *Dress up prettily,*
> *They wash and dry themselves*
> *With lilies and roses.*
>   *As the number of grasses*
> *In the flowery meadows,*
> *As the number of drops*
> *In the great ocean*
>   *So many blessings*
> *For our dear . . . . . .*

CHAPTER 20

1. (Extracts from D. Berzsenyi: "My portion"):

> *Peace is my portion. I have moored my boat;*
> *No fairy dream shall, lure me to cast loose;*
> *Place of retirement, to thy breast receive*
>   *Th' aspiring youth.*
> *Wherever fate shall cast my lot in life,*
> *I am free from penury and care,*

289

> *Always and everywhere in calm content*
> *To heaven I look.*

(Transl. by W.N. Loew. From: "Hungarian Poetry" ed. E. F.
Kunz, Pannonia Publ. Co. Sydney, 1955).

2. (From: M. Csokonai-Vitéz: "To the Rose-bud"):

> *Open, Rose-bud, sweetly smiling,*
> *Open up at last;*
> *Open to the vagrant breeze*
> *Whose kisses are awaiting you.*
> *Oh, how this weedy garden*
> *Will take pride in you!*
> *Oh, how dare they take*
> *This precious garment from you.*
> *Let me pick you, elegant stalk;*
> *Already you are beautiful.*
> *How many pert, coquettish,*
> *Cheeky girls await you!*
> *No, no! let no one of these*
> *Undo her clasps at your sight;*
> *Dear Julia, who planted you*
> *Will grant you a new garden.*
> *There you may parade your purple*
> *Among more precious robes;*
> *There you may parade your perfume*
> *Among her dearer scents.*

(Transl. by Paul Desney.

3. (Extract from the song "To Hope" by M. Csokonai-Vitéz):

> *Why do you flatter me with your honied lips?*
> *Why are you smiling at me?*
> *Why do you still raise in my bosom a dubious heart?*
> *Keep to your own devices, you encouraged me once,*
> *I had believed your pretty words, yet you have deceived me.*

4. (Two stanzas from S. Kisfaludy's "Lamenting Love"):

> *(No. 75) O thou stream, that springing*
> *from the cold hill's side*
> *tears down sadly ringing*
> *where dark pine trees bide*
> *with hesitant windings*
> *between rock and tree,*

till, loosing your bindings,
you reach the sea,
art the image of my life,
which sobs its tortured way
snared by endless strife
towards its final bay.

(No. 126) Days come, days go back,
but sorrow does not range;
the hours fly and pass,
but my destiny does not change.
Volcanoes tire;
Rivers, lakes run dry:
but not my fire
or tears from my eye;
forests, meadows, come alive;
star-clusters turn and swill;
fortune revolves and thrives;
only my misery stands still.

(Transl. by Paul Desney).

5. (First verse of "National Anthem" by F. Kölcsey):

God, bless the Hungarian
With abundance, gladness,
Graciously protect him when
Faced with foes or sadness.
Bring for people torn by fate
Happy years and plenty:
Sins of future, sins of late,
Both are paid for amply.

(Transl. by E. F. Kunz. From: "Hungarian Poetry", ed. by E. F. Kunz).

6. ("The Sorrowing Husband" by Ch. Kisfaludy):

At Szatmár village is an inn,
Fair Mistress Therese lives within.
Her eyes are lustrous, black her hair,
Her form all grace, beyond compare,
She is the fairest of the fair.
But woe! — the truth, — it must be told, —
Though beautiful, she was a scold.
Just now a quarrel she began;

To chide, to brawl, to rail — it ran
As but an angry woman can.
This time it was the husband who
Upon himself her anger drew.
He meekly sat behind the stove
From whence she with a broomstick drove,
When sudden, in the noisy hum,
A cry is heard: "The Tartars come!"
Though each one trembles, runs, hides, weeps;
Still, our good Mistress Therese keeps
Her courage, goes into the street
For boldly any man to meet,
A splendid weapon is her tongue.
As said before, she's fair and young,
Her face all rosy from the flare
She had been in; her neck, arms are bare,
Her heaving breast, her fiery eye
Her usual good looks amplify.
The Tartar comes. His eyes are fire,
And burning with brute desire
When Mistress Therese he espies
He realises what a prize
She would be. So with no ado
Up comes to her the Tartar foe
And taking hold around her waist,
With one strong pull he had her placed
Beside himself, and then with haste
He into the far distance raced.
No woman more his saddle graced
Than now he, drunk with joy, embraced.
The spouse, whose wife had just been stolen,
Feels, that his eyes with tears are swollen;
Looks up the road on which they fled
"Poor Tartar!" is all that he said.

(Transl. by W. N. Loew. From: "Hungarian Poetry", ed. by
E. F. **Kunz**).

7. (A prose rendering of the concluding lines of "Fair Helen"
by M. Vörösmarty):
. . . Pale as a snow-white statue stands fair Ilonka, speechless,
numb.

"Shall we indeed go to the huntsman at the court of Mátyás, dear child? It is better for us in the wilds of Vértes; our little home there will give us peace". The grandfather spoke with understanding grief, and the sad pair went on their way, their steps stricken with care.

If you have seen a fair flower in bloom drop through inner sickness — so did fair Ilonka, fearing the light, droop beneath her secret sorrow. Her companions were feelings aflame, painful memories, dead hopes. Her life, brief yet an agony, passed away, fair Ilonka languished to the grave; her languishing was the fall of lilies: her face of innocence and grief. The King comes and stands in the deserted house; they rest in their eternal home.

(From: "Five Hungarian Writers", D. M. Jones).

8. (From "To the Daydreamer" by M. Vörösmarty):

Into what place does the world of your eyes now lapse?
What do you look for in the doubtful distance there?
Can it be past time's dark flower perhaps
Upon which, trembling, clings your wondrous tear?
Clad perhaps in the future's veil you see
Nightmarish apparitions which come your way.

He who wants a flower does not bear a bush;
He who would have vision gazes not into the sun;
He who would seek after pleasure loses out.
Only the humble are not brought pain through desire.
. . . Don't look, don't look into the distance of desire
The entire world is not our land to hold;
Only that which the heart alone can encompass,
That only can we hold as our own.

(Transl. by Paul Desney).

9. (From "Thoughts in the Library" by M. Vörösmarty):

What can we do here? struggle — each one
according to his strength — for the noble aim.
Before us a nation's destiny lies.
When we have raised that from its sunken state
and placed it as high as possible by
the clear rays of spiritual struggle,
we can say, turning to our ancestors'
ashes: Thanks be, Life! To your health!
we've had a good time — we've done a man's work!

(Transl. by Paul Desney).

10. (From "Appeal" by M. Vörösmarty)
Be true to the land of thy birth,
Son of the Magyar race;
It gave thee life and soon its earth
Will be thy resting place.
Although the world is very wide,
This is thy home for aye;
Come weal or woe on fortune's tide,
Here you must live and die.
This is the dear, hallowed soil
On which our fathers bled;
This, where a thousand years of toil
Has bound the mighty dead.

(Transl. by W. Jaffray. From: "Hungarian Poetry").

11. (From "The Old Gypsy" by M. Vörösmarty:)
Gypsy, strike up! You've gulp'd your wine for pay.
. . . Strike up! Who knows how soon the day will come
When fiddle-bow is bent and music dumb?
Grief's in your heart, but wine is in your glass:
Play, gypsy, play, and let your troubles pass!
Your boiling blood should eddy like the tide,
The marrow of your brain be stirr'd and warm,
Your eyes should glitter like a meteor,
Your sounding string be like a thunderstorm.
Strike up? But no! In silence leave the strings
Until that day when earth shall join in feast,
Till all the storm and darkness shall be past,
And war's abhorrent discords shall have ceas'd
When that day comes, play on with new-found cheer
Until the very gods rejoice to hear!

(Transl. by W. Kirkconnell. From: "Hungarian Poetry").

CHAPTER 21

1. (Prose rendering of the first verse of "Shepherds' Dance")
I wish I had woken up sooner. I have just heard the angels'
voice telling us that Jesus was born in a humble stable. Now
I want to go there, hoping to see Little Jesus. Come, dear
friend, let us go, our old shepherd friend will play the flute.
We shall entertain Jesus and Mary while you catch a lamb.

(Recorded in Pest county, Central Hungary).

2. (Extracts — in prose — from "Gloria . . .")
Gloria in excelsis — wake up, shepherds, wake up! Today your Lord was born in Bethlehem. You find Him in a humble stable there. . . (Recorded in Northern Hungary).

3. (Variant of the carol "Herdsmen. . .")
Herdsmen, when in Bethlehem, they were
Tending herds in the night on the fields,
God's angels appeared before them.
With great fear their hearts grew heavy.
"I bring you good news, don't be afraid,
For today was born your Lord and Saviour. . ."
(Recorded in the Jász district, Great Plain).

4. (Variant of the carol "Kirje. . .")
Kyrie, Kyrie, Little Baby,
Little Prince of Bethlehem,
You became our Saviour,
You have saved us from damnation.
   There is no cover on Jesus' bed
The poor Dear must be cold!
He has no warm wintercoat,
He has lost His little lamb.
   Little Jesus, golden apple,
The Holy Virgin's His mother.
She swaddles Him with her own hands
Rocks His cradle with her own feet.
(Recorded in a Great Plain village).

5. (Variant of "Shepherds. . .")
Shepherds, wake up,
Let's go at once
To the town of Bethlehem
To the humble, little stable!
Let's go, let's not tarry,
Let's get there tonight,
To pay our respects to our Lord.
(Recorded in Zala county, Transdanubia).

6(a) (From: "A Beautiful Rose"):
She could find no shelter in the town,
They will have to stay in the desert,
Oxen and the ass stand around the manger,
They look down on Little Jesus.

If I were your cradle I would rock you gently,
I would not let you catch cold,
I would cover you and look after you,
I would serve you, my Master.
  (Recorded in a Great Plain village).

  (b) (Another carol with the same theme):

> *O, if you had been born*
> *In our town, Bicske,*
> *In Hungary you would have found*
> *A warmer home and better people . . .*

  (Recorded in Komárom county, Transdanubia).

7. (Extracts from a "Bethlehem play"):

(All): Bethlehem, Bethlehem,
  In your vicinity
  Mary arrived and went
  Into a humble stable.
  There she was sitting
  Like a forsaken turtle — dove,
  Making ready for the blessed birth.
(The Angels): God's Lamb is crying,
  There she is who takes pity on Him.
  The Holy Mother is rocking Him:
  Aye, aye, aye, Jesus, sleep!
(Mary): Don't cry, my sweet,
  Thou art my ornament!
  Beautiful lullaby they sing,
  The heavenly host, aye, aye, aye, sunshine of my soul.
(Joseph): Alas, this manger is very hard,
  My dear Son, alas, Thou art cold.
  There is no shelter here against cold
  Except Saint Joseph's cloak.
  Aye, aye, aye, Jesus, sleep!
  (Recorded in Sopron county, Transdanubia).

8.
> *Our Gracious Lady,*
> *Great Patron of our nation,*
> *Being in great, dire need,*
> *We address you thus:*
> *Do not forget in her peril*
> *Hungary, our beloved country,*
> *And us, poor Hungarians!*

CHAPTER 22

1. (Extracts from the address given by Louis Kossuth in Harrisburg, Pennsylvania in 1852. He looks back on the achievements of Hungary's freedom struggle in 1848-1849 then appeals for American moral and political support for Hungary's continued struggle to regain her independence).

". . . In Hungary (before 1848) the people of every race were equally excluded from all political right — from any share of constitutional life. The endeavours of myself and my friends for internal improvement — for emancipation of the peasantry — for the people's restoration to its natural rights in civil, political, social and religious respects — were cramped by the Habsburg policy. But the odium of this cramping was thrown by Austria upon our conservative party: and thus our national force was divided into antagonistic elements.

Besides, the idea of Panslavism and of national rivalries, raised by Russia and fostered by Austria, diverted the excitement of the public mind from the development of common political freedom. And Hungary had no national army. Its regiments were filled with foreign elements and scattered over foreign countries, while our own country was guarded with well disciplined foreign troops. And what was far worse than all this, Hungary, by long illegalities, corrupted in its own character, deprived of its ancient heroic stamp, Germanized in its salons, sapped in its cottages and huts, impressed with the avoidable fatality of Austrian sovereignty and the knowledge of Austrian power, secluded from the attention of the world, which was scarcely aware of its existence, — Hungary had no hope in its national future, because it had no consciousness of its strength, and was highly monarchial in its inclinations and generous in its allegiance to the King. . ."

(This logical, unemotional analysis of the deeper causes of Hungary's defeat in 1848-49 from an address given in English to an American audience compares interestingly with a highly emotional speech given to the Hungarian Parliament in July 1848. On this occasion Kossuth, the Finance Minister of the first Hungarian government, asked for an appropriation to enable the government to set up a national defence force of 200,000 soldiers (Cf. Chapter 19). The following are the introductory and concluding sentences of the speech):

"Gentlemen, in ascending the Tribune to call upon you to save the country, I am oppressed with the greatness of the moment; I feel as if God had placed in my hands the trumpet to arouse the dead, that if sinners and weak, they may relapse into death, but that if the vigour of life is still within them, they may waken to eternity. The fate of the nation at this moment is in your hands; with your decision on the motion which I shall bring forward, God has placed the decision on the life or death of Hungary. . ."

. . . (After having explained the need for a strong defence force, he concluded:) ". . . I here solemnly and deliberately demand of this House, a grant of 200,000 soldiers and the necessary pecuniary assistance. . ."

(When Kossuth reached this part of his speech, Paul Nyáry, the leader of the opposition, stood up, and raising his right hand, as if in the act of taking an oath, exclaimed: "We grant it . . ." As one man the deputies repeated the words of Nyáry. Kossuth continued with a voice trembling with emotion):

"(Gentlemen). . . you have all risen to a man, and I bow before the generosity of the nation, while I add one more request: let your energy equal your patriotism, and I venture to affirm that even the gates of hell shall not prevail against Hungary. . ."

(Hollister, W.C. "Landmarks. . . ", J. Wiley and Sons New York, 1967; Headley: Life of Kossuth, quoted in "Hungary and its Revolutions" by E. O. S., London, G. Bell, 1896).

CHAPTER 23

1. (From: S. Petöfi: "National Song):

> *Magyars up! your country calls you!*
> *Break the chain which now enthralls you.*
> *Freemen be, or slaves for ever.*
> *Choose ye, Magyars, now or never.*
> *For by the Magyar's God above*
> > *We truly swear*
> *We truly swear the tyrant's yoke*
> > *No more to bear!*

(Transl. by W. N. Loew, From: "Hungarian Poetry").

2. (a) (From: "The bush is trembling. . . ":)

> *The bush is trembling for*
> *A bird alighted upon it;*
> *My soul is trembling for*
> *You have come into my mind,*
> *My lovely little girl,*
> *Of this world you are*
> *The brightest diamond. . .*

(Transl. by Paul Desney).

(b) (From: "I'll be a tree. . .":)

> *I'll be a tree if you are its flower,*
> *Or a flower, if you are the dew;*
> *I'll be the dew, if you are the sunbeam,*
> *Only to be united with you.*

(Transl. by E. F. Kunz).

(c) (From: "Autumn is here, here again. . .":)

> *Darling, sit down by my side,*
> *Sit and make no sound,*
> *While my song departs over the lake*
> *Like a whispering wind.*
> *—Slowly place your lips to mine,*
> *If kiss me you would deem,*
> *So as not to awaken Nature*
> *And so disturb its dream.*

(Transl. by Paul Desney).

3. ("The cottage door. . .")

> *The cottage door stood open wide,*
> *To light my pipe I stepped inside,*
> *But, oh! behold, my pipe was lit,*
> *There was indeed a glow in it.*
> *But since my pipe was all aglow*
> *With other thoughts inside I go,*
> *A gentle winning maiden fair*
> *That I perchance saw sitting there,*
> *Upon her wonted task intent*
> *To stir the fire aflame, she bent;*
> *But, oh! dear heart, her eyes so bright*
> *Were shining with more brilliant light.*

She looked at me as in I passed
Some spell she must have on me cast.
My burning pipe went out, but oh!
My sleeping heart was all aglow.

(Transl. by C. H. Wright. From "Hungarian Poetry").

4. (From: "The Hungarian Plain":)

What, O ye wild Carpathians, to me
Are your romantic eyries, bold with pine?
Ye win my admiration, not my love;
Your lofty valleys lure no dream of mine.

Down where the prairies billow like a sea,
Here is my world, my home, my heart's true fane,
My eagle spirit soars, from chains released,
When I behold the unhorizoned plain.

Upwards I mount in ecstasies of thought
Above the earth, to cloud-heights still more near,
And see, beneath, the image of the plain,
From Danube on to Tisza smiling clear.

Stampeding herds of horses, as they run,
Thunder across the wind with trampling hoof,
As lusty herdsmen's whoops resound again
And noisy whips crack out in sharp reproof.

Far, far away, where heaven touches earth,
Blue tree-tops of dim orchards tower higher,
Like some pale fog-bank, and beyond them still
A village church projects a simple spire.

Fair art thou, Alföld, fair at least to me!
Here I was born, and in my cradle lay.
God grant I may be buried 'neath its sod,
And mix my mouldering cerements with its clay!

(Transl. by W. Kirkconnell. From: "Hungarian Poetry").

5. (From: "One Thought torments me. . . ":)

One thought torments me: that I lie
Upon a featherbed to die!
Slowly wither, slowly waste away,
Flowerlike, the furtive earthworm's prey;
Like a candle slowly to be spent
In an empty, lonely tenement.
My life, let me yield
On the battlefield!

'Tis there that the blood of youth shall flow from my heart,
And when, from my lips, last paeans of joy but start.
Let them be drowned in the clatter of steel,
In the roar of the guns, in the trumpet's peal,
And through my still corpse
Shall horse after horse
Full gallop ahead to the victory won,
And there shall I lie to be trampled upon.

(Transl. by E. B. Pierce and E. Delmár).

6. (From: "Bor the Hero" by J. Arany:)

Shadows of the dying day
On the quiet valley fell,
Bor, the Hero rode away —
"Sweet and fair one, fare thee well."
Wind-swept branches stir and strain,
Lo! a lark is singing near,
Bor, the Hero rides amain,
Silent falls the maiden's tear.
Whither wends that soaring flight?
Darkness mingles earth and sky
"Daughter, haste, thy troth to plight!"
There is none to make reply.
Darkness mingles earth and sky,
Ghostly shapes the forest fill,
There is none to make reply,
"Come!" 'Tis Bor that whispers still.
Spirit lips a chant intone,
Ghostly whispers stir her mood,
"My dear spouse, O! mine alone,
Take me wheresoe'er you would."
Near the fane of hoary stone
Gleams a light transcending day,
Spirit lips a chant intone,
Festal robes the priest array.
With a light transcending day,
Ruined aisle and altar shine,
Festal robes the priest array,
"Now, Beloved, thou art mine."
Darkness mingles earth and sky
Hark! frightened owlet cried!

Cold in death, the altar nigh,
Lay the young and lovely bride.

(Transl. by C. H. Wright. From: "Hungarian Poetry").

7. (From: "The Bards of Wales":)

Edward the king, the English king,
Bestrides his tawny steed,
"For I will see if Wales" said he,
"Accepts my rule indeed."

"In truth this Wales, Sire, is a gem,
The fairest in thy crown:
The stream and field rich harvest yield,
And fair are dale and down."

"And all the wretched people there
Are calm as man could crave;
Their hovels stand throughout the land
As silent as the grave."

Edward the king, the English king,
Bestrides his tawny steed;
A silence deep his subjects keep
And Wales is mute indeed.

The castle named Montgomery
Ends the day's journeying;
The castle's lord, Montgomery,
Must entertain the king.

"Ye lords, ye lords, will none consent
His glass with mine to ring?
What! Each one fails, ye dogs of Wales,
To toast the English king?"

All voices cease in soundless peace,
All breathe in silent pain;
Then at the door a harper hoar
Comes in with grave disdain:

"Harsh weapons clash and hauberks crash,
And sunset sees us bleed,
The crow and wolf our dead engulf —
This, Edward, is thy deed!"

"Now let him perish! I must have"
(The monarch's voice is hard)
"Your softest songs, and not your wrongs!" —
In steps a boyish bard:

302

"The breeze is soft at eve, that oft
From Milford Haven moans;
It whispers maidens' stifled cries,
It breathes of widows' groans.
    Ye maidens bear no captive babes!
Ye mothers rear them not!"
The fierce king nods. The lad is seiz'd
And hurried from the spot.
    "No more! Enough!" cries out the king.
In rage his orders break:
"Seek though these vales all bards of Wales
And burn them at the stake!"
    In martyrship, with song on lip,
Five hundred Welsh bards died;
Not one was mov'd to say he lov'd
The tyrant in his pride.
        . . .

    " 'Ods blood! What songs this night resound
Upon our London streets?
The mayor should feel my irate heel
If aught that sound repeats!"
    Each voice is hush'd; through silent lanes
To silent homes they creep.
"Now dies the hound that makes a sound;
The sick king cannot sleep."
    "Ha! Bring me fife, drum and horn,
And let the trumpet blare!
In ceaseless hum their curses come . . .
I see their dead eyes glare. . ."
    But high above all drum and fife
And trumpets' shrill debate,
Five hundred martyr'd voices chant
Their hymn of deathless hate.

(Transl. by W. Kirkconnell. From: "Hungarian Poetry").

8. (From: "The Death of Buda", Canto Six: "The Legend of
the Wonder Hind").
    The bird flies on from bough to bough;
    The song is pass'd from lip to lip;
    Green grass grows o'er old heroes now,
    But song revives their fellowship.
        . . .

Across the waste now faintly come
The sounds of distant fife and drum;
In darksome loneliness they seem
Like heavenly music in a dream.

   Here mystic state the fairies keep,
Along the wilderness they dance,
Or 'neath the cloudy vapour sleep;
And revel in the vast expanse.

   No man is near, but there are seen
Earth's maids of fair and noble mien;
The daughters of Belár and Dúl,
Apt students in the fairy school.

   A test severe they must endure;
Must hold enslav'd in amorous chains,
To hapless fate nine youths allure;
While fancy-free each maid remains.

   'Tis thus they learn the fairy art,
To wield false hope's heart-piercing dart;
Each eve recount the feats of day,
Then dance the darksome hours away.

(Transl. by E. D. Butler. From: "Hungarian Poetry").

9. (From: "I lay the lute down. . .")

   . . . O my orphaned song, what thing art thou? —
Perhaps the spectre of departed lays
That issues from the tomb with pallid brow
To whisper down the graveyard's grassy ways?. . .
Art thou a coffin garlanded with flowers? . . .
A cry of anguish in a wilderness? . . .
Youth of my soul, bereft of golden hours,
Ah, whither hast thou stray'd in thy distress! —
I lay the poet's lute down. Dull as lead,
It irks the hand. And who still asks for song?
Who can rejoice in flowers that are dead?
Who seeks their mouldering fragrance to prolong?
If men destroy the tree, the bloom it bore
In shrivelling beauty perishes anon.
Youth of my soul, returning nevermore,
Ah, whither, tell me, whither hast thou gone!

(Transl. by W. Kirkconnell. From: "Hungarian Poetry").

10. (Extracts from I. Madach: "The Tragedy of Man").

(Scene One:)

Lucifer (to God):
> A corner is all I need,
> Enough to afford a foothold for Negation,
> Whereon to raise what will destroy
> Thy World . . .

(Scene Three:) (Adam and Eve have just been expelled from Paradise)

Eve (to Adam): I am making such an arbour
> As we had before, and so can conjure up
> The Eden we have lost . . .

(Scene Eleven: Eve looks at a grave:)

Eve: Why dost thou yawn before my feet, grim Death?
> Dost thou believe I fear thine awful gloom?
> The dust of Earth is thine. But not the breath
> Of radiant life. I'll shine beyond the tomb!
> While Love and Poetry and Youth endure,
> Upon my homeward way I still will go.
> My smile alone the ills of Earth can cure . . .

(Scene Thirteen: Adam, though disgusted with the frustrations of mankind, realises that he has a task to perform:)

Adam: Though Science may redeem the Earth, in time
> It too will pass away, like everything
> Which has fulfilled its end. But the Idea
> Which gave it life, again will rise triumphant.

(Scene Fifteen: Adam, having seen in his dream the tragedies and frustrations of human history, decides to prevent it all by committing suicide:)

Adam: Before me is that cliff — below the gulf.
> One jump, the last act, the curtain comes down,
> And I say: the comedy has ended . . .

Eve: . . . I am a mother, Adam . . .

(Adam falls upon his knees and turns to the Lord again, but he still fears for the future:)

Adam: . . . My heart on high I'll set!
> But, ah, the end! If that I could forget

The Lord: Man, I have spoken! Strive and unfalteringly, trust!

(Transl. by C. P. Sanger. From: Madach: "The Tragedy of man", Ed. Pannonia, Sydney, 1953).

11. ("In Twenty Years", by János Vajda).

Like the ice that caps the peak of Montblanc,
That neither sun nor wind can warm,
My quiet heart does no longer burn
No new suffering can do it harm.

Around me the stars in their millions
Winking lead me on as they revolve
Scattering over my head their shine;
Even so, still I will not dissolve.

But sometimes on a quiet, quiet evening
– As I slide ·alone into my dreams
Upon the enchanted lake of youth
Your swan-like form appears.

And when the rising sun arrives
Then my heart is again alight
Like Montblanc's eternal snows
After a long winter's night.

(Transl. by Paul Desney).

12. (From the last chapter of "The Dark Diamonds" by M. Jókai: Ivan, the owner of a coal-mine, finds the girl of his dreams — working in his coal-mine)

The girl stood still on top of the coal. . . The next moment Iván was at her side . . .

"You are here! You have come back here!"

"I have been here, sir, for almost a year, and if you will keep me on, I should like to stay."

"You can stay, but only on one condition — as my wife," cried Iván, pressing her hand to his heart.

Evila shook her head, and drew away her hand. "No, no. Let me be your servant, a maid in your house, your wife's maid. I shall be quite happy; I want nothing more . . . if you knew all, you would never forgive me."

"I know everything, and I can forgive everything."

His words proved that Iván knew nothing. If he had known the truth, he would have known that there was nothing, nothing to forgive. As it was,–he pressed his love to his heart, while she murmured:

"You may forgive me, but the world will never pardon you."

"The world!" cried Iván, raising his head proudly. "My world is here," laying his hand on his breast. "The World!

Look around from this hill. Everything in this valley owes its life to me; every blade of grass has to thank me that it is now green. Hill and valley know that, with God's help, I have saved them from destruction! I have made a million, and I have not ruined any one... My name is known all over the world, and yet I have hidden myself here, not to be troubled with their praises."

"Oh, sir," she whispered, "if I do not die, I shall always love you, but I feel that I shall die."

As she spoke she fell back in a faint. Her brilliant colour faded to a wax pallor, her flashing eyes closed; and her body, which a moment before was like a blooming rose, crumpled lifeless, like an autumn leaf.

Ivan held her lifeless body in his arms.

The woman whom he had loved for so long, for whom he had suffered so much, was his, just as her pulse ceased to beat, just as she said: "I shall always love you, but I feel that I shall die."

But she did not die.

- A diamond is a diamond for ever.

(Transl. by F. Gerard. From: "The Dark Diamonds". Corvina Press, Budapest, 1968).

13. (From: K. Mikszáth's novelette, "The Gentry": a Budapest journalist has been a guest at a wedding attended by Hungarian-Slovak gentry in the northern county Sáros. After the wedding he asks his friend about the luxury and pomp displayed by the guests)

"And those four-in-hands," I exclaimed, "the pomp, the splendour and brilliance, the Havana cigars and everything, everything?"

"So much eyewash. The four-in-hands were borrowed from one place; the trappings here, the first pair of horses there, the second pair from another place. . ."

"But this is sheer deceit!"

"Poppycock," Bogozy interrupted passionately. "Who would be deceived? Everyone knows that the other hasn't got four horses. These good boys, myself included, simply keep up form. . . beautiful, ancient form. Why, all this is so charming. . . This is the custom with us and customs must be respected at all costs. . . But as regards the merits

of the case, even if the brilliance and pomp, the splendour
and liveliness, the refined and easy manners, the joviality
and aristocratic airs. . . the horses, the silver cutlery. . .
don't belong to one or the other. . . by all means they
belong to somebody — to all of us. These things happen
to be scattered among us and whose business is it if, on
certain occasions, we artificially pool them on one spot? . . ."

(Transl. by L. Halápy. From: "Hungarian Short Stories",
Oxford Uni. Press, London, and Corvina, Budapest, 1967).

CHAPTER 26

1. ". . . (Károlyi) thought that he was going to assure a better
armistice for the new, pro-Allied Hungary, so he went, probably following Czech advice, to Belgrade, to receive what
he thought more generous terms from General Franchet
d'Espérey. . . Their humiliation, indeed, was complete. . .
When a socialist member of the delegation was introduced
to the French commander, the latter exclaimed, "Etes-vous
tombés si bas?" (Have you sunk to such depths?). . ." (From
"History of the Hungarian Nation" S. B. Várdy, Danubian
Press, Astor Park, 1969).

2. On March 20, 1919, Károlyi addressed the following proclamation to the people of Hungary:
"To the people of Hungary!

The government has resigned. Those who had been govern-
ing by the will of the people with the support of the Hungarian
proletariat, have now realised that the compelling force of
circumstances demands new directions. . . The Paris peace
Conference has decided to place almost the entire territory
of the country under military occupation. . . The aim of the
military occupation is to use Hungary as the operational and
supply area against the Russian Soviet army which is now
fighting on the Soviet-Rumanian border. The territories taken
from us are to be the reward given to the Rumanian and
Czech troops to be used against the Russian-Soviet army.

As the provisional President of the Hungarian People's
Republic I turn to the proletariat of the world for justice
and assistance against this decision of the Conference of
Paris. I resign and hand the power to the proletariat of the
peoples of Hungary.

Mihály Károlyi."

In his "Memoirs", published in 1956 (J. Cape, London), Károlyi asserts that he never signed this proclamation, and that in fact he was removed from office by a "coup d'etat" staged by the Social Democrats and instigated by the Entente (!). (Pp. 156-157). He fails to explain, however, why his regime was replaced by Kun's Communists, not the Social Democrats who had — allegedly — ousted him, why he remained in Budapest during the Kun regime (in the fashionable Svábhegy district), on very friendly terms with the "usurpers" (Communist Kun and Socialist Kunfi), and why he left Hungary in a hurry a few days before the downfall of the Kun regime (July, 1919). He also fails to explain why he had to wait until 1956 to repudiate the famous (and fatuous) proclamation.

3. After a counter-revolutionary uprising in Budapest, the Kun government issued a proclamation urging the Communists to "retaliate by the Red Terror of the proletariat. . ." (Hungarian text quoted in "Magyarország Története Képekben", Gondolat publ. Budapest, 1971).

4. General H. H. Bandholtz, U.S.A. member of the Inter-Allied Military Mission in Budapest wired to Paris on August 16, 1919: ". . . the Rumanians were doing their utmost to delay matters in order to complete the loot of Hungary. . . (after having carted away locomotives, railroad cars, machine tools and other equipment) they proceeded also to clean the country out of private automobiles, farm implements, cattle, horses, clothing, sugar, coal, salt and, in fact, everything of value. . . dismantled telephones even in private residences." Another member of the U.S.A. Mission reports that the "total amount of rolling stock taken by them (Rumanians) from the Hungarian State Railways was 1,302 locomotives and 34,160 railroad cars." The Rumanian occupation caused damage, as it was officially estimated, of almost three billions of gold crowns (equivalent to the same amount in US dollars).

In another telegram, addressed to the Supreme Allied Council in Paris (October 13), General Bandholz states that "in all towns occupied by the Rumanians we found an oppression so great as to make life unbearable. Murder is common: youths and women are flogged, imprisoned without trial, and arrested without reason. . ." (Quoted in S. B. Vardy: "History of the Hungarian Nation" pp. 214-215. Ed. Danubian Press.

Astor Park, 1969.) (Cf. also: H. H. Bandholtz, "An Undiplomatic Diary", ed. by F. K. Kruger, New York, 1933).

5. The "White Terror" myth was born in the imagination of Károlyi and his emigré friends in Paris and London. The ex-president substantiated his accusations by grossly misstating the date of Horthy's entry into Budapest. In his "Memoirs" he writes: "On *August 12th* Admiral Horthy, having waited for the departure of the looting Rumanian troops, made his entry into the city (Budapest). . . and started his punitive White Terror". (Károlyi: Memoirs, J. Cape, London, 1956, p. 174). It is a historic fact that Horthy entered Budapest on *November 16th* (1919), by which time the worst of the lawless acts of individual revenge against Kun's henchmen was over. During the months of the "legal vacuum" (August-November, 1919), Horthy and his collegues of the Counter-Revolutionary Government (Bethlen, Teleki etc.) lived under the watchful (and somewhat suspicious) eyes of the Allied (French) commander in Szeged and had therefore neither the authority nor the opportunity to commit (or to stop) "atrocities."

Thus Horthy and the Hungarian governments of two decades (and, indirectly, the entire Hungarian nation) were branded "fascists", "white terrorists" (and worse) because of the blatant distortion of facts by a confused ex-politician trying to excuse his own blunders.

Regrettably, most foreign historians (and politicians) repeated uncritically these accusations without bothering to check their dates or to read the reports of the members of the Allied Military Mission in Budapest, who were closely observing Horthy's actions in 1919 and 1920 (while Károlyi and his friends collected their "evidence" in Paris and London). Thus the British High Commissioner P. B. Hohler, the leader of the Inter-Allied Military Mission, Brig. Gen. R. N. Gorton, and Admiral Sir E. Troubridge stated in their reports of *February and March 1920:* "There is nothing in the nature of terror in Hungary. . . life is as secure here as in England. . ." (Quoted by Károlyi in his "Memoirs", p. 377). Similarly, the U.S. observer, Col. Horwitz (himself Jewish) attested: "Horthy's forces had done everything within reason to prevent such persecutions (of the Jews and Communists). . . as to there being a real "White Terror", there was nothing of the kind. . ." (Quoted in Várdy: History of the Hungarian Nation, p. 215).

6. The 10th of the "Fourteen Points" of President Wilson states that: ". . . the peoples of Austria-Hungary, whose place among the nations we wish to see safeguarded and assured, should be accorded the freest opportunity of autonomous development. . ." The Hungarians were one of the "peoples" of the Austro-Hungarian Monarchy. . .

7. Historic Hungary — including Croatia — had, in 1910, an area of 325,000 sq. km. and a population of 21.800.000. An area of 232.500 sq. km. (71.4%) and a population of 13.280.000 (63.5%) were transferred to the succession states by the Trianon Treaty. Counting Hungary proper — without Croatia — the 1910 area of the country was 283.000 sq. km. with a total population of 18,300,000. The following detailed statistics refer to Hungary proper — without Croatia.

Total losses by the Trianon Treaty:
Area: 190.000 sq. km. (67%)
Population: 10.700.000 (58%)
Left to Hungary after 1920:
Area: 93.000 sq. km., population: 7,600,000
Gains by the succession states:
Rumania: area: 103.000 sq. km. population: 5,260,000
Czechoslovakia: area: 62.000 sq. km. population: 3,520,000
Yugoslavia: area: 21.000 sq. km. population: 1,510,000
Austria: area: 4.000 sq. km. population: 290,000
Poland: area: 600 sq. km. population: 25,000
Italy: area: 21 sq. km. population: 50,000.

The number of Magyars transferred to each succession state was about 1/3 of the population of each detached territory, i.e.: to Rumania 1,700,000; to Czechoslovakia: 1,100,000; to Yugoslavia 550,000.

Each detached area had also a large population of non-Magyar tongue who were alien to the nation to which the area was transferred (e.g. Germans). Thus the area annexed by Rumania had a Rumanian population of 55% only, the Czechoslovak area a Slovak population of 60%, the Yugoslav area a South-Slav population of about 33%.

For comparison, here are the data of the last Hungarian census before Trianon — the census of 1910. These data refer to Hungary proper (without Croatia):

Magyars: 9,950,000 (54%)
Rumanians: 2,950,000 (16%)
Slovaks: 1,950,000 (10.4%)
Serbs: 460,000 (2.5%)
Other South Slavs: 150,000 (1.1%)
Others: Germans, Ruthenes etc.: 2,840,000 (16%).

The proportion of foreign nationalities in the newly created succession states was very similar to the Hungarian situation in 1910. Thus the Trianon Treaty created three new states with similar minority problems.

Though the Wilsonian "Fourteen Points" guaranteed "self-determination" and "autonomous development" to "the peoples of the Austro-Hungarian Monarchy", only one act of "self-determination" was allowed in connection with the Trianon Treaty: the western Hungarian town Sopron, claimed by Austria, was retained by Hungary after a plebiscite in 1921. No plebiscite and no "autonomous development" was granted to any Magyar-speaking region in the territories occupied by the victorious succession states, though large Magyar-speaking areas were contiguous to the Trianon frontier.

CHAPTER 28

1. (E. Ady: "The White-Lady":)

An old, fearful castle is my soul,
A mossy, lofty, forlorn spot.
(Behold! how enormous are my eyes,
Yet sparkle not, and sparkle not).
The lone, forsaken rooms ring hollow.
From the walls so sad, so dreary,
Black windows look down on the valley, —
(So weary are my eyes, so weary!)
Eternal are here apparitions,
The stench of vaults, the shroud of fog;
And shadows rustle in the darkness
And unforgiven phantoms sob.
(But rarely at the hour of midnight
My large eyes begin to flare —)
The white-lady roams then the castle
And smiles, standing at the window there.
(Transl. by R. Bonnerjea. From: "Hungarian Poetry").

2. (From: "Up flew the Peacock. . .")

> New winds are shaking
> The old Magyar maples,
> Waiting we wait for
> The new Magyar miracles.
> Either we are madmen and
> All of us shall perish.
> Or what we believe in
> Shall verily flourish.
> —New flames, new faiths,
> New kilns, new saints
> Exist, or anew void mist
> The future taints.
> Either the Magyar words
> Shall have new senses,
> Or Magyar life will stay sad,
> Ever changeless.

(Transl. by C. W. Horne).

3. ("Autumn came to Paris")

> Yes, Autumn came to Paris yesterday,
> Gliding in silence down Rue Saint-Michel;
> Here in the dog-days, soft beneath the leaves
> She met and hail'd me well.
>
> I had been strolling toward the slumbering Seine,
> Deep in my heart burn'd little twigs of song:
> Smoky and strange and sad and purple-hued.
> I knew for death they yearned.
>
> The Autumn understood and whisper'd low;
> Rue Saint-Michel grew tremulous and grey;
> The jesting leaves cried out along the street
> And flutter'd in dismay.
>
> One moment: then the Summer shone again,
> And laughing Autumn left on tripping toe;
> And I alone, beneath these whispering leaves,
> Beheld her come and go.

(Transl. by W. Kirkconnell. From: "Hungarian Poetry").

4. (From: "The horses of Death"):

> On the white road of the moonlight
> The winds, wild shepherds of the sky,

313

Drive on their flocks of scudding cloud
And towards us, towards us, without sound,
Unshod, Death's horses onward fly.
  He before whom those horsemen rein
Into that saddle mounts, his breath
Catching, grown pale, and with him fast
Along the white road of the moon
Seeking new riders, gallops Death.

(Transl. by J. C. W. Horne).

5. (From: "A half-kissed kiss"):

  This kiss consumed we should peacefully
Die without sorrow.
 — *We long for that kiss, we crave for that fire,*
But sadly we say: tomorrow, tomorrow.

(Transl. by R. Bonnerjea. From: "Hungarian Poetry").

6. (From: "A Kinsman of Death"):

  I am akin to death, his kinsman,
Fleeting to the love I love, swift burning;
Her lips to kiss I love who goes
Not returning.
  Roses I love, the sick, the languid,
Women whose passion fears the morrow,
Years of the past, radiant years,
Years of sorrow.

(Transl. by J. C. W. Horne).

7. ("Craving for Affection"):

  No gay forefathers, no successors,
No relatives and no possessors.
I belong to nobody,
I belong to nobody.
  I am what every man is, Grandeur,
A North, Secret, and a Stranger,
Distant will o'the wisp,
Distant will o'the wisp.
  Alas, but I cannot thus remain,
I must make myself to all quite plain,
That seeing they may see me,
That seeing they may see me.

Therefore all: Self-torture, melody!
I want to be loved by somebody,
And to be somebody's,
And to be somebody's.

(Transl. by R. Bonnerjea. From: "Hungarian Poetry").

8. (From: "A familiar lad"):

A little lad came to me last night,
Who once was I, now dead, beguiling,
Gently smiling.
At my wrinkling face he stares and stares,
And sheds many a tear in surprise
Upon my eyes.

(Transl. by R. Bonnerjea).

9. (From: "Detestable, lovable nation"):

If thousand times I turn from thee,
'Tis but a dance, an illusion.
In Magyarland things are awry,
I shall wait till the conclusion,
My loving, beloved and loathsome nation.

(Transl. by R. Bonnerjea. From: "Hungarian Poetry").

10. ("The Magyar Messiah"):

Our weeping is more bitter,
More piercing torments try us.
A thousandfold Messiahs
Are Hungary's Messiahs.
A thousandfold they perish,
Unblest their crucifixion.
For vain is their affliction,
Ah, vain is their affliction.

(Transl. by W. Kirkconnell).

11. (From: "Gog and Magog"):

Through Verecke's immortal pass came I.
Old Magyar songs still clamour in my ears,
Yet may I through Déveny break in here
With new melodies of newer years?

(Transl. by R. Bonnerjea).

12. (From: "Reminiscences of a Summer-night"):
I thought, at that time, I thought,
that some neglected God
would come to life and take me away;
and right up to now here I live
as the somebody that that night made of me
and waiting for God I reminisce
over that terrible night:
it was a strange,
strange summer's night.
(Transl. by Paul Desney).

13. ("In Elijah's Chariot"):
God, as with Elíjah, elects those
Whom he most loves, whom most he hurts.
He gives them quick-beating, fiery hearts
Which are like burning chariots.

This Elijah-tribe flies towards heaven
And stops where snow eternal is.
On top the ice-capped Himalayas
Crumble, rumble their carriages.

'Twixt earth and heaven, sad and homeless,
The winds of Fate them onwards chase,
And their chariots gallop on towards
Vile forms of beauty, cold and base.

Their hearts burn, their brains are icicles,
The world mocks them and rocks with fun,
But with diamond dust their cold highway
Is sprinkled by the pitying sun.
(Transl. by R. Bonnerjea).

14. (From: "The Lord's arrival"):
When all deserted,
When I bore my soul crumbling violently,
The Lord took me in His embrace,
Unforeseen. silently . . .
(Transl. by R. Bonnerjea).

15. (From: "Adam, where art thou?"):
'Tis only because God with flaming sword
To clear my human path has marched before.
I hear His footsteps walking in my soul
And His sad query: "Adam, where art thou?"

My breath replies in throbbing past control,
I have already found Him in my heart,
I've found Him and have clasped Him in my arms,
In death we'll be united, ne'er to part.

(Transl. by W. Kirkconnell).

16. (From: "Gypsy Song", by M. Babits):

"Here the meadow, there the wood,
countries bad and countries good,
although all the same to you:
everywhere the skies are blue.
If a Jew walks woodland way,
without looking, thus you prey.
If a girl goes meadow ways,
without asking you embrace.
That's because you sprang from branch
born beneath a tree in trench
and as fruit falls far from tree
so your mother shall lose thee;
fatherless, motherless,
homeless, landless, countryless."

(Transl. by E. F. Kunz. From: "Hungarian Poetry").

17. (From: "They sang long, long ago in Sappho's day...")

The world is selfish grown:
Just common hunger, common fever, faint
Confusion stammering, — and beyond that crew
Lies loneliness and silence. Song has flown,
And love, like doves' soft kiss, is silent too.
In our own hearts, my dear, song's word is rife.
They sang long, long ago in Sappho's day.
Kiss me! For song is dead, and grieving life
Takes refuge where two hearts own single sway.
Once men were truly men; but now, a herd
Of tired beasts that chew the cud of care.
Be thou an island till the fens that gird
Thee round grow red with sunrise! Learn to con
Cocoons that breed bright moths! Who need despair?
The old gods pass and go, but man lives on.

(Transl. by W. Kirkconnell. From: "Hungarian Poetry").

18. (From: "The lyric poet's epilogue"):

So I remain my own prison walls:
the subject and the object both, alas,
the Alpha and Omega both, am I.

(Transl. by A. Kramer).

19. ("I have forgot" by Gy. Juhász):

I have forgot the fairness of her hair;
But this I know, that when the flaming grain
Across the rippling fields makes summer fair,
Within its gold I feel her grace again.

I have forgot the blueness of her eyes;
But when Septembers lay their tired haze
In sweet farewell across the azure skies,
I dream once more the sapphire of her gaze.

I have forgot the softness of her voice;
But when the spring breathes out its softest sigh,
Then I can hear her speak the tender joys
That bless'd the springtime of a day gone by.

(Transl. by W. Kirkconnell. From: "Hungarian Poetry").

20. (From: "The pendulum", by A. Tóth):

Hoarse is the husky tickling's muffled chant
As often through the night my sad eye sees
Eternity (it seems) sway there aslant
And whittle futile Time to atomies.

Only a myriad pendulums are awake:
Blind, swaying splendors and mysterious miens,
Relentless sickles, golden guillotines.

(Transl. by W. Kirkconnell. From: "Hungarian Poetry").

21. (From: "Trees of Üllöi-út" by D. Kosztolányi):

The yellowed fields are withering,
trees of Üllöi-út.
My moods like suns of autumn sink;
soughing and slowly blows the wind
and kills the past spring's root.
O where, O where does fly the youth?
You sad leaved trees, O tell the truth,
trees of Üllöi-út.

(Transl. by E. F. Kunz. From: "Hungarian Poetry").

22. (From: "To my wife"):

> *You came in my room telling something odd;*
> *so after years of years I realised*
> *that there you are and scarcely listening*
> *surprised I looked at you. I closed my eyes.*
> *And this to myself I repeated mumbling:*
> *"I am used to her as I am used to air.*
> *She is giving me the breath."*

(Transl. by E. F. Kunz. From: "Hungarian Poetry").

23. (A. József: "Mama")

> *For one week I haven't stopped to think*
> *always of Mama, at the sink,*
> *bearing a creaking basket of soft*
> *clothes at her lap up to the loft.*
>
> *I was still a plain-spoken lout —*
> *I shouted, stamped my feet about:*
> *let her leave the clothes in a heap*
> *and take me up the stairs so steep.*
>
> *She went on dumbly hanging clothes,*
> *not scolding, nor even looking on*
> *and the clothes, shining, swishing,*
> *wheeled and soared up high.*
>
> *I should not wimper — it's too late —*
> *I now see how she was great —*
> *grey hair flowing on the sky,*
> *dissolving blue starch there up high.*

(Transl. by Paul Desney).

24. (From: "Ars Poetica"):

> *Ferment is fine to lose oneself in!*
> *Repose and tremors embrace*
> *and clever charming chit-chat*
> *arises from the foam.*
>
> *Other poets? of what concern are they?*
> *Let them all mime their intoxication*
> *up to their necks*
> *in phoney images and wine.*
>
> *I go past today's pub*
> *to meaning and beyond!*
> *A free mind will never serve*
> *the scurrilous modes of drivel . . .*

(Transl. by Paul Desney).

25. (From: "Lullaby"):

> *The sky is closing his blue eyes,*
> *the houses' eyes close one by one,*
> *the fields sleep under eiderdown —*
> *so go to sleep my little son.*
>
> *On the armchair sleeps the coat,*
> *dozes the tear, his job is done,*
> *he won't tear further, not to-day —*
> *so go to sleep, my little son.*
>
> *The dream like glassball will be yours,*
> *you will be giant, mighty one,*
> *but only close your little eyes —*
> *and go to sleep, my little son. . .*

(Transl. by E. F. Kunz).

26. (From: "The three Kings"):

> *Jesus, Jesus, God greet you, God greet you!*
> *Three kings are we well and true.*
> *Flaming star stood round our place,*
> *so we came on foot in haste.*
>
> *Lord Saviour, God bless you, God bless you!*
> *Far and warm lands crossed we through.*
> *All our bread and cheese is gone,*
> *all our shining boots are worn,*
> *but we brought you gold a lot,*
> *incense in an iron pot.*
>
> *Blushes, blushes Mary red, Mary red,*
> *happy mother bends her head.*
> *Through the tears which fill her eyes*
> *scarcely sees her Jesus Christ.*
> *All around the shepherds sing. —*
> *Time to feed the little thing.*
>
> *Dearest three Kings, kind and true,*
> *now good night, good night to you!*

(Transl. by E. F. Kunz. From: "Hungarian Poetry").

27. (From: "A painter in the Village" by G. Gárdonyi):

> *"I'd like to beg you, Mr. Picture-maker, to paint*
> my little daughter, my Ilonka. . ."*
>
> *"Which one is your daughter?" asked the painter.*
>
> *"She's dead, Sir, she's dead," the woman said with*
> tears in her eyes.*

"She was an only daughter," I explained as the mother faltered, "a lovely creature, with blue eyes."

"It's a difficult business," the painter answered. "Have you got some photograph of her?"

"No, I haven't, my dear Sir, that's why I want her to be painted, because I haven't got a picture of her."

On our way home the painter suddenly asked:

"Did the little girl look like her mother?"

"She'd have grown up to be just like her, if she'd lived."

"I'm going to try something," he said merrily. "I'll paint that woman as though she were seven years old."

And the following day he began to paint the portrait of the dead child. The mother posed zealously, though she did not quite know what for . . . When the picture was ready, the artist took a large green shawl and from it improvised a frame around the painting. Then he called the woman.

No sooner had she glanced at the picture than she burst into tears.

"Do you recognise her?" I asked, deeply moved.

"Of course I do, Sir," she answered, "although the poor thing has changed a lot in the other world."

(Transl. by L. Halápy. From: "Hungarian Short Stories").

CHAPTER 29

1. The *"First Jewish Law"* decreed that, in the future, only 20% of the persons engaged in certain professions (Journalism, Medicine, Theatre, Law, Engineering) and salaried commercial employment could be Jewish.

According to the 1930 census, 5% of Hungary's population belonged to the Jewish faith. At the same time, the proportion of Jews in certain professions was the following: lawyers: 49%, journalists: 32%, doctors in private practice: 55%, salaried employees in commerce: 42% etc. (Cf. Macartney: "October the Fifteenth" and contemporary statistical publications).

2. ". . . Horthy warned Hitler not to undertake the operation (the attack on Czechoslovakia), because in his belief it would lead to a world war, and Germany would be defeated, because she would find the British Navy against her. Britain would assemble a coalition, and although she often lost battles, she

321

always ended by winning the war. . ." (Macartney: "October Fifteenth" vol. I. p. 242, Edinburgh Uni. Press. 1957).

3. The Munich Agreement of Sept. 29, 1938, signed by Hitler, Chamberlain, Daladier and Mussolini, stated that: " . . . the problems of the . . . Hungarian minorities in Czechoslovakia. . . if not settled within three months by agreement between the respective governments, shall form the subject of another meeting of the Heads of Governments of the four Powers here present. . ."

4. The *"Second Jewish Law"* decreed that the proportion of Jewish persons in the free professions should be reduced to 6% gradually, (without dismissing those already employed) and in commerce to 12%. There were many exemptions.

5. ". . . On the 9th (September, 1939), Ribbentrop asked Csáky (Hungarian Foreign Minister), requesting passage of German troops through Hungary against Poland. . . in return he offered Hungary . . . the oil wells of the (Polish) Sambor region. . . The next morning the meeting (of the Hungarian Cabinet) agreed unanimously to reject the request. . . Horthy added a rider that the Germans should be told that he was having the railways mined and would have them blown up if the Germans tried to use them. . ."
". . . during the brief campaign (September 1939) Hungary had given Poland all active assistance that the laws of neutrality allowed. . . In fact a trifle more, for a legion (of Hungarian volunteers), some 6000 strong, had fought on the Polish side. . ." (Both quotations from Macartney: "October Fifteenth" vol. 1. pp. 366-367).

6. By June 26, 1941, Italy, Finland, Rumania, Slovakia, and Croatia had followed Germany in declaring war on Soviet Russia whilst Hungary had only broken off diplomatic relations. The Germans kept urging Hungary to join the campaign, adding veiled hints to the territorial claims of Slovakia and Rumania (which were already belligerents on the German side). After the attack on Kassa (26 June), Bárdossy saw Horthy who demanded "reprisals" (but not a declaration of war). A cabinet meeting was inconclusive, though the majority of the ministers seemed to be in favour of a statement that "Hungary regards herself as being in a state of war with Russia". Without returning to the Regent or consulting the Parliament, Bárdossy informed

the German Legation and issued a press communiqué (June 27) that "Hungary was at war with the Soviet Union." Only then did he announce to the Lower House of the Parliament that "the Royal Hungarian Government concludes that in consequence of these attacks (the bombing of Kassa) a state of war has come into being between Hungary and the Soviet Union".

The Hungarian Constitution reserved the right of the declaration of war to the Regent — but only after Parliament had previously given its consent. There is no doubt therefore that Bárdossy disregarded the Constitution. Prof. Macartney suggests a typically "Magyar" reason: Bárdossy wished that if things went wrong, all responsibility should fall on himself, not on the Regent or the individual members of the Parliament. (Macartney: "October Fifteenth" vol. II. pp. 28-30. Cf. also N. Horthy: "Memoirs", New York, 1957).

7. ". . . the policy adopted by all the 'democratic' and 'left-wing' leaders alike was to shelter behind the Government, support it unobtrusively, and let it play their game for them. . . The stories spread abroad of heroic resistance by these elements to the 'German Fascists' and their 'Hungarian abettors' were pure fiction. Hungarian resistance to Germany throughout the war was directed from the top: its key figures were the Regent, Kállay and Keresztes-Fischer (Minister of the Interior in several governments)." (Macartney: "October Fifteenth" I. p. 379).

8. Horthy's instructions to Kállay were: to defend, preserve and (if necessary) to restore the complete independence (internal and external) of Hungary, to develop toward the Germans spiritual and moral resistance and to keep the concessions to the minimum, short of provoking a German occupation. To keep the Army as intact as possible. . . To seek contact with the British and to call a halt to the anti-Semitic measures. Later Horthy authorised Kállay to initiate armistice negotiations with the western powers but insisted, as a point of honour, on giving Germany previous notice of an eventual armistice agreement. (Kállay: "Hungarian Premier", Oxford Uni. Press, 1959. Also: Macartney and Horthy op. cit.).

9. The *"Third Jewish Law"* (1941, Bárdossy) prohibited marriage between Jews and non-Jews but imposed no other restrictions.

The *"Fourth Jewish Law"* (1942, Kállay) provided for expropriation, against compensation, of all Jewish-owned land. (There were very few Jewish landowners in Hungary). Another measure, introduced later, excluded the Jews from active armed service in the Defence Forces. Instead, they served in labour formations as auxiliaries.

10. Prof. N. Rich (a Jewish historian) in his work "Hitler's War Aims" I-II (London, Deutsch, 1974) praises Horthy for having preserved Hungary as a refuge (for Jews) until the Germans took over the country in 1944. Other (non-Hungarian) historians support this opinion (Macartney etc.).

11. After 17 days of fierce fighting the Hungarian IIIrd Army Corps was surrounded by strong Russian armoured formations. The German commander, general Siebert, ordered the Corps to "attack the Russians". The Hungarian Corps commander, general count Marcel Stomm issued the following order to his troops: "Krasznoje Olim, February 1, 1943.

The Roy. Hungarian IIIrd Army Corps, having been separated after the Uryv breakthrough (13 January) from the Roy. Hungarian 2nd Army, was placed under the orders of the German Group Siebert. In this position, the Corps has been protecting the withdrawal of the German 2nd Army for the last 12 days. During this time, the Hungarian soldiers had to suffer the horrors of the Russian winter nights outdoors, without food, ammunition, without cover in the open snowfields. . . Today I received the order to lead you in an attack to break through the Russian lines. . . through the Russian army which even the well equipped and armed German troops were unable to stop. . . I can not pass this order to you, as it would be senseless to expect the half-starved, half-frozen Hungarians to go to their deaths by the thousands. . . After this I must allow everybody to look after himself as well as possible. . . God be with you, Hungarian soldiers!"

On issuing this order, general Stomm said good-bye to his staff and began to walk. . . in the direction ordered by his commanding officer, toward the Russians. He could hardly walk as both his legs were frozen. He was captured later — with his service revolver in his hand — the only general captured armed by the Russians. . . (The author's own information. The general's order was published in the Hungarian newspapers after the war).

12. In the middle of 1944 about 1,100,000 men were on active service in the Hungarian Defence forces (out of a total population of 14 million) — a remarkable effort after the horrendous losses at the Don in 1943. However, only one Army, the 1st (successfully defending the eastern Carpathians under generals Lakatos and Farkas) was fully equipped. The makeshift 2nd (northern Hungary) and 3rd (Transylvania) Armies consisted of troops without heavy equipment, modern transport, armour, air support or anti-tank defences. Moreover, several divisions were still on occupation duty employed by the German Command in distant sectors of the eastern front.

The suspicious Germans refused to equip the Hungarians with heavy and modern weapons even though the production of the Hungarian war industry (still working at full capacity) had been almost entirely requisitioned by the German command. Only a few new units could be provided with modern equipment, such as the elite "Szent László" division (general Z. Szügyi) — destined to become the last defender of Hungarian soil in 1945.

13. Budapest was defended by about 70,000 troops — more than half of them Hungarians — against 20 Russian divisions supported by 2000 planes.

It is impossible to give an estimate of the military and civilian losses, but we know that some units suffered very high casualties. The Budapest Guard Battalion fought to the last man and the University Regiment lost 80% of its effectives. Thousands of civilians died during the house-to-house fighting and in consequence of indiscriminate shelling, bombing, lack of food, fuel and medical help. The water, gas and electricity services broke down completely at the beginning of January (during the coldest winter in living memory). The districts occupied by the Russians were subjected to a reign of unbridled violence by armed gangs of Soviet army "deserters" (a term used by Russian Marshal Voroshilov).

On the 14th of February the pale winter sun rose behind a pall of smoke and red haze over the ruins of the city once called the "Queen of the Danube". The guns were silent at last and the screams of the wounded soldiers in the burning Buda hospital had stopped.

It was the dawn of Ash Wednesday, the first day of Lent, 1945.

BIBLIOGRAPHY

(This is the list of the main English language works consulted by the author. Works written in other languages are not mentioned here, neither are articles, pamphlets and chapters in comprehensive works or encyclopaedias).

ALVAREZ, A. (intr.) Hungarian Short Stories, Oxford Uni. Press, (The World's Classics), New York, Toronto, 1967.

BANDHOLTZ, H. H. An Undiplomatic Diary, Columbia Uni. Press, New York, 1933.

BARTÓK, B. Hungarian Folk Music, Oxford Uni. Press, London, 1931.

BOLDIZSÁR, I. (ed.) Hungary — a Comprehensive Guidebook, Corvina, Budapest, 1959.

BOWRING, J. Poetry of the Magyars, Print Smallfield, London, 1830.

CSICSERY-RÓNAI, I. The First Book of Hungary, Franklin Watts Inc. New York, 1967.

DE DARUVAR, Y. The Tragic Fate of Hungary, "Nemzetör" and American Hungarian Literary Guild, Astor Park, 1974.

DEGH, L. (ed.) Folktales of Hungary, Uni. of Chicago Press, 1965.

DESNEY, P. Hungarian poems in English translation, (manuscript), Sydney, 1972-1974.

DOBSZAY, L. The Kodály Method and its Musical Basis, Akadémiai Kiadó, Budapest, 1972.

DOMJÁN, J. Hungarian Heroes and Legends, D. Van Nostrand Co. Inc. Princeton, 1963.

DONALD, R. The Tragedy of Trianon, Thornton Butterworth Ltd. London, 1928.

ENDREY, A. Sons of Nimrod (The Origin of Hungarians), Hawthorn Press, Melbourne, 1975.

E.O.S. Hungary and its Revolutions (with a Memoir of L. Kossuth), London, 1896.

ERDEI, F. (ed.) Information Hungary, Pergamon Press, Oxford, (Countries of the World, vol. 2), 1968.

FEKETE, M. Eminent Hungarians, Aurora, München, 1966.

FÉL, E. and HOFER, T. Proper Peasants, Corvina, Budapest — New York, 1969.

FÉL, E., HOFER, T. and CSILLÉRY, K. Hungarian Peasant Art, Corvina, Budapest, 1969.

FENYŐ, M. Hitler, Horthy and Hungary (German-Hungarian Relations, 1941-1944), Yale Uni. Press, 1972.

FOLDVÁRY, Z. G. An outline of the History of Hungary between 890 A.D. and 1146 A.D. (manuscript), Sydney.

GÁBORJÁN, A. Hungarian Folk Costumes, Corvina, Budapest, (Series Hungarian Folk Art)

GALLUS, S. (ed.) Studies for a New Central Europe, Mid-European Institute, New York, 1968-1972.

GINK, K., KISS, I. S. Folk Art and Folk Artists in Hungary, Corvina, Budapest, 1968.

GOÓR, Gy. The Hungarian Soldier, (manuscript), Sydney, 1972.

326

GROSZ, J. and BOGGS, W. A. Hungarian Anthology, (a collection of poems), Pannonia, Toronto, 1966.

HARASZTI, E. The Ethnic History of Transylvania, Danubian Press Inc. Astor Park, Florida, 1971.

HORTHY, N. The Confidential Papers of Admiral H., Corvina, Budapest, 1965.

HORTHY, N. Memoirs, Hutchinson, London, 1956.

HUNGARIAN PAST, periodical, ed. by the Hungarian Historical Society, Sydney.

HUNGARIAN RHAPSODY: The Hungarian State Folk Ensemble, Corvina, Budapest, 1956.

HUNGARY: edited by the Hungarian Rotarians, Budapest, 1931.

ILLYÉS, Gy. Once upon a Time (Forty Hungarian Folk Tales), Corvina, Budapest, 1964.

JONES, D. M. Five Hungarian Writers, Clarendon, Oxford, 1966.

KÁLLAY, M. Hungarian Premier, Oxford Uni. Press, London, 1954.

KAMPIS, A. The History of Art in Hungary, Corvina, Budapest-London, 1966.

KÁROLYI, M. Memoirs (Faith without Illusion), J. Cape, London, 1956.

KERTESZ, St. Diplomacy in a Whirlpool: Hungary between Nazi Germany and Soviet Russia, Univ. of Notre Dame Press, Notre Dame, 1953.

KIBÉDI-VARGA, A. The Hungarians, Amerikai Magyar Könyvkiadó, Köln, 1956.

KIRKCONNELL, W. The Magyar Muse. (An Anthology of Hungarian Poetry) Kanadai Magyar Ujság, Winnipeg, 1933.

KLANICZAY, T. History of Hungarian Literature, Collet's, London, 1964.

KODÁLY, Z. Folk Music of Hungary, Barrett and Rockliff, London, 1960.

KOSSUTH, L. Memoirs of my Exile, Cassell, London, 1886.

KUNZ, E. F. Blood and Gold (Hungarians in Australia), Cheshire, Melbourne, 1969.

KUNZ, E. F. (ed.) Hungarian Poetry, Pannonia, Sydney, 1955.

KUNZ, E. F. (intr.) I. Madach: The Tragedy of Man (transl. by C. P. Sanger), Pannonia, Sydney, 1953.

LEADER, N. Hungarian Classical Ballads and their Folklore, Cambridge Uni. Press, 1967.

LOEW, W. N. Magyar Poetry, New York, 1899.

MACARTNEY, C. A. Hungary (A Short History), Edinbourgh Uni. Press, 1962.

MACARTNEY, C. A. Hungary and her Successors 1919-1937, Oxford Uni. Press, London, 1937.

MACARTNEY, C. A. October Fifteenth. A History of Modern Hungary, 1929-1945. I-II, Edinburgh Uni. Press, Edinburgh, 1956.

MANGA, I. Hungarian Folksong and Folk Instruments, Corvina, Budapest.

MENCZER, B. A Commentary on Hungarian Literature, Amerikai Magyar Kiadó, Castrop-Rauxel, 1956.

MINDSZENTY, J. Card. Memoirs, Macmillan, New York, 1974.

MONTGOMERY, J. F. Hungary, the Unwilling Satellite, New York, 1947.

MUSICA HUNGARICA ed. by B. Szabolcsi and M. Forrai, Qualiton, Musica, Budapest, 1970.

NEW HUNGARIAN QUARTERLY (THE), monthly periodical, editor: I. Boldizsár, Budapest.

NYERGES, A. N. Poems of E. Ady, Hungarian Cultural Foundation, Buffalo, 1969.

ORTUTAY, Gy. Hungarian Peasant Life, Officina, Budapest, 1948.

PADÁNYI, V. Dentumagyaria, Transylvania, Buenos Aires, 1963.

PAPP, A. Hungary (A Guide Book), Corvina, Budapest, 1971.

RAJETZKY, B. (ed.) Hungarian Folk Music I-II, UNESCO-Hungarian Academy of Sciences, Qualiton, Budapest.

327

REMÉNYI, J. Hungarian Writers and Literature, ed. by A. J. Molnar, Rutgers Uni. Press, New Brunswick, 1964.
RICH, N. Hitler's War Aims I-II. A. Deutsch, London, 1974.
RIEDL, F. History of the Hungarian Literature, Heinemann, London, 1906.
SINOR, D. History of Hungary, G. Allen and Unwin, London, 1959.
SMITH, L. S. Hungary, Land and People, Athenaeum, Budapest, 1933.
SNYDER, L. L. Fifty Major Documents of the Twentieth Century, Van Nostrand, New York, 1955.
SZABOLCSI, B. A Concise History of Hungarian Music, Corvina, Budapest, 1964.
TÁBORI, P. The Real Hungary, Skeffington, London, 1939.
TÓTH, J. C. Sing out and Go (Hungarian Folk Songs), K. and J. Tóth, Lorain, Ohio, 1969.
VÁRDY, B. and KOSÁRY, D. History of the Hungarian Nation, (The Hungarian Heritage Books, Astor Park, Danubian Press, Florida, 1969.

VARSÁNYI, J. (ed.) Quest for a New Central Europe (A Symposium), Australian Carpathian Federation, Adelaide, 1976.
VISKI, K. Hungarian Dances, Dr. Vajna, Budapest, 1937.
VISKI, K. Hungarian Peasant Customs, Dr. Vajna, Budapest, 1937.
WANKLYN, H. G. The Eastern Marchlands of Europe, G. Philip and Sons, London, 1941.
WARREN HOLLISTER, C. (ed.) Landmarks of the Western Heritage I - II, J. Wiley and Sons, New York, 1967.
WASS, A. (ed.) Selected Hungarian Legends, Danubian Press, (Hungarian Heritage Books), Astor Park, Florida, 1971.
WEISSBERG, A. Advocate for the Dead, A. Deutsch, London, 1958.
YOLLAND, A. B. Hungary, T. C. and E. C. Jack London, 1917.
ZAREK, O. The History of Hungary, London, 1939.
ZATHURECZKY, J. Transylvania, Anderson-Hall Research Centre, Uni of Florida, 1963.

ACKNOWLEDGMENTS

Grateful thanks are due to the following authors and publishers for their permission to reproduce extracts from copyright works:

Cambridge University Press, Cambridge, J. Cape Publishers, London, Corvina Press, Budapest, Danubian Press Inc. Astor Park, Flo., Mr. Paul Desney of Sydney, NSW, Edinburgh University Press, Edinburgh, Dr. E. F. Kunz of Canberra, ACT, Oxford University Press, Oxford, Pannonia Publishing Co. Sydney, NSW, K. and J. C. Tóth Publishers, Lorain, Ohio, University of Chicago Press, Chicago, Amerikai Magyar Kiadó, Köln, John Wiley and Sons New York.

INDEX

LIST OF ILLUSTRATIONS

CONTENTS